IMAGES
of America

MORRIS PLAINS

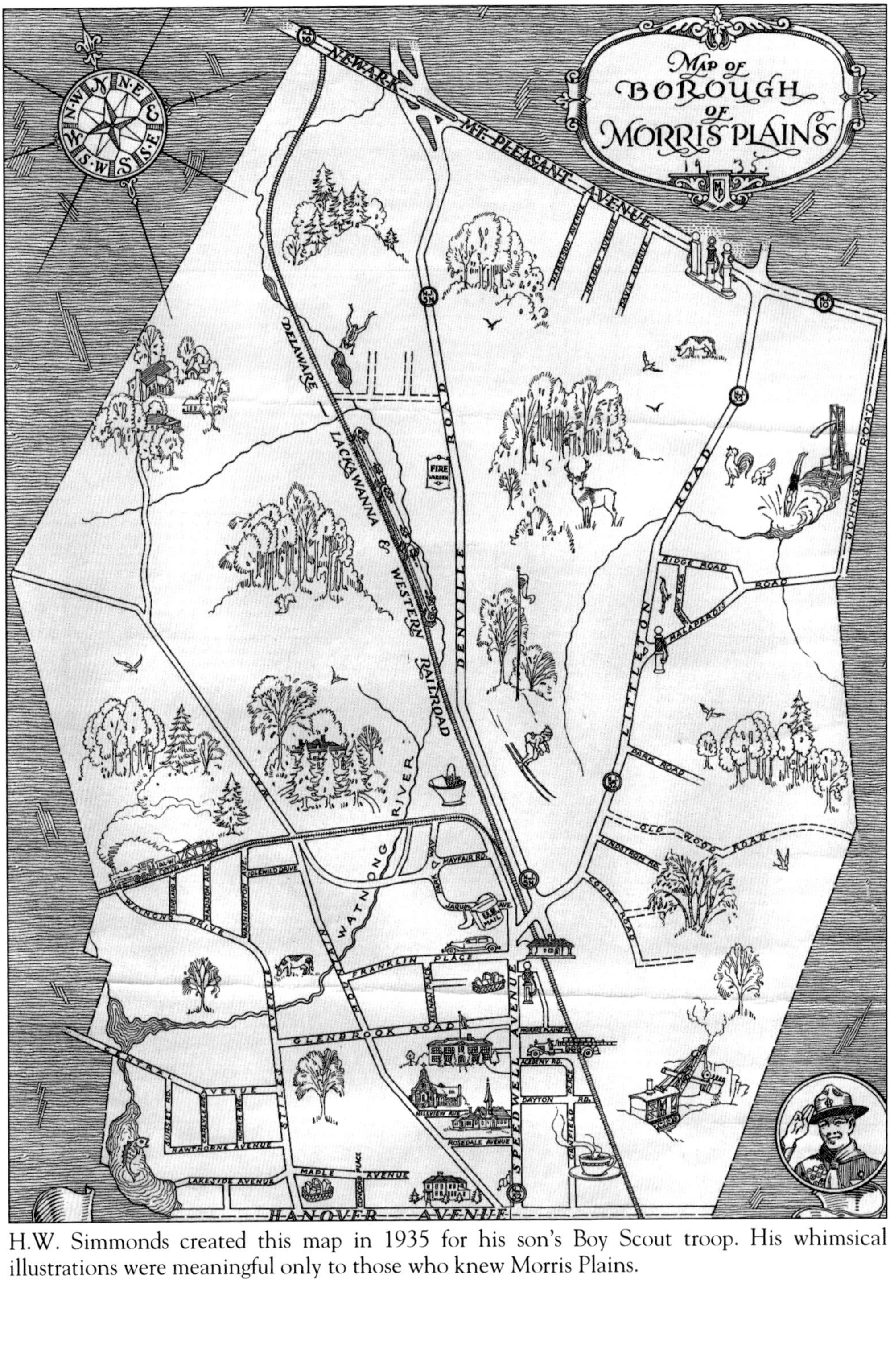

H.W. Simmonds created this map in 1935 for his son's Boy Scout troop. His whimsical illustrations were meaningful only to those who knew Morris Plains.

IMAGES
of America

MORRIS PLAINS

Virginia Dyer Vogt and Daniel B. Myers

ARCADIA
PUBLISHING

ISBN 978-0-7385-0482-7

Published by Arcadia Publishing
Charleston, South Carolina

Printed in the United States of America

Library of Congress Catalog Card Number: 00-105707

For all general information contact Arcadia Publishing at:
Telephone 843-853-2070
Fax 843-853-0044
E-mail sales@arcadiapublishing.com
For customer service and orders:
Toll-Free 1-888-313-2665

Visit us on the Internet at www.arcadiapublishing.com

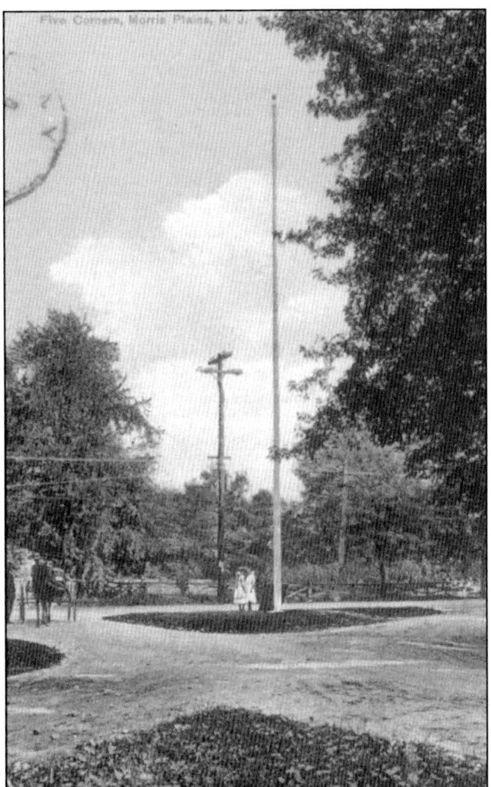

AT THE CROSSROADS, 1911. Five Corners in Morris Plains has existed since the Union Turnpike (today's Mountain Way) was laid out in the late 18th century, running diagonally northwest between West Hanover and Speedwell Avenues. Two hundred years ago this five-pointed crossroads was the hub of a small settlement that extended westward along both sides of Hanover.

Contents

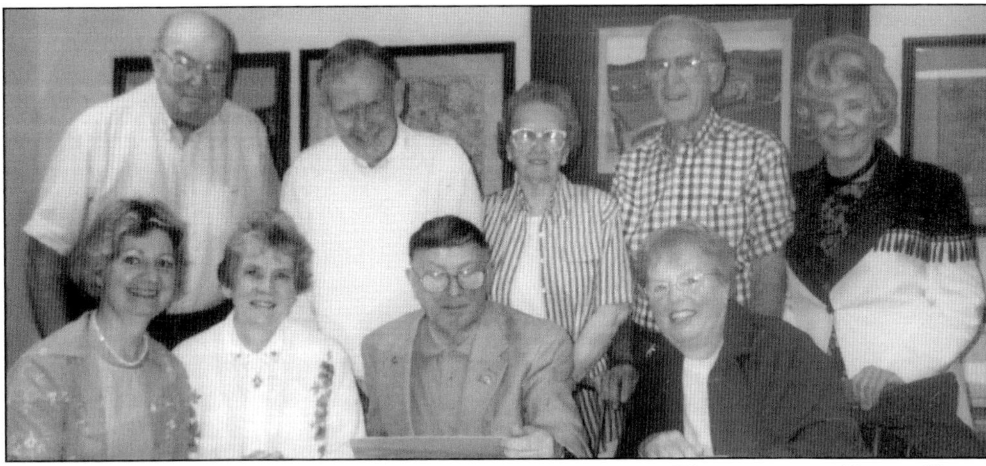

Members of the Morris Plains Museum Association at Work on the Book. Shown working on this book, from left to right, are the following: (front row) Virginia Vogt, president; Maryclare Myers, treasurer; Hank Sawoski, assistant historian; and Jean Johnson, secretary; (back row) John Vilven; Daniel Myers, town historian; Anita Carroll; Robert Carroll; and Helen Hildebrant Schnack. Mary Palmer is missing.

Acknowledgments

We wish to thank every individual and institution that donated or loaned pictures for this book: The American Red Cross, Harold Armstrong, F. Paine Baldwin, Jean Bartron, George Burns, Florence Bush, Bob Byrnes, the Campbell family, Gerald Coursen, Edward Coss, Charles Craver, Hildreth Cronshey, John Drake, Foster Ensminger, Alan Florin, Mrs. John Harper, Walter Hutton, Jean Johnson, Virginia Grove Kenworthy, Donald Kyle, Alex Laurie, Adelaide Layer, Kay Leary, MacLean Drug Store, Warren Ming Jr., Joan and Roger Morgan, the Morris County Historical Society, Mary Murdician, Peter Olin, Jean Dobbins Osborne, Mary Mills Palmer, Gordon Parsons, Robert Pease, St. Virgil's Archives, Helen Hildebrant Schnack, Charles Sebelle, the Signorelli family, Pat Sipple, Ruth Totten, Mattie Tunis, Virginia Dobbins VanNess, Alice VanWinkle, Lee Vogt, G. Vorsheim, Elizabeth White Weisert, Mary Elzerman Whitehead, and E. Wilson.

A special thanks goes to the Joint Free Public Library of Morristown and Morris Township for sharing its excellent photographic resources and research assistance. The photographs borrowed from the JFPLMMT are also acknowledged in the captions.

We are grateful to eminent historian John T. Cunningham for his experience, encouragement, and advice.

We especially thank Maryclare Myers for cataloging the hundreds of pictures involved in the project and for her excellent research assistance.

We are grateful for two fine books on Homer Davenport: *Homer Davenport of Silverton* by Leland Huot and Alfred Powers (West Shore Press: Bingen, Washington, 1973) and Charles and Jeanne Craver's *The Annotated Quest: Homer Davenport and His Wonderful Arabian Horses* (Seauphah Publishing Association: Hillview, Illinois).

Finally, thanks to Robert and Anita Carroll, Jean Johnson, Maryclare and Dan Myers, Mary Palmer, Maryclare Procanik, Hank Sawoski, Helen Schnack, John Vilven, and Lee Vogt for proofreading.

Introduction

In the late 17th century, land in Nova Caesaria (New Jersey) began to pass from a handful of British Crown grantees to settlers willing to bet their future on the undeveloped wilderness across the Hudson. The first settler in what would become Morris Plains was Thomas Pierson, the son of a Newark constable. In 1685, Pierson built a small sawmill on what is now Thompson's Pond on Central Avenue.

The flat plateau between the low mountains where Pierson settled was first known as Watnong Plains, the Native American name for the brook that ran diagonally through it. It was also simply known as the Plains. In the next century, it would become Morris Plains, under the jurisdiction of Hanover Township.

For 200 years, the tiny village of Morris Plains consisted of a small cluster of homes near the intersection of Speedwell Avenue and Walnut Grove Road (today's West Hanover Avenue). After the Union Turnpike (Mountain Way) was laid out in the late 18th century, this crossroads became known as Five Corners. Beyond the settlement at Five Corners was a handful of outlying farms. There were also a few small mills and forges drawing power from the Watnong Brook.

In 1848, the Morris and Essex Railroad was extended from Morristown to Morris Plains, and a small group of dwellings and commercial enterprises slowly began to grow up around the station in the upper reaches of town. Still, 200 years after Thomas Pierson, only a few dozen homes and farms were scattered over the Plains. Most of the land was in the hands of several large landowners: South of Granniss Avenue were Fairchild, Roberts, Gregory, Johnson, Jaqui, Stiles, Thompson, and Whitney. To the north were McCurdy, Granniss, Sires, and Marsh.

In 1871, Morris Plains was selected as the site for the New Jersey State Asylum for the Insane (soon called Greystone for the color of the local rock of which it was built). This huge enterprise, almost a town unto itself, brought jobs and increased commerce to the Plains. Also at this time, Morris Plains began to attract wealthy and powerful men who built large estates in the pristine countryside. A new wave of immigrants found work on these estates, fueling the need for more non-farm tract homes. Several far-thinking Plainsmen anticipated this need. F.W. Jaqui laid out plans for the Plains's first subdivision before 1889. On the other side of town, Fr. James J. Brennan acquired land north of West Hanover that he developed as small building lots for his growing body of Irish Catholic parishioners.

Changing times finally caught up with Morris Plains in the years just before World War I. The Speedwell Avenue business extension was greatly expanded, led by the many commercial enterprises of Daniel M. Merchant. Trolley lines were laid in 1909, and the railroad underpass was constructed in 1915. In the years between the wars, the population of Morris Plains doubled to 2,000 as many of the old farm tracts were developed into suburban neighborhoods. Between 1950 and 1964, the population doubled again.

In 1926, Morris Plains broke its ties to Hanover Township, and the little town began to follow its own destiny. Today, what was once a tiny farming settlement is a thriving community of 5,200, most of whom leave Morris Plains each day for jobs in all parts of the tristate area. Yet Morris Plains remains rich in the community spirit of earlier days, generously supporting its local schools, churches, and other civic organizations. Morris Plains, the "community of caring," is widely known as a vibrant place to live and raise a family.

And, if you know where to look, you can still catch a fleeting glimpse of old Watnong Plains.

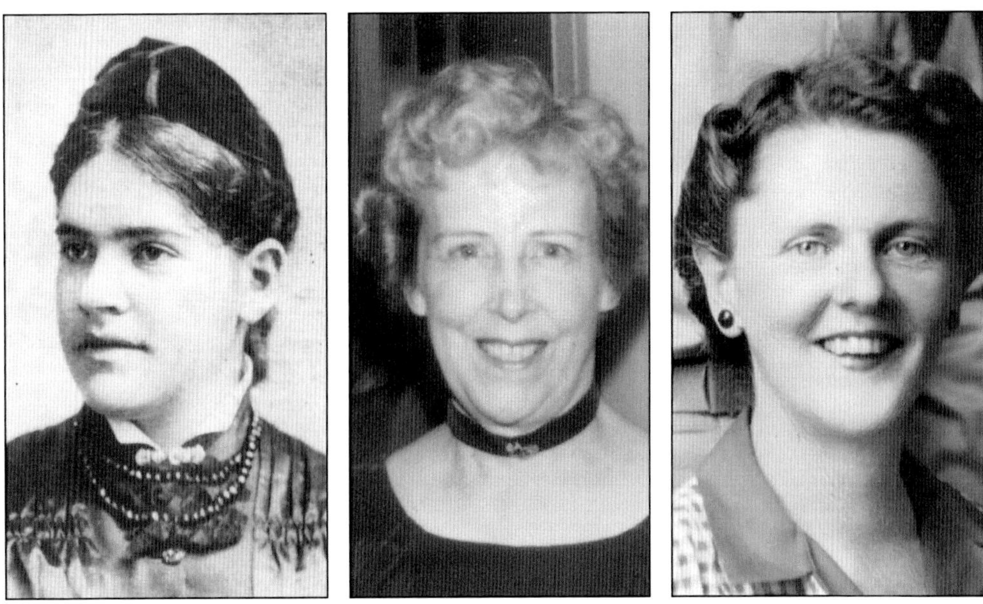

MORRIS PLAINS'S THREE MUSES OF HISTORY. Julia Beers (left, 1862–1955), the town's first librarian, wrote a history of early Morris Plains. Muriel Rennie (center, 1913–1992) became the first town historian in 1954 and founded the Morris Plains Museum. Mary Byrnes (right, 1912–1994) assisted Muriel for many years in organizing the museum's growing collections.

One

Five Corners and a Brook

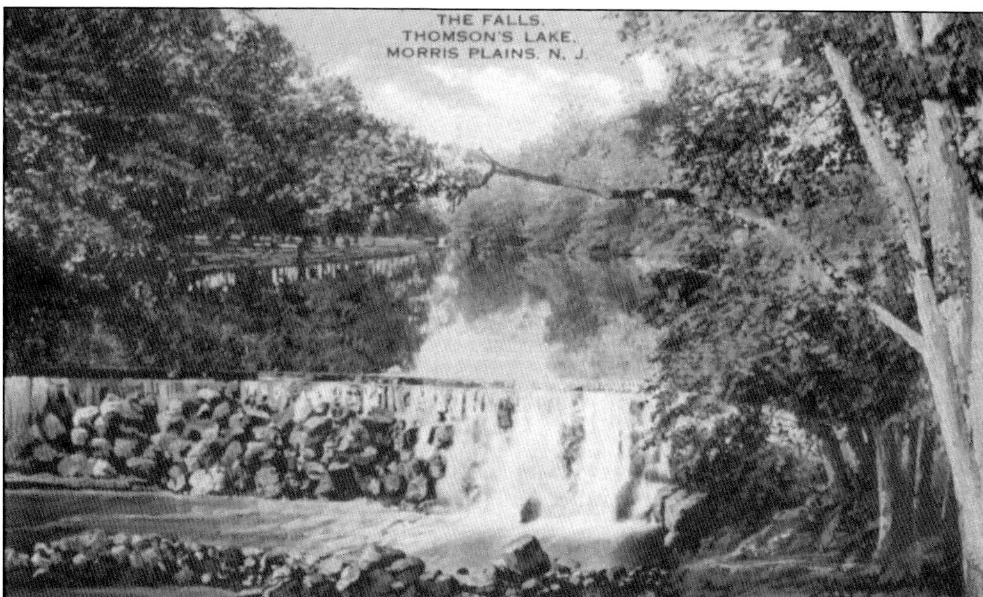

Thompson Pond: Where Morris Plains Started. Thomas Pierson came to Watnong Plains in 1685 and built a sawmill on what is now Thompson Pond near Central Avenue. The Pierson family had a mill on that spot for 200 years, until 1882, when the land was taken to pay taxes. Two large estates soon rose on the former Pierson tract: Brookbank, built by wealthy businessman Arthur Thompson and Fairlawn, the seat of the Stephen Whitney family. In the 1940s, Fairlawn was razed to make way for a housing development called Glenbrook Park.

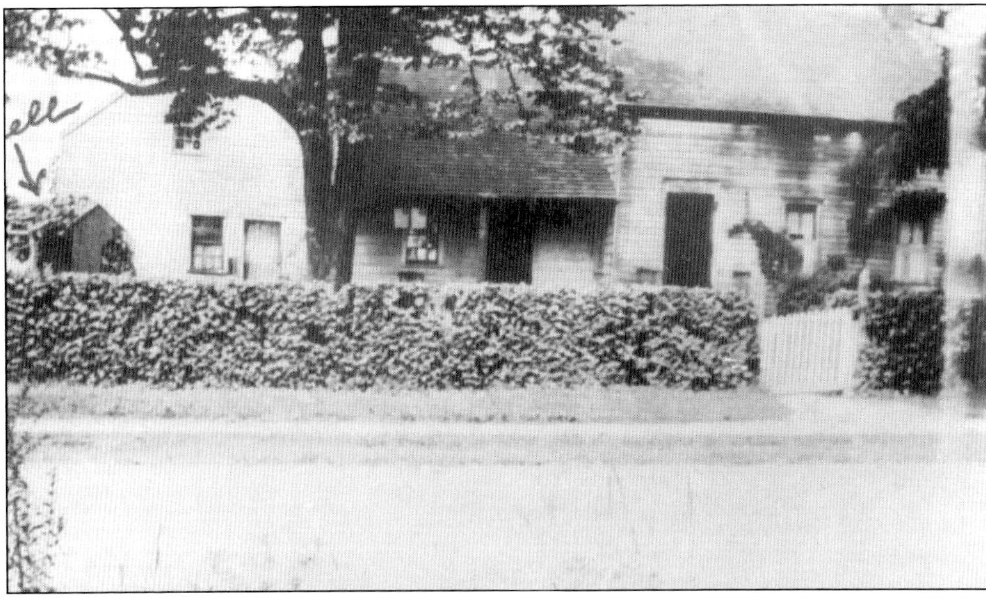

THE GODDEN-PEASE HOUSE. Robert Pease's research on his home at 30 Stiles Avenue establishes it as one of the oldest in Morris Plains. The house was owned in the mid-18th century by David Godden, who left it to his son in 1790. Pease's research did not preclude that David's father, Samuel, may have lived there even earlier. Note the well and the kitchen shed to the left in this picture from the 1920s—both long gone.

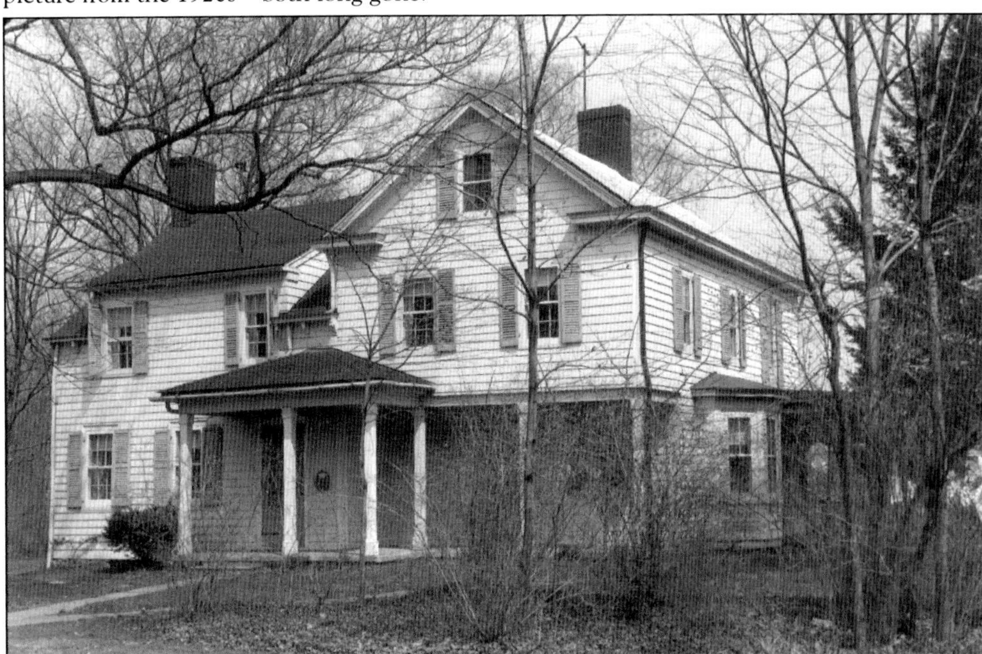

THE GODDEN-STILES HOUSE. David Godden left the house that now stands at 45 Stiles Avenue to another son after his death. By the mid-1800s, it was owned by J. Hazen Stiles, who called it the Homestead. It was owned by the Stiles family until 1986. The old house is still occupied, but the surrounding property is soon to be a new housing development.

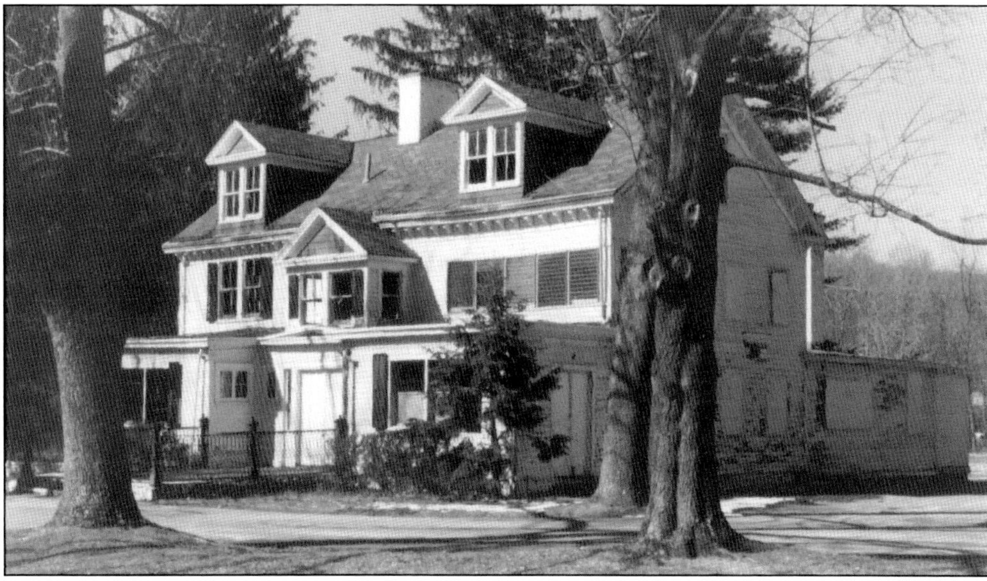

Another Early Site. In 1736, Timothy Peck built a cottage and forge on Watnong Brook, where today Granniss Avenue meets Sun Valley Way. The property passed through many generations of Turners and Vails. In the 1940s, it was an experimental chicken farm. It became Ashbrook Farms after renovation in the 1960s by the Armitage family. The old house was the temporary home of the library during construction of the new wing in 1982. In 1990, it was demolished, and the site became a recycling center. Today, the lovely brookside setting is Watnong Park.

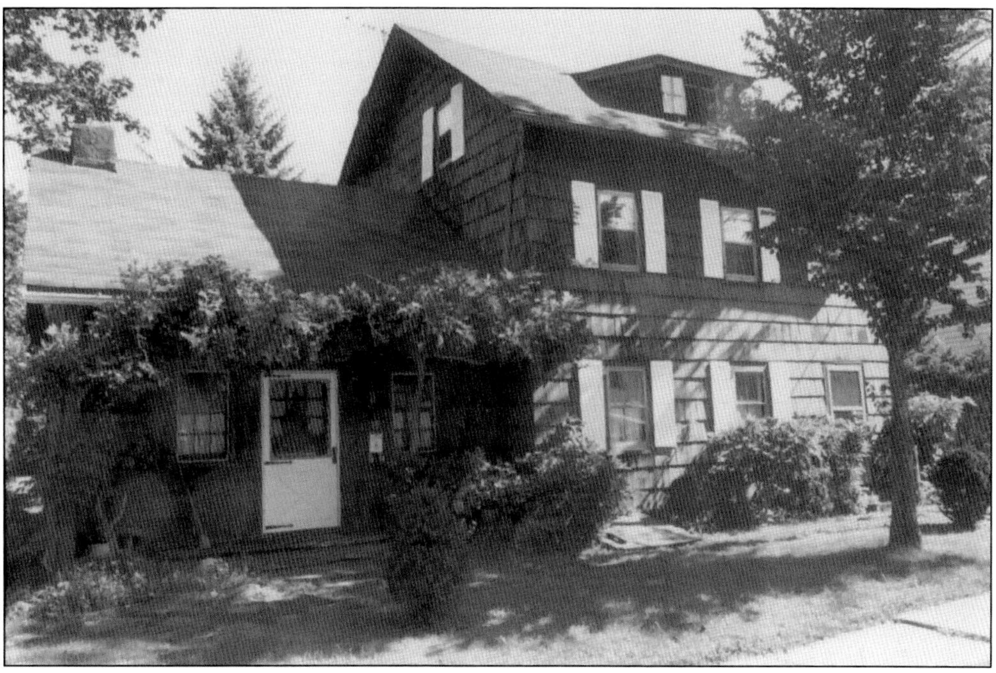

Sherman's Gardener's Cottage. This home at 23 West Hanover Avenue was built in 1854 and was originally owned by Gordon Burnham. In 1932, Julia Sherman left the cottage to her gardener, Michael Hyland. Recently, the house was extensively remodeled.

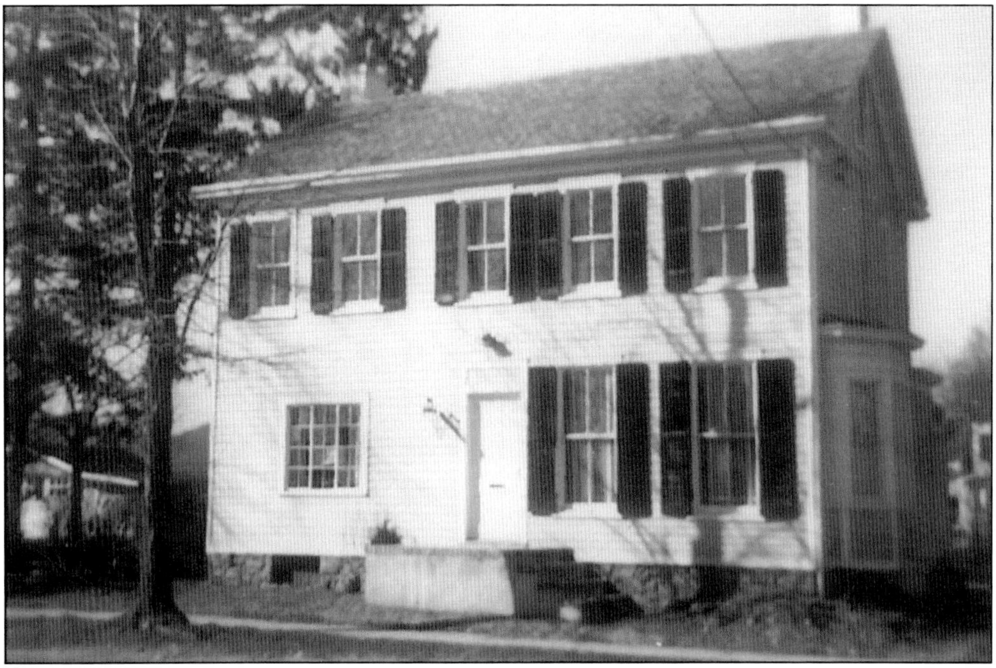

The Loper-Devine House near Five Corners. This old house at 17 West Hanover Avenue was built in the middle of the 19th century. James Devine had a grocery store on the property. Daniel Merchant sold it to Warren Ming in the mid-1900s.

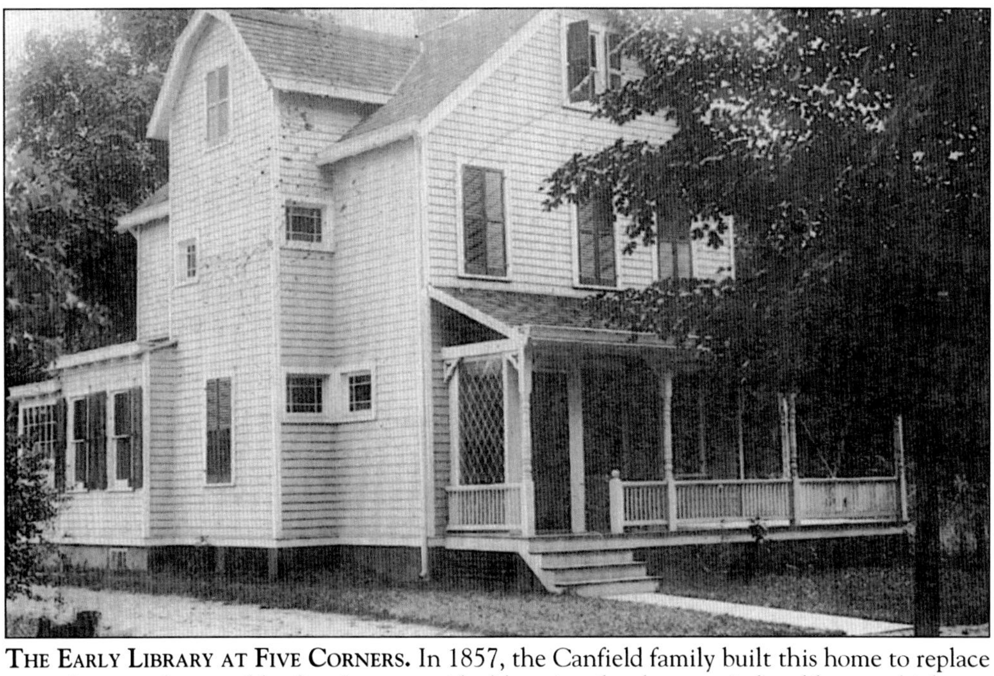

The Early Library at Five Corners. In 1857, the Canfield family built this home to replace an earlier one destroyed by fire. It was an ideal location for the town's first library, which was organized there in the late 1800s by Margaret Caldwell Canfield. In 1910, the house became the convent of the Sisters of St. Dominic. The structure was razed to build the current convent in 1930.

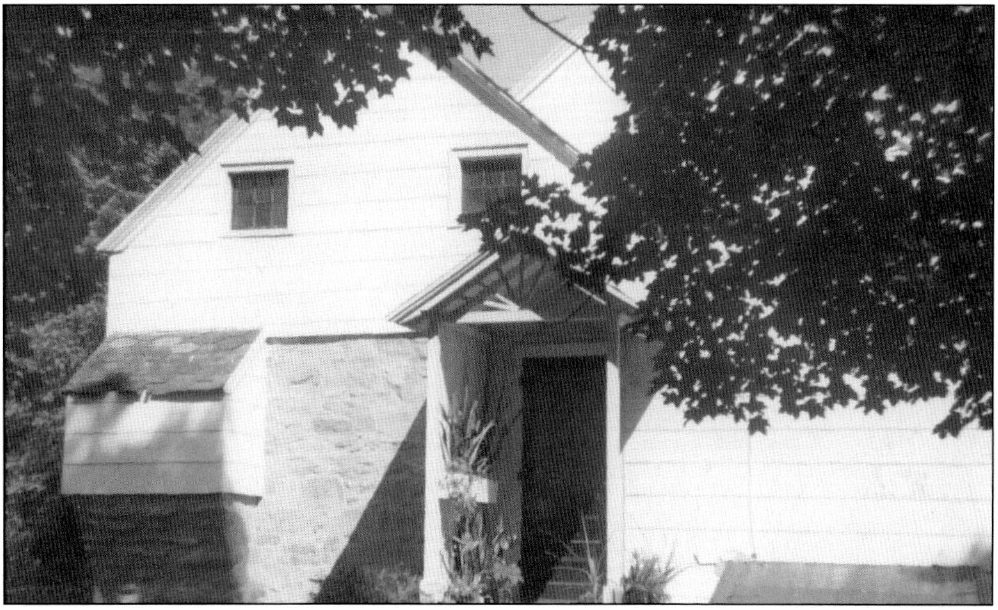

The Gregory House. Seth Gregory bought an 84-acre farm near Five Corners for his son, Jedidiah, in 1801. Research done on behalf of the current owner, Jean Johnson, indicates that the farmhouse on the property dates to the early 1700s, which would make it the oldest documented dwelling in town. The bake oven on the left is still functional. Seth Gregory also owned an inn across the road where drovers and their herds spent the night on their way to market in Newark.

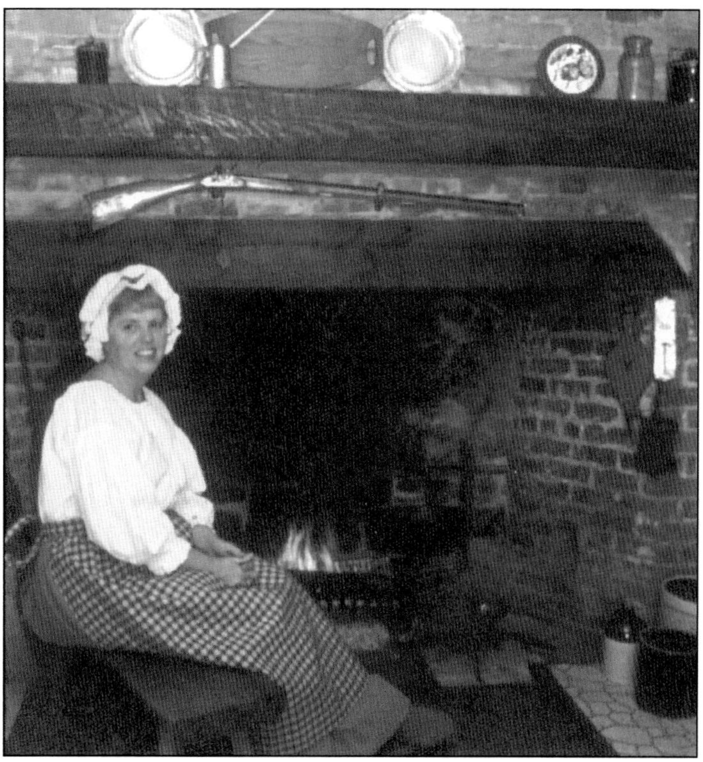

An Interior View of the Gregory House. In 1977, Jean Johnson poses in colonial dress in front of a fireplace nearly 280 years old. During a renovation, Jean found a child's old shoe in the wall above the door, an 18th-century custom thought to bring good luck. The Johnson family has owned the house for several generations.

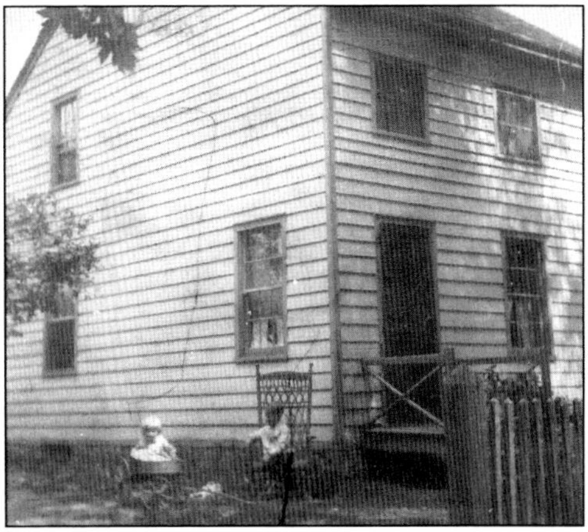
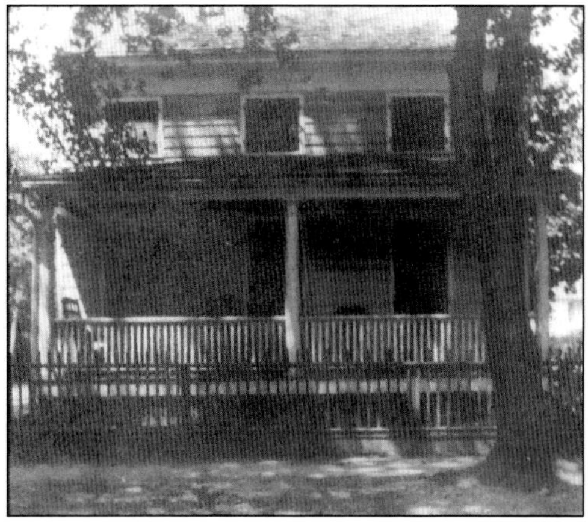

THREE VIEWS, 190 YEARS. The Loper-Patterson-Mills house near Five Corners at 21 West Hanover Avenue was likely built in the late 1700s and is now owned by Mary Mills Palmer. William Loper and his daughter Anna had a private school here in the late 1800s. The house is pictured in 1893 (above left), sometime before 1930 (above right), and recently (below).

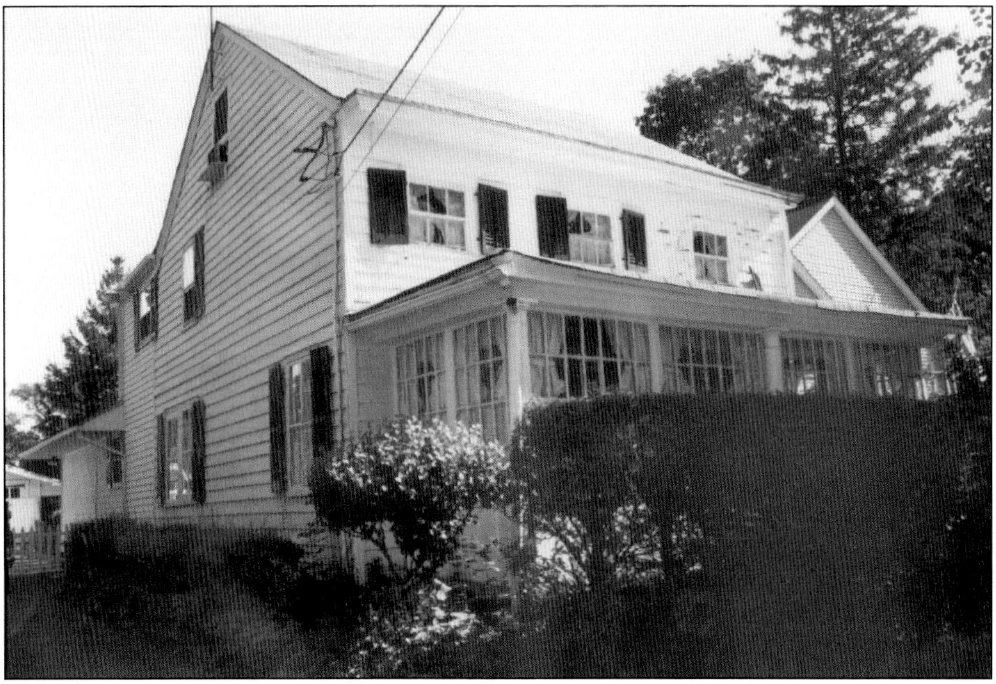

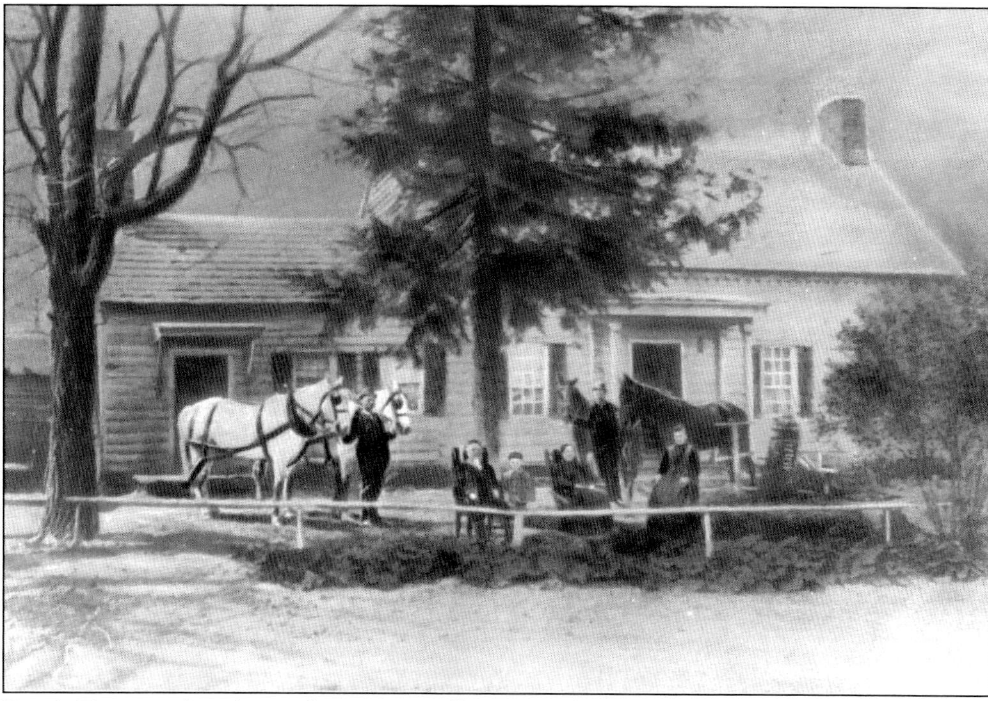

PUFF'S TAVERN. Another early inn was Puff's Tavern, built by James Puff Losey in 1740 on the south side of West Hanover Avenue near Puff's Brook. This undated picture has an ethereal quality of times past and seems more a picture of a family proud of its lovely, shaded front yard and pairs of matched horses than a rough drover's stopover.

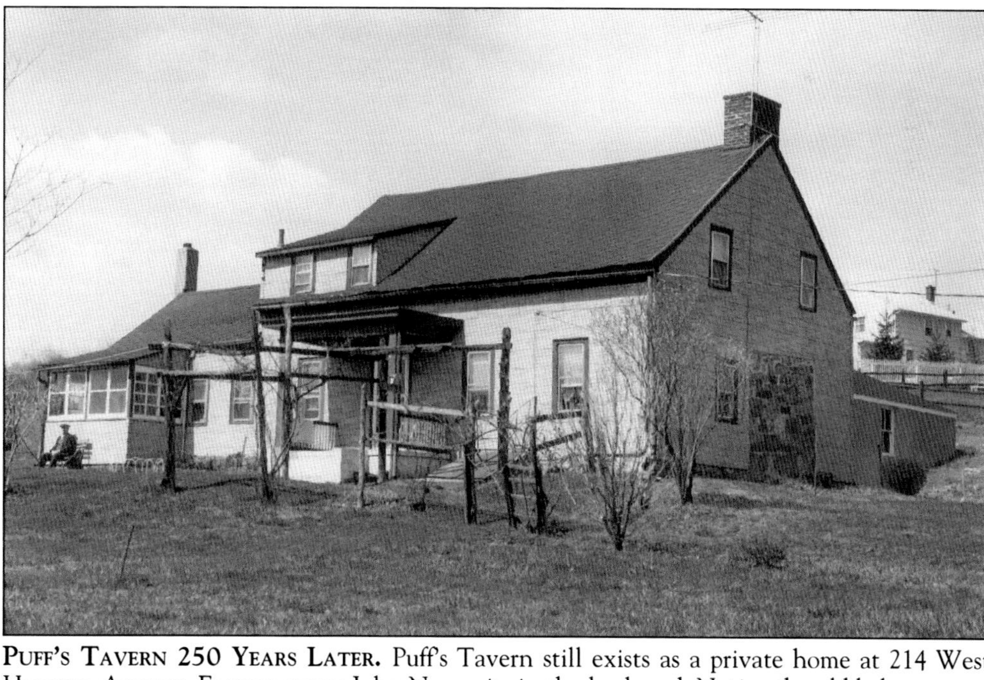

PUFF'S TAVERN 250 YEARS LATER. Puff's Tavern still exists as a private home at 214 West Hanover Avenue. Former owner John Nunn sits in the backyard. Notice the old bake oven to the right.

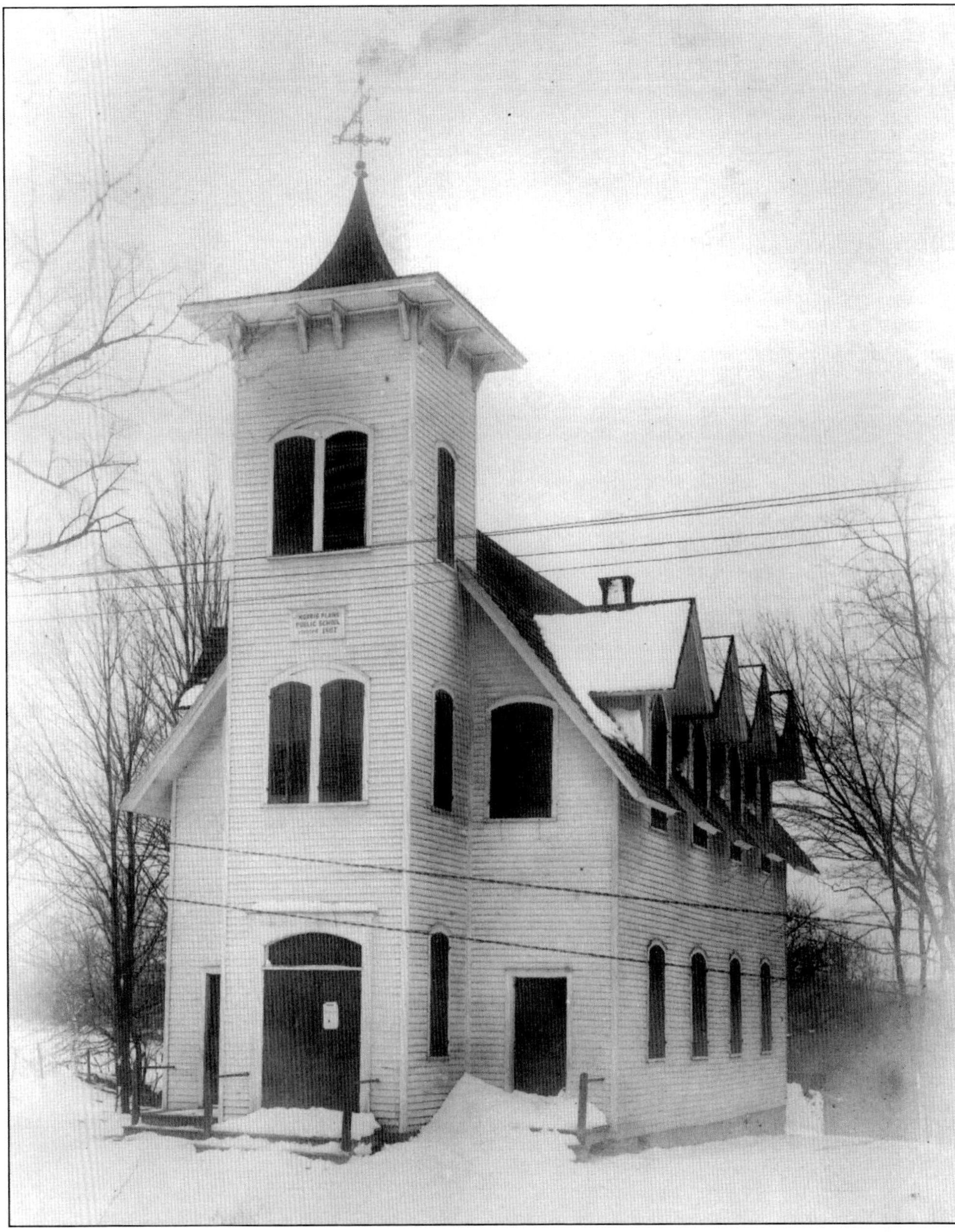

From Sheep Pen to School to Apartments. This school was built in 1866 to replace the "old stone schoolhouse," which dated from the early 1800s. It was subsequently referred to as the "new frame schoolhouse." On the site before the schools was a stone sheep pen which held sheep for shearing after they were cleaned in the "sheep washing pond" behind the pen. The 1866 school is still there. It was once Meeker's Paint Shop and is now a trim apartment building at the corner of West Hanover Avenue and Irondale Road. (Courtesy JFPLMMT.)

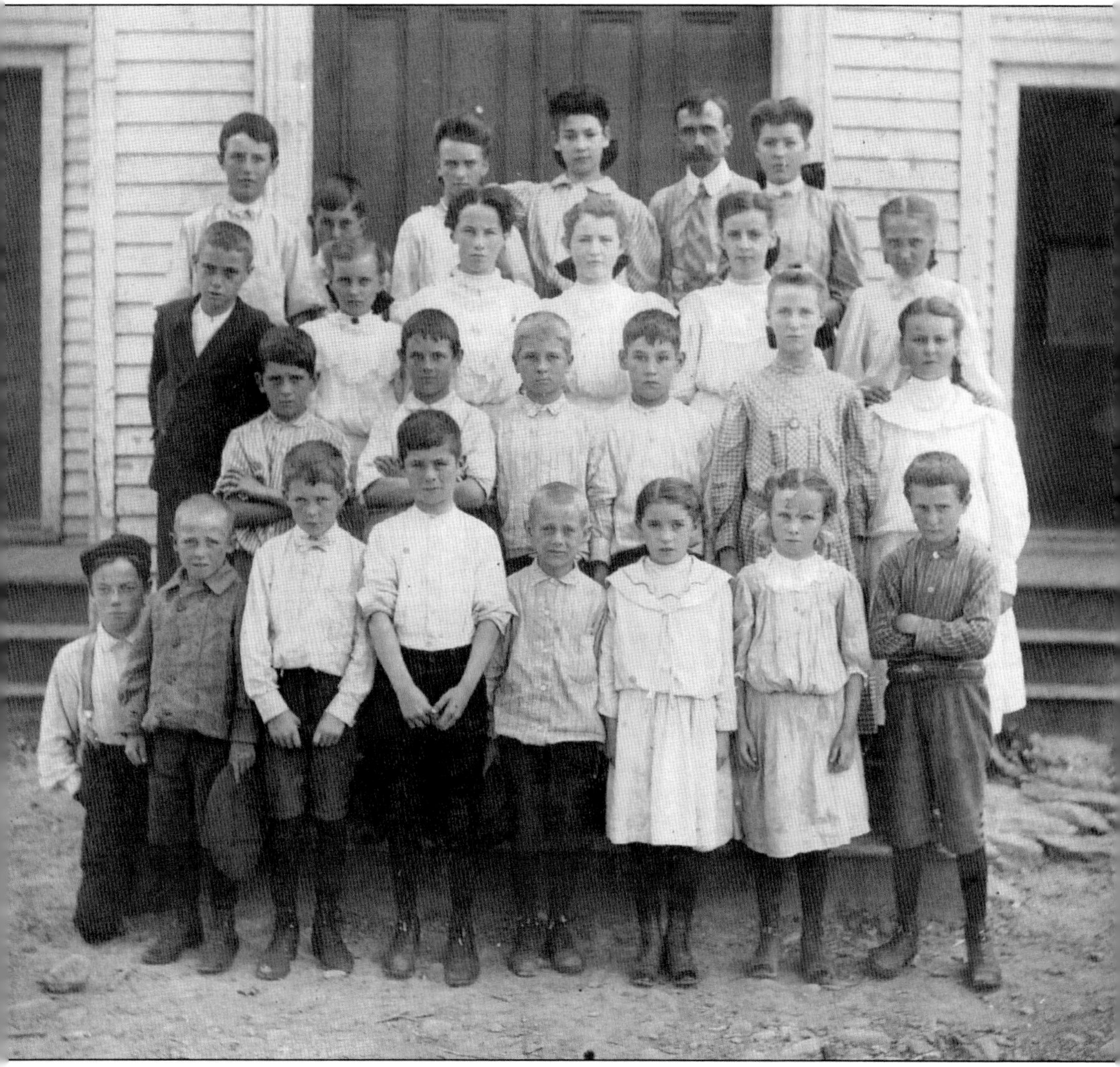

CHILDREN OF THE "NEW FRAME SCHOOLHOUSE." The class of 1906 or 1907 poses in front of the school. Shown, from left to right, are the following: (first row) Joseph Gilligan (who lost his legs in a streetcar accident), Raymond Evans, Madison Drake, Andrew Murphy, Arthur Olin, Sarah Meyers, Carrie Ramsey, and Peter Searing; (second row) Irving Bartron, Charles Bartron, Winfield Monez, Edward Murphy, Florence Monez, and Freda Nunn; (third row) Guy Hill, Janet Ramsey, Agnes Murphy, Janet Fraser, Margaret O'Grady, and Lillian Ayers; (fourth row) Henry Parsons, Herman Garrabrant, Mollie Ramsey, Mollie Murphy, Mr. Albert Gordon (teacher and principal), and Edith Parsons. One hopes these children were generally happier than they look on this day, especially young Peter Searing on the right.

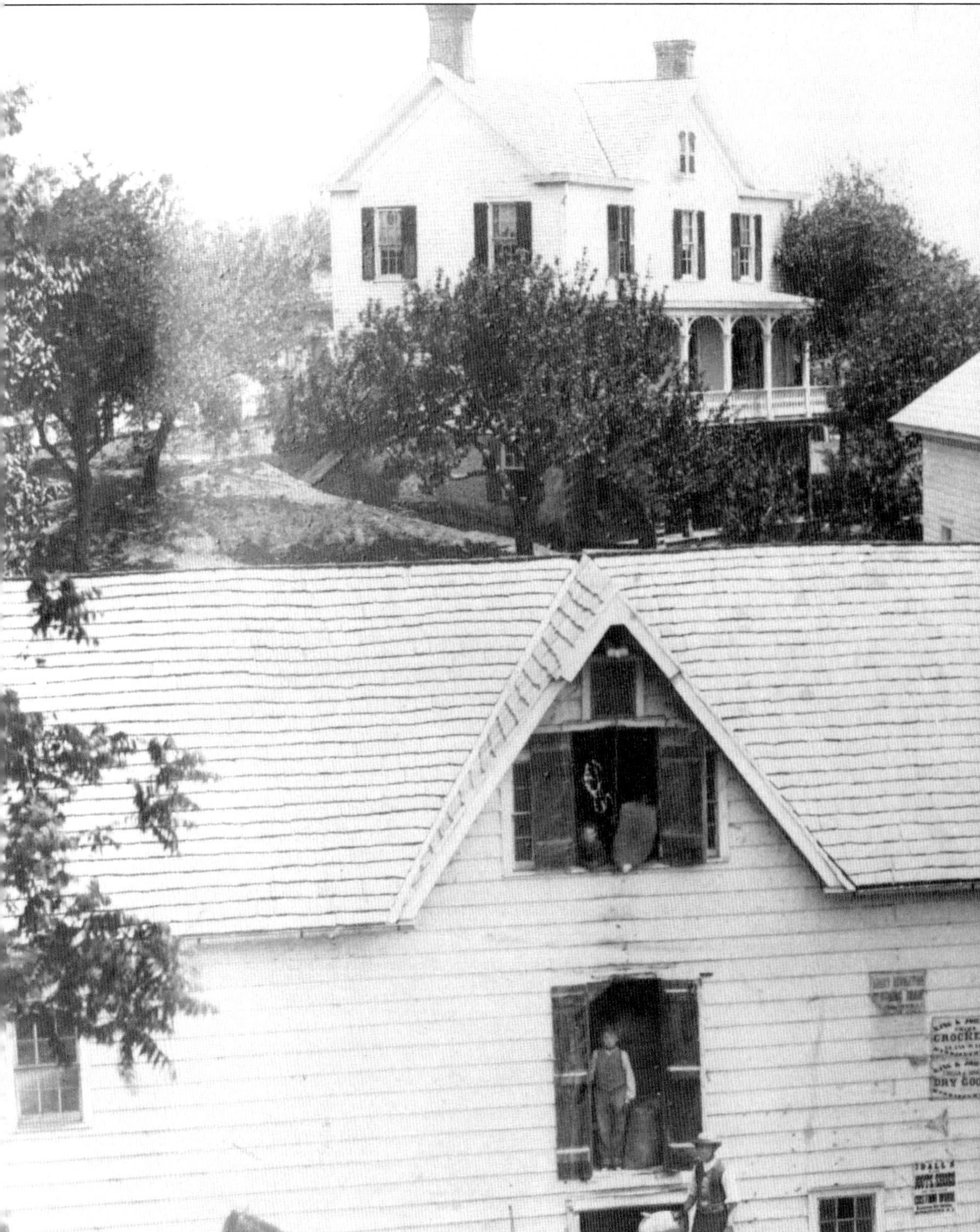

Jaqui's Gristmill, 1864. Early settlement on the Plains occurred along today's placid Watnong Brook, which provided power to run at least six forges and mills in the area. Shown is Jaqui's Gristmill at Hanover Avenue and Lake Valley Road. F.W. Jaqui's house is seen above the mill

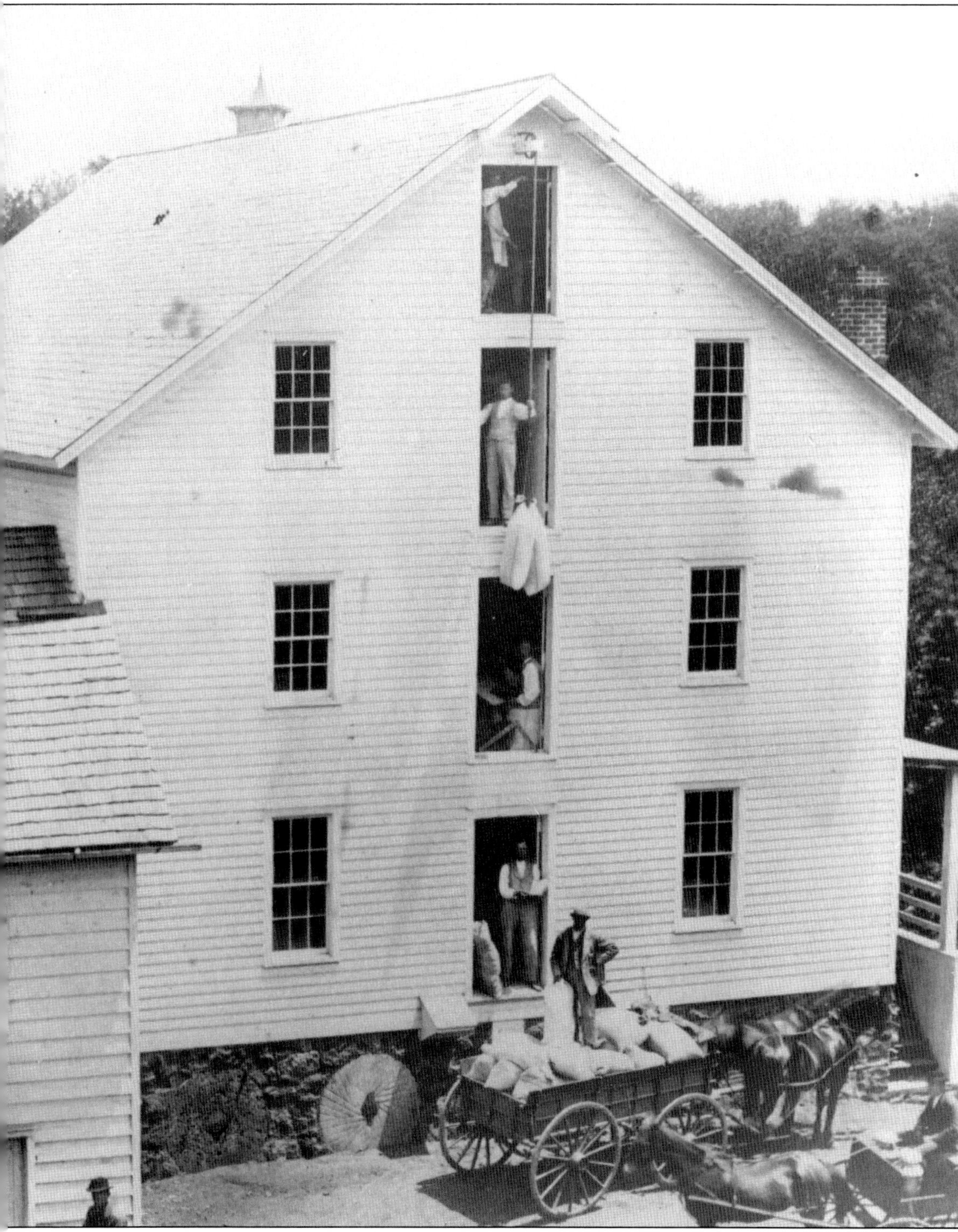

(later Dr. Edward Kessler's home). The mill is a hive of activity, with horse-drawn wagons being loaded with flour and feed. The mill's old foundation can still be seen today.

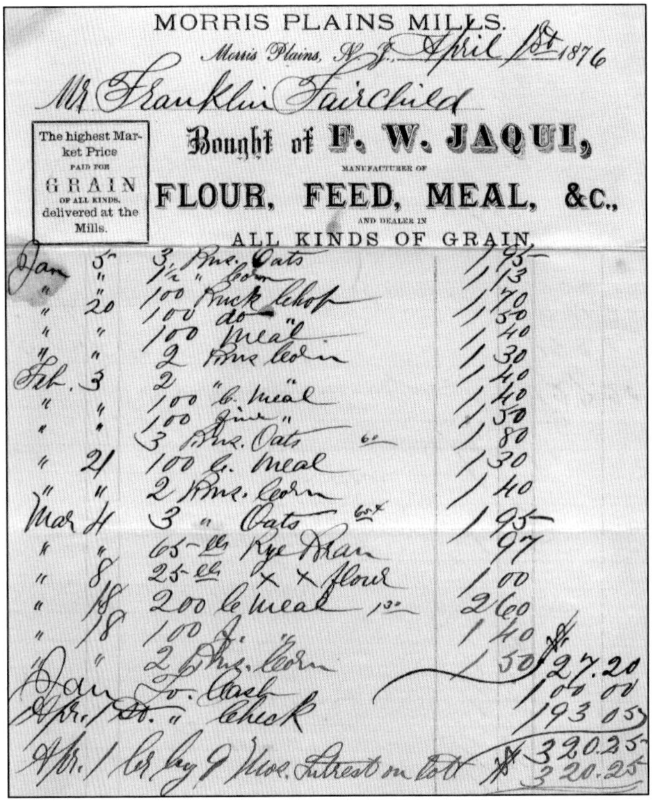
MORRIS PLAINS MILLS.
Morris Plains, N.J. April 1st 1876
Mr Franklin Fairchild
Bought of F. W. JAQUI,
MANUFACTURER OF
FLOUR, FEED, MEAL, &c.,
AND DEALER IN
ALL KINDS OF GRAIN.

The highest Market Price paid for GRAIN of all kinds, delivered at the Mills.

Date		Item	Amount
Jan	5	3 Bus. Oats	1 95
"	"	1/2 " Corn	1 13
"	20	100 Buck chop	1 70
"	"	100 do	1 50
"	"	100 Meal	1 40
"	"	2 Bus Corn	1 30
Feb.	3	2 "	1 40
"	"	100 C. Meal	1 40
"	"	100 fine "	1 50
"	"	3 Bus. Oats 60	1 80
"	21	100 C. Meal	1 30
"	"	2 Bus. Corn	1 40
Mar	4	3 " Oats 65	1 95
"	"	65 lbs Rye Bran	97
"	8	25 lbs x x flour	1 00
"	18	200 C. meal 130	2 60
"	18	100 f. "	1 40
"	"	2 Bus. Corn	1 50
			$27.20
Jan		To Cash	100 00
Apr. 1		To " Check	193 05
Apr. 1		Cr. by 9 Mos. Interest on "	$320.25
			320.25

"Bought of F.W. Jaqui." In 1876, Franklin Fairchild purchased more than 100 pounds of flour, feed, and meal for less than $10. His account was apparently in arrears, and he was charged interest on the unpaid balance—an early example of buying on credit.

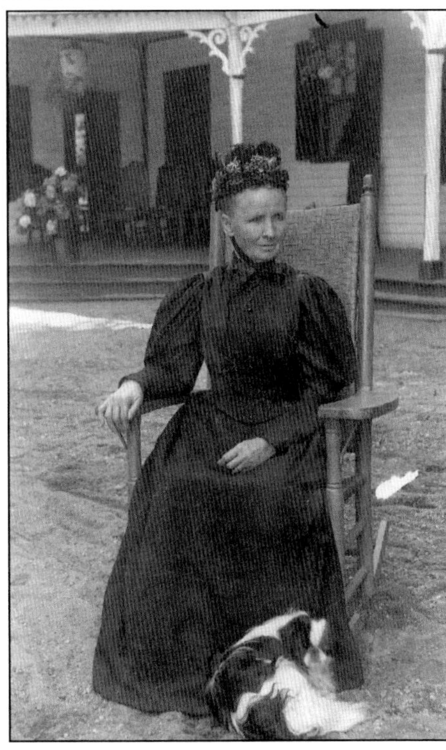

Granny Elliott. The lovely Granny Elliott poses for this picture on a visit to the Sires Farm in 1870. She is beautifully dressed and coiffed, and the fancy dog at her feet belies a modern conception of farm life in a small village. Today, Grannies often go visiting in blue jeans.

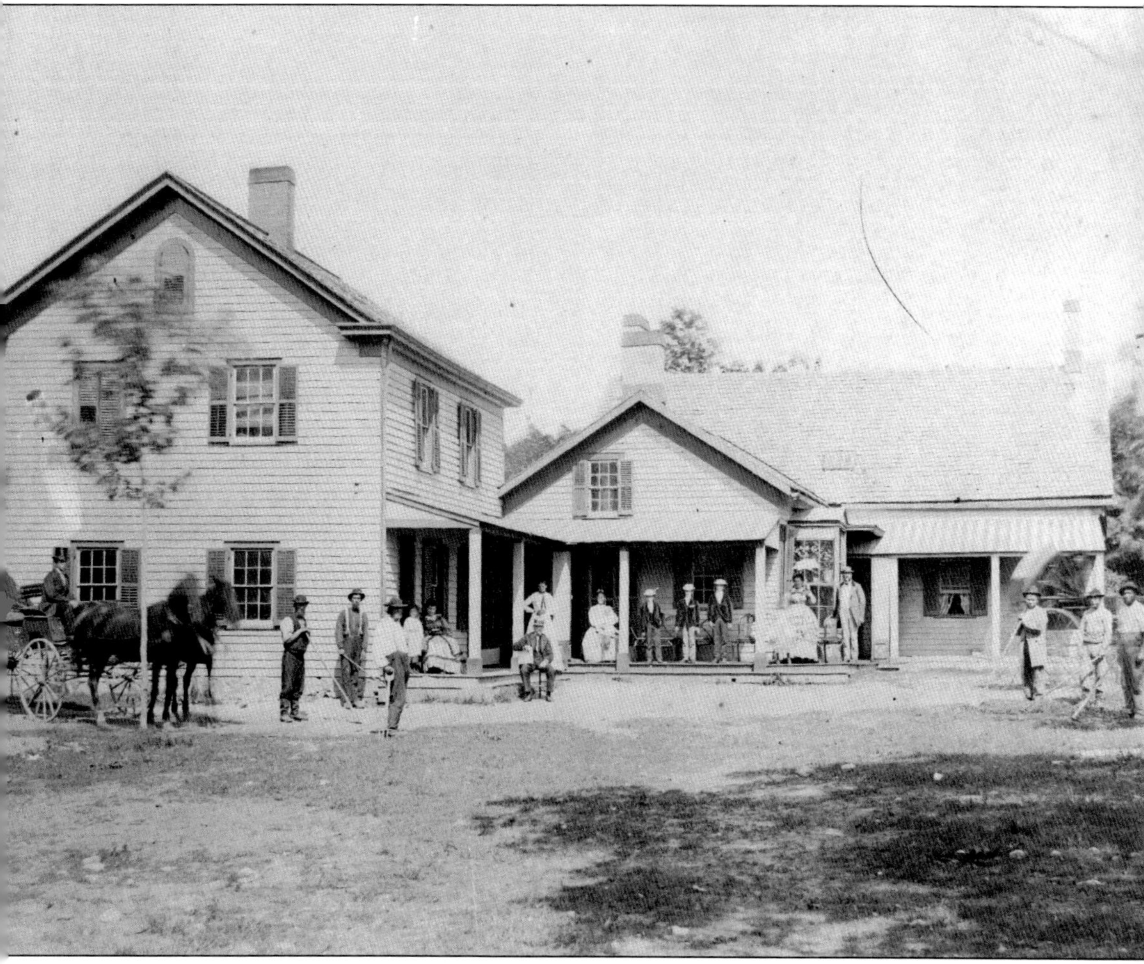

The Benjamin Sires Farm, 1871. The Sires farm was more luxurious than most farms of the era. It was located where Warner-Lambert now sits, just north of town on Tabor Road. Sires began his career as an itinerant peddler and ended up amassing a real estate empire, at one time holding 99 deeds in and around Morris Plains alone. He is pictured seated at center with his wife. His sons are standing in a row. Friends Mr. and Mrs. Henry B. Saline are at the right. Sires would later build a large mansion on this site.

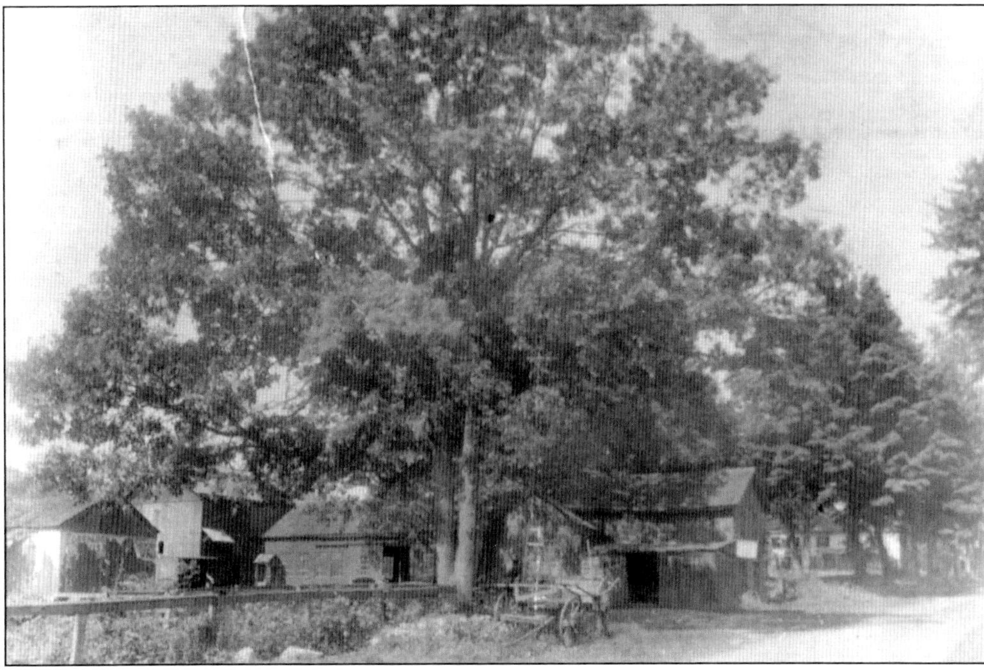

"UNDER A SPREADING CHESTNUT TREE THE VILLAGE SMITHY STOOD." The old poem by Longfellow might have been inspired by Peter Tunis's blacksmith shop, built in the mid-1800s. The shop and his home were located on Littleton Road near the corner of Mount Pleasant Turnpike (Route 10).

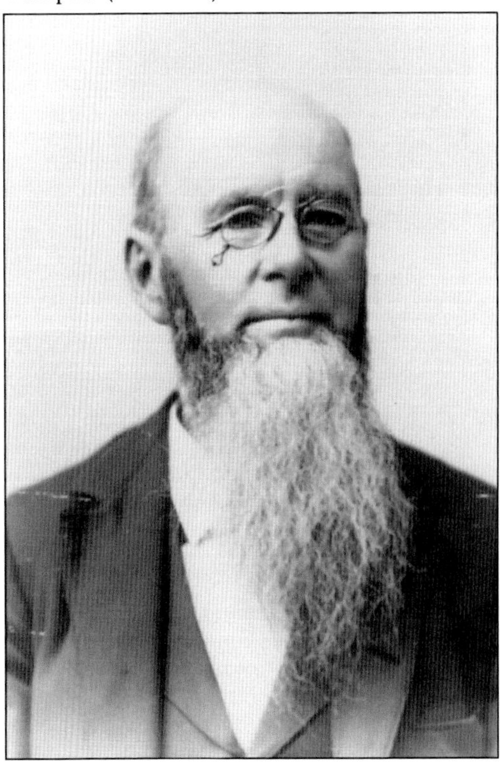

THE TUNIS MYSTERY. One day Peter Tunis, with his smithy days behind him at the age of 82, went on a walk and never came home. Advertisements were placed and handbills were circulated, but there was no response. Months later, a hunter found a body in southern New Jersey. "That's grandpa for sure," the family declared. "You can tell by the shape of his head." But at the funeral, a woman showed up to claim the body as that of her husband. That was the end of the matter for 60 years, until 1974, when a sewer excavation turned up a long-dead body on Watnong Drive. Could it be Peter Tunis, after all this time? Local historian Carl Scherzer thought so. But this was long before DNA testing, and no one can know for sure what happened that fateful day when Grandpa Tunis strolled into the mists of history without a trace.

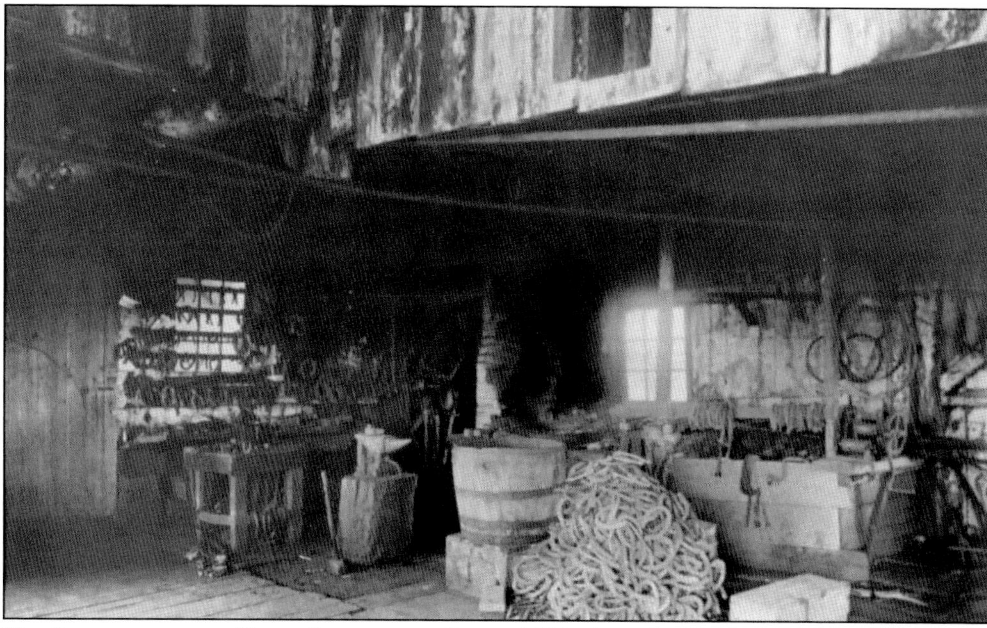

THE INTERIOR OF THE TUNIS BLACKSMITH SHOP, 1870. A stack of horseshoes is somehow more poetic than a pile of old tires.

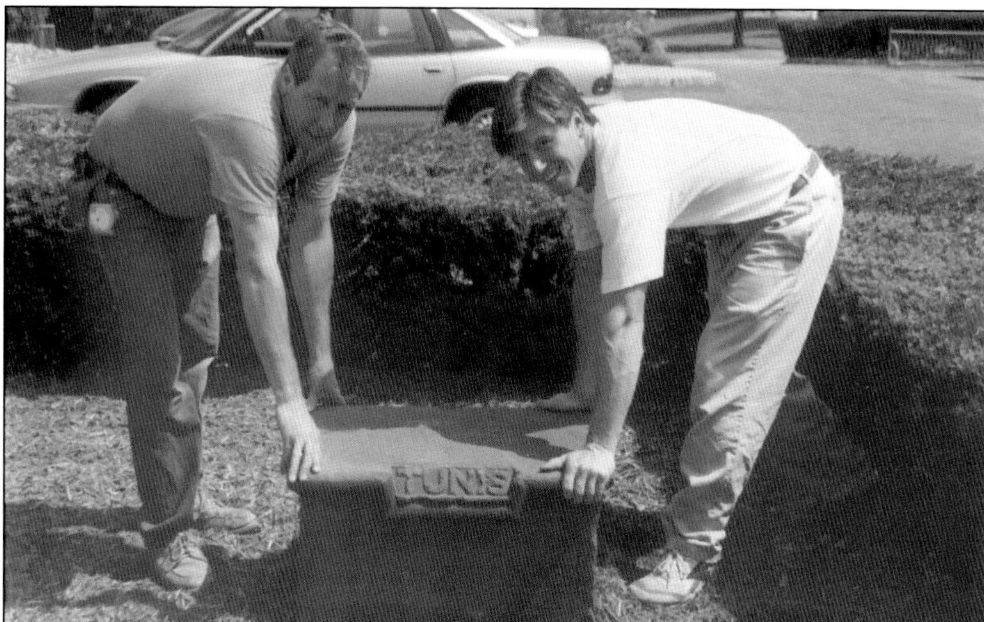

GOODBYE TO LITTLETON. In 1997, town historian Dan Myers, longtime Plainsman Bob Carroll, and museum president Virginia Vogt set out to record what was left of the tiny village of Littleton before it was plowed under to make way for the Edwards Supermarket. Five or six falling-down structures with dank, boarded-up rooms were duly photographed. Then, smothered in tall weeds, this carriage stone was found. With the help of Jimmy and Eric Maw, the only remaining trace of the Tunis family in Littleton was moved to the grounds of the Morris Plains Library and Museum.

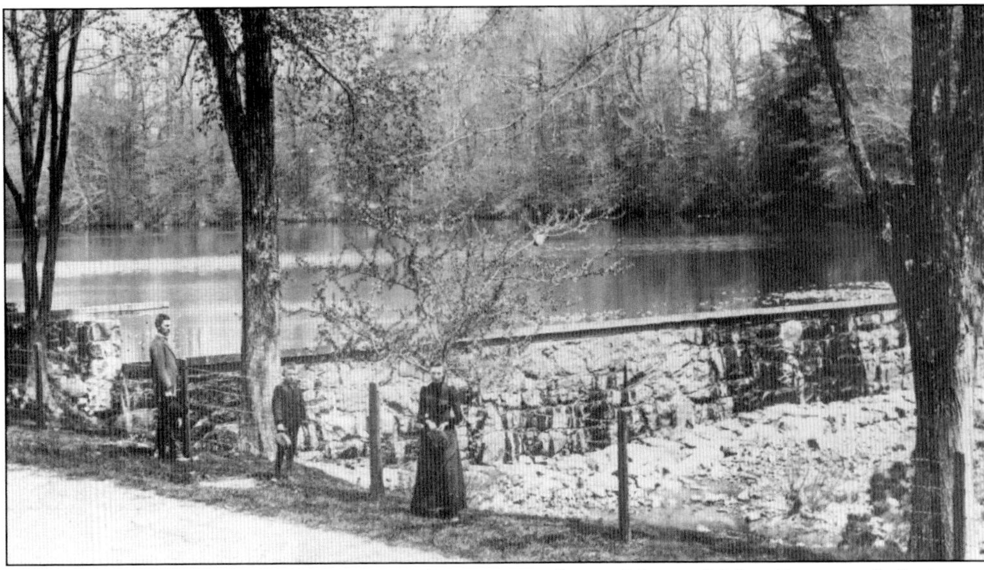

BRANT'S POND, TODAY A BALLPARK. This picture shows Mr. and Mrs. Brant and their son, James, by their peaceful mill pond *c.* 1900. Brant's mill lay below F.W. Jaqui's mill on the Watnong Brook. In 1919, a raging "hundred-years storm" caused Jaqui to open his floodgates to save his dam. The unrestrained Watnong barreled downstream, destroying Brant's dam and sweeping away the pond. The flood permanently changed the course of the brook. There is now a ballpark on the former site of Brant's Pond (at Lake Valley Road near Mill Road).

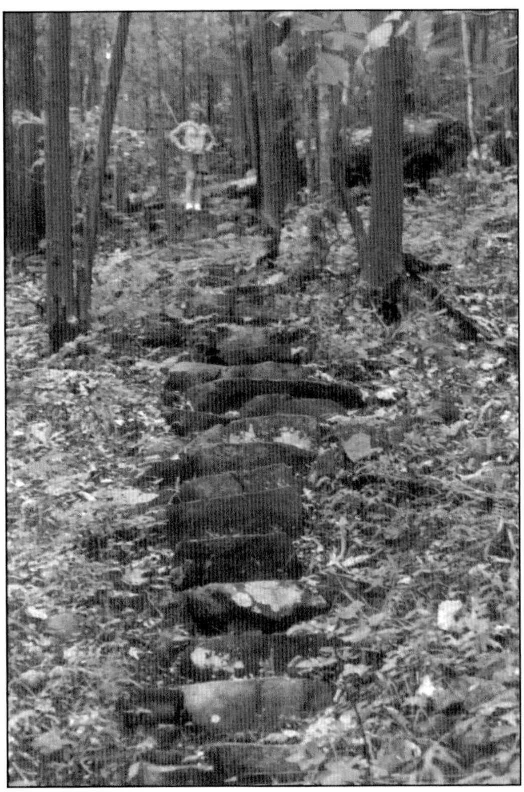

THE STONE STEPS TO THE TOP OF WATNONG MOUNTAIN. The "300 stone steps" have attracted Morris Plains children for generations. But who built them? Was it Native Americans? Did revolutionaries build them as part of a mountain-to-mountain warning system for George Washington? Some historians credit the latter theory, as there may be similar sites on other high points all the way to New York Harbor, where American spies once watched for an expected British invasion.

Two

A Certain House

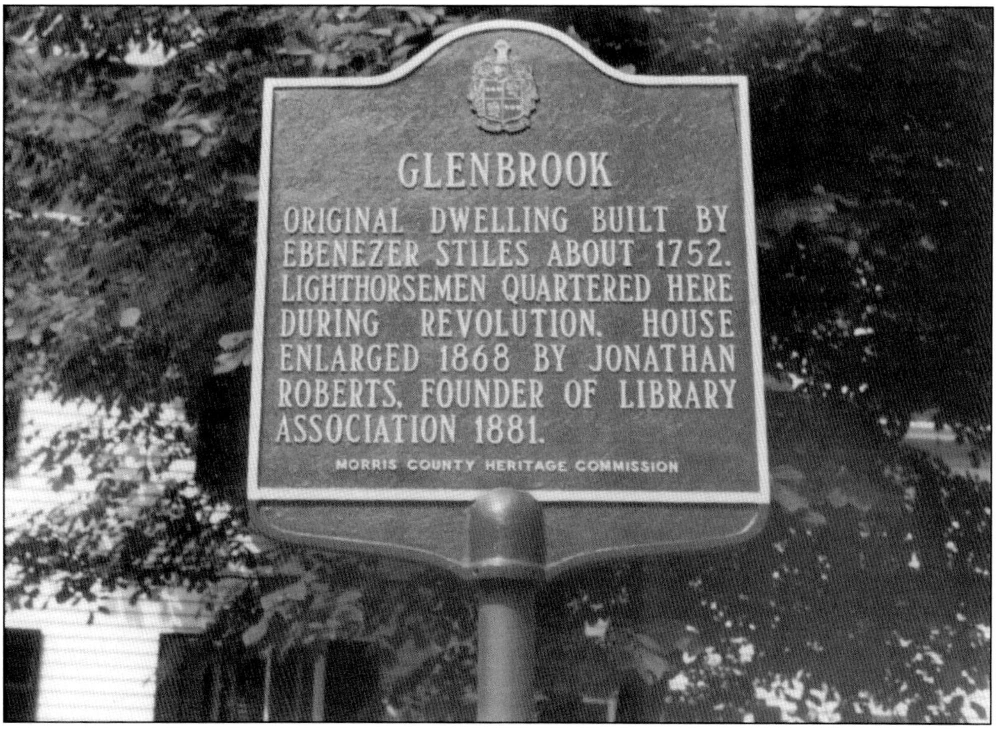

On This Spot. About 250 years ago, Ebenezer Stiles acquired 80 acres of Timothy Peck's original land grant and built a country home to house his wife and 11 children. After his death in 1814, Ebenezer's property was divided among his many sons. Two generations later, Lewis Stiles reassembled the pieces of the original farm, buying land from the other heirs and extending the farm's economic activities to include a tannery. But his only child was not interested in the farm, and that was the end of the Stiles family in the old homestead at the bend of the road.

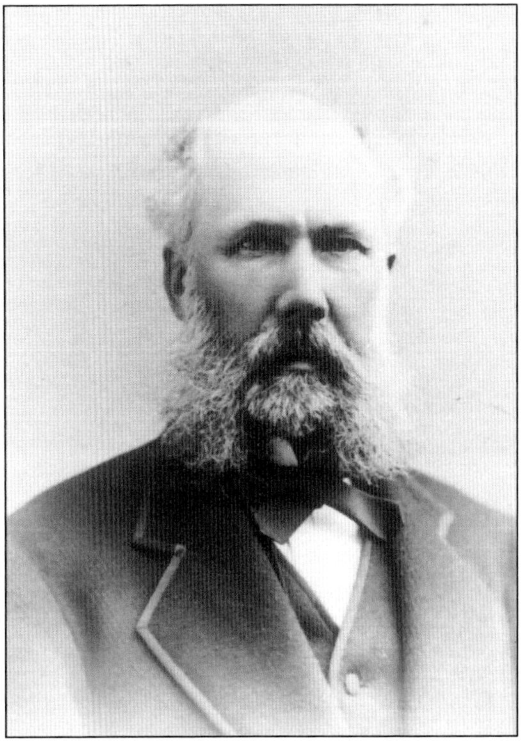

JONATHAN W. ROBERTS "RETIRES" TO THE PLAINS. In 1867, a stranger came to Morris Plains. Jonathan W. Roberts had been a successful businessman before his doctor ordered him to retire to the country for health reasons at age 45. Thus Roberts's fate became entwined with a certain old house. He decided to buy the Stiles farm from the moment he saw it. But first he had to sell the idea to his wife.

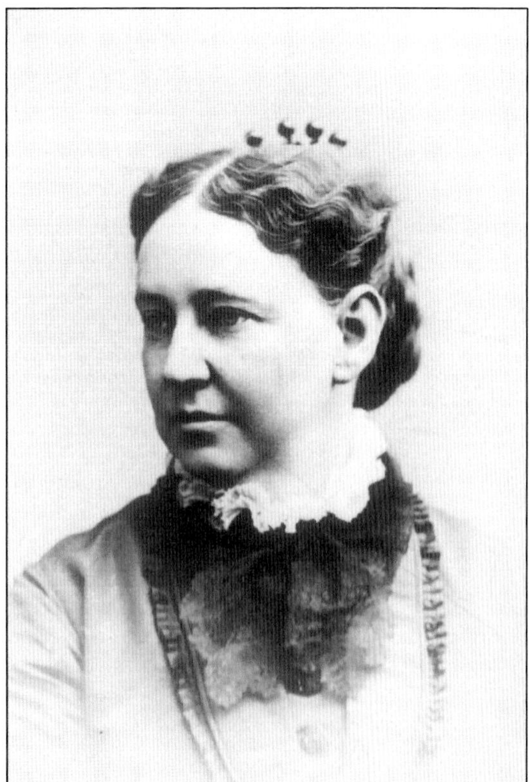

MARY KING ROBERTS CAPITULATES. Jonathan Roberts's wife had no interest in living on a farm. But Jonathan, talented salesman that he was, led Mary along an overgrown path where the Watnong Brook gradually revealed itself in all its long-ago glory. Tradition states that Mary Roberts sealed her fate with the exclamation, "I want that brook."

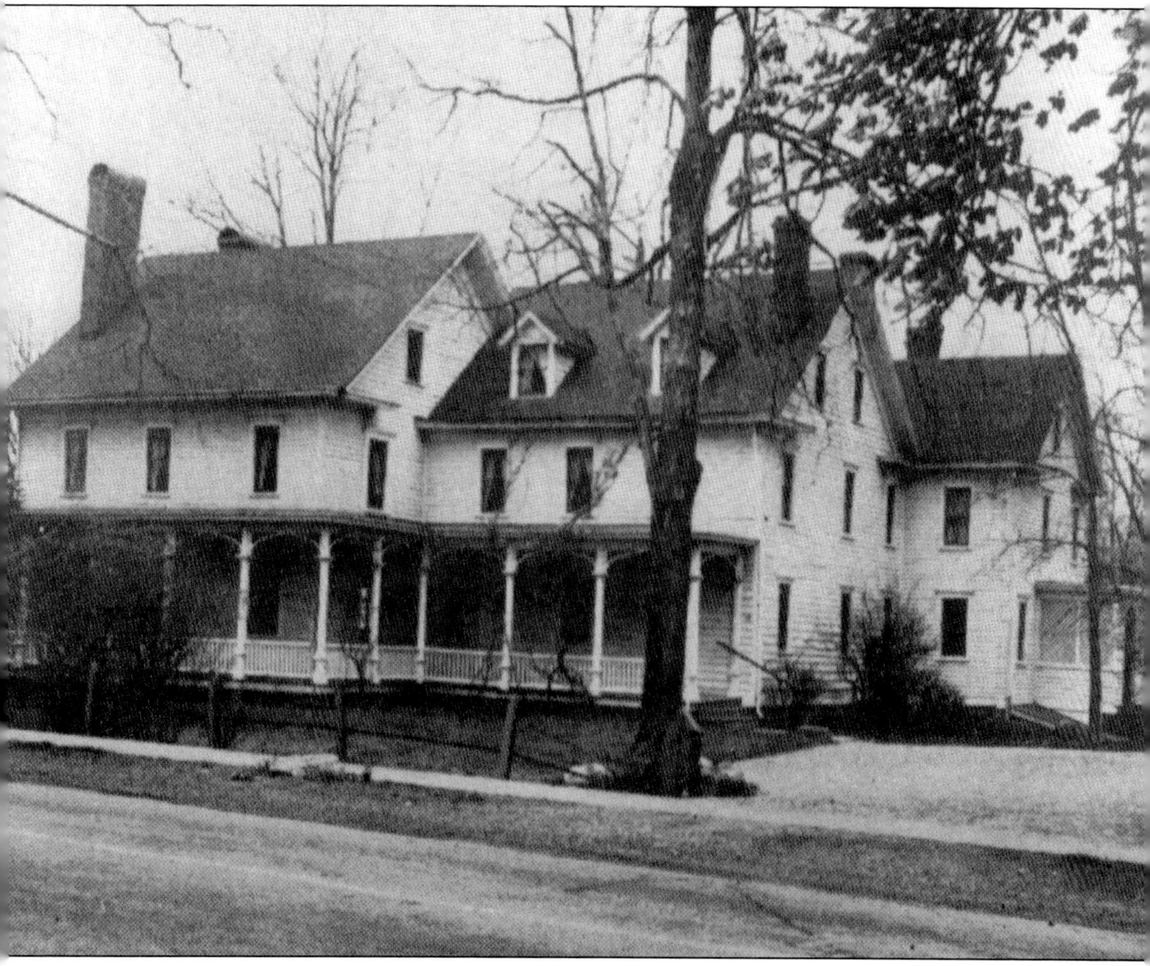

What Jonathan Roberts Wrought. Upon taking possession of the old Stiles place, Roberts went into action. He moved another Stiles home from across the road and attached it to the main house. A new kitchen wing and large porches were then added. He altered the course of the Watnong and moved the dam. In all, Roberts changed the locations of 17 buildings. Mary Roberts named the farm-cum-country estate Glenbrook. In this late-1800s picture, the original homestead is on the left, Lewis B. Stiles's former residence is to the front right, and the Roberts wing is in back.

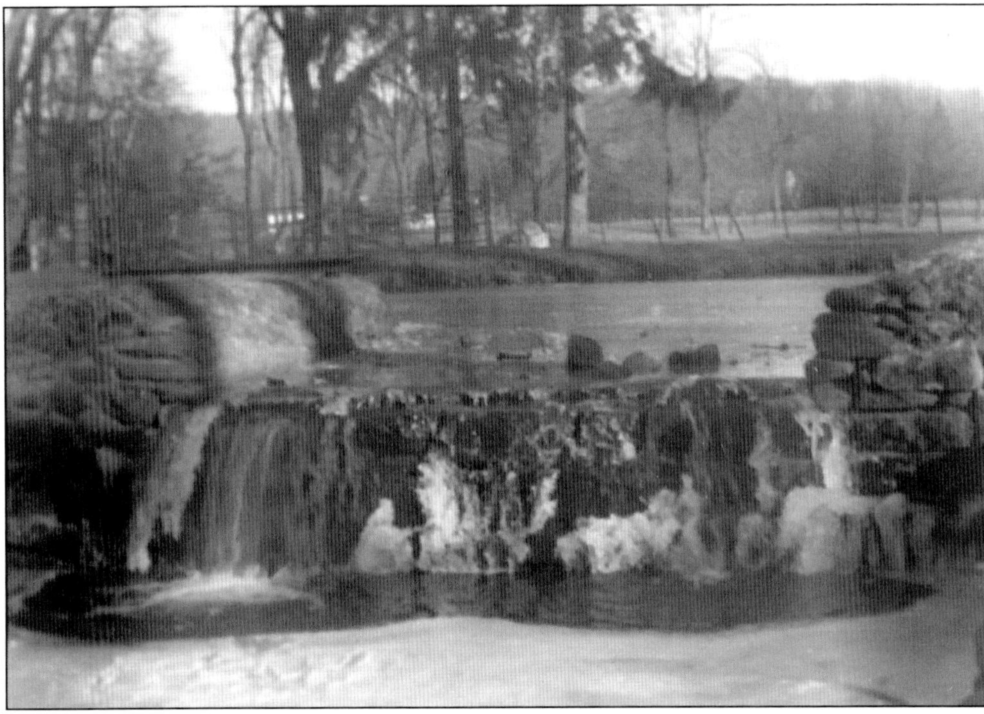

The Pond at Glenbrook. This view of the pond and dam at Glenbrook was taken in the winter of 1939–1940. It suggests that the Watnong Brook had considerably more flow then.

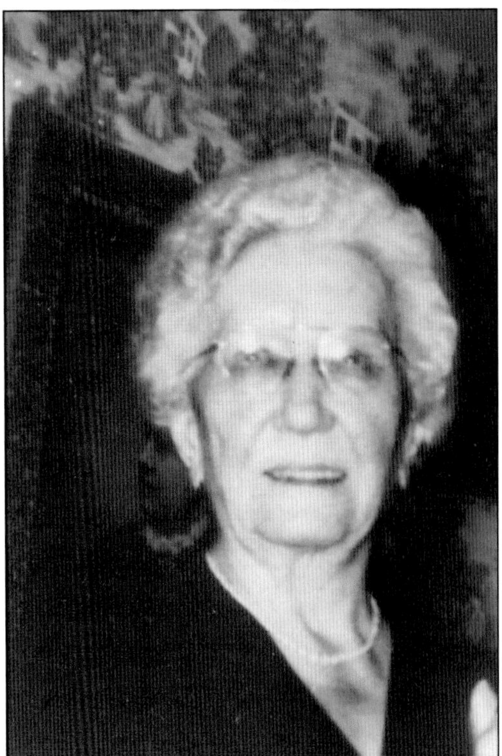

Mrs. Altha Hatch Cutler. After years of contributing generously to her adopted community, Mary Roberts died in 1894. Jonathan Roberts asked his niece, Altha Hatch, to help him manage Glenbrook. When Roberts died in 1912, his niece inherited the property. Miss Hatch later married Judge Willard Cutler and was active in charity work and historical preservation. She was an honorary member of the Washington Association and curator of the Ford Mansion, among many other achievements.

Mrs. Cutler's Field, 1936. An unidentified boy stands in front of Mrs. Cutler's field. In the background are Mrs. Cutler's cow, Babe, and James McNeil's horse, Peter Pan. (McNeil was the caretaker at Glenbrook.)

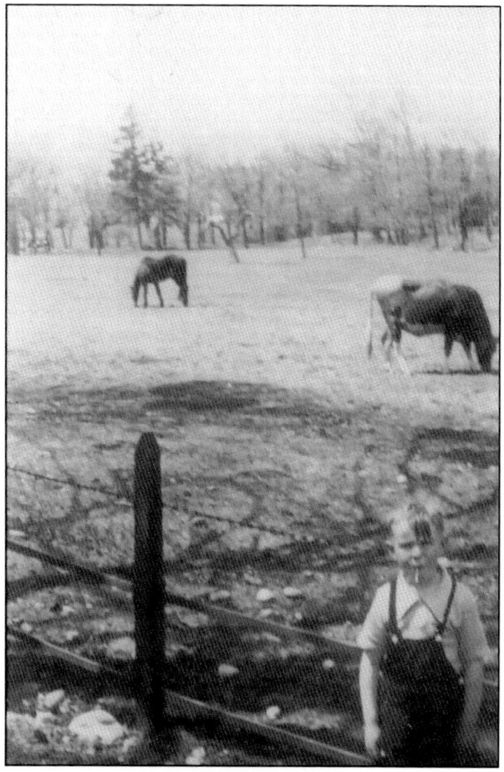

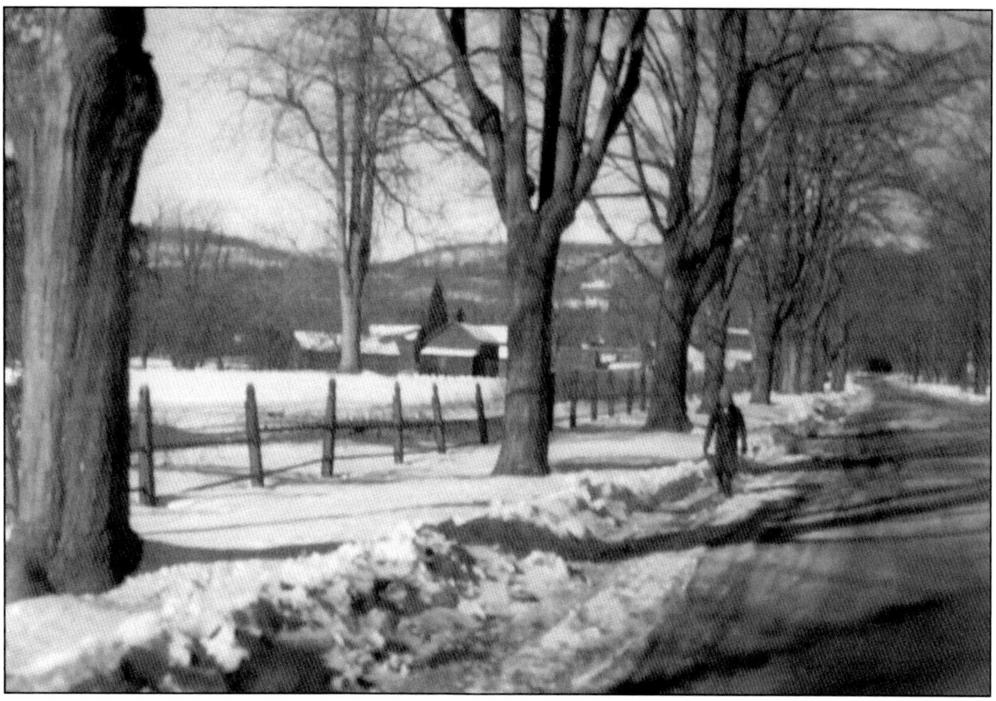

A Long-Ago Snowy Day. A boy who is identified as "Mr. E. Wilson's son" is walking toward Glenbrook Road along Mountain Way. Note the Roberts-Cutler barns in the back of the field.

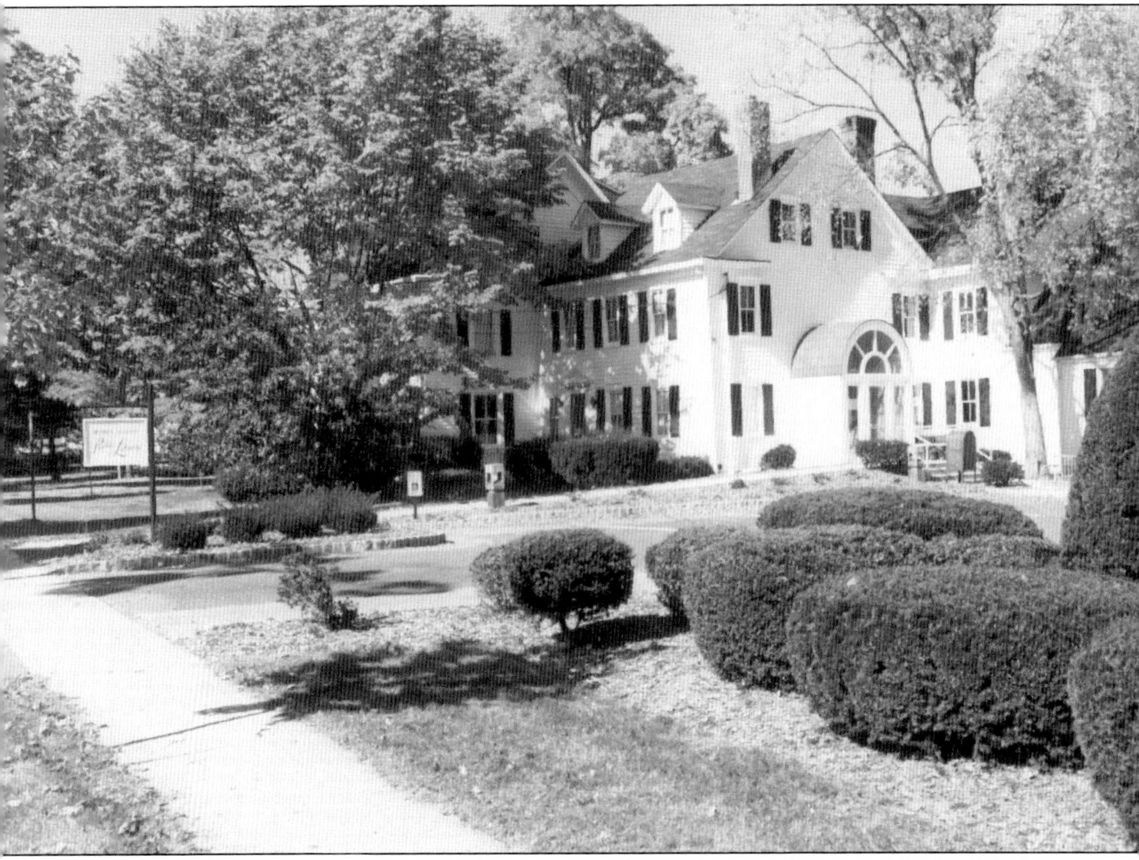

THE ROBERTS-CUTLER LEGACY. When Mrs. Cutler died in 1963 at age 95, she left the old Stiles homestead, transformed into Glenbrook by the Robertses, to the Morris Plains Library Association. Mrs. Cutler's field became Roberts Garden, a lovely town park. Jonathan and Mary Roberts would surely be pleased at the fate of their beloved Glenbrook, as they were both avid supporters of early libraries in Morris Plains. (Mrs. Roberts died while tending the library she started in the old tannery building on Glenbrook's grounds.)

Three

A Sleepy Village Stirs

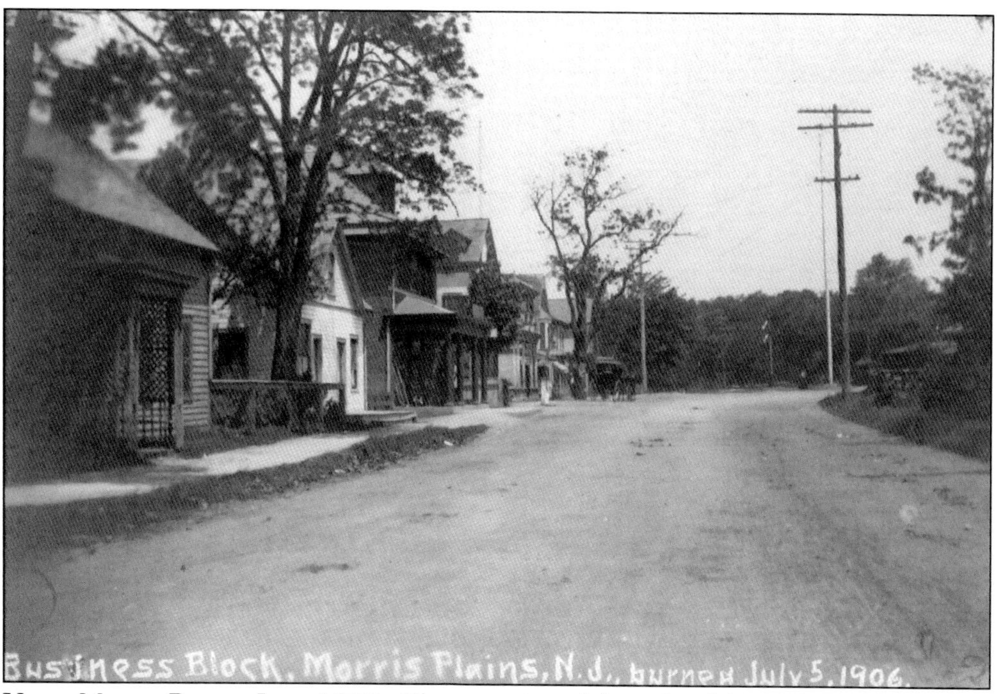

Upper Morris Plains, Late 1800s. The extension of the railroad from Morristown in 1847 focused attention on upper Morris Plains, and a small business section slowly began to develop across from the station. Jacob Young's provisions store was on the corner of Jaqui Avenue by 1780. By the time of this picture, Young's store had passed to Isaac Clark, and Clark had sold it to his clerk, Daniel M. Merchant. It is the farthest building in the distance. Other businesses were the Wiese Hotel and the J.C. Layer Butcher Shop.

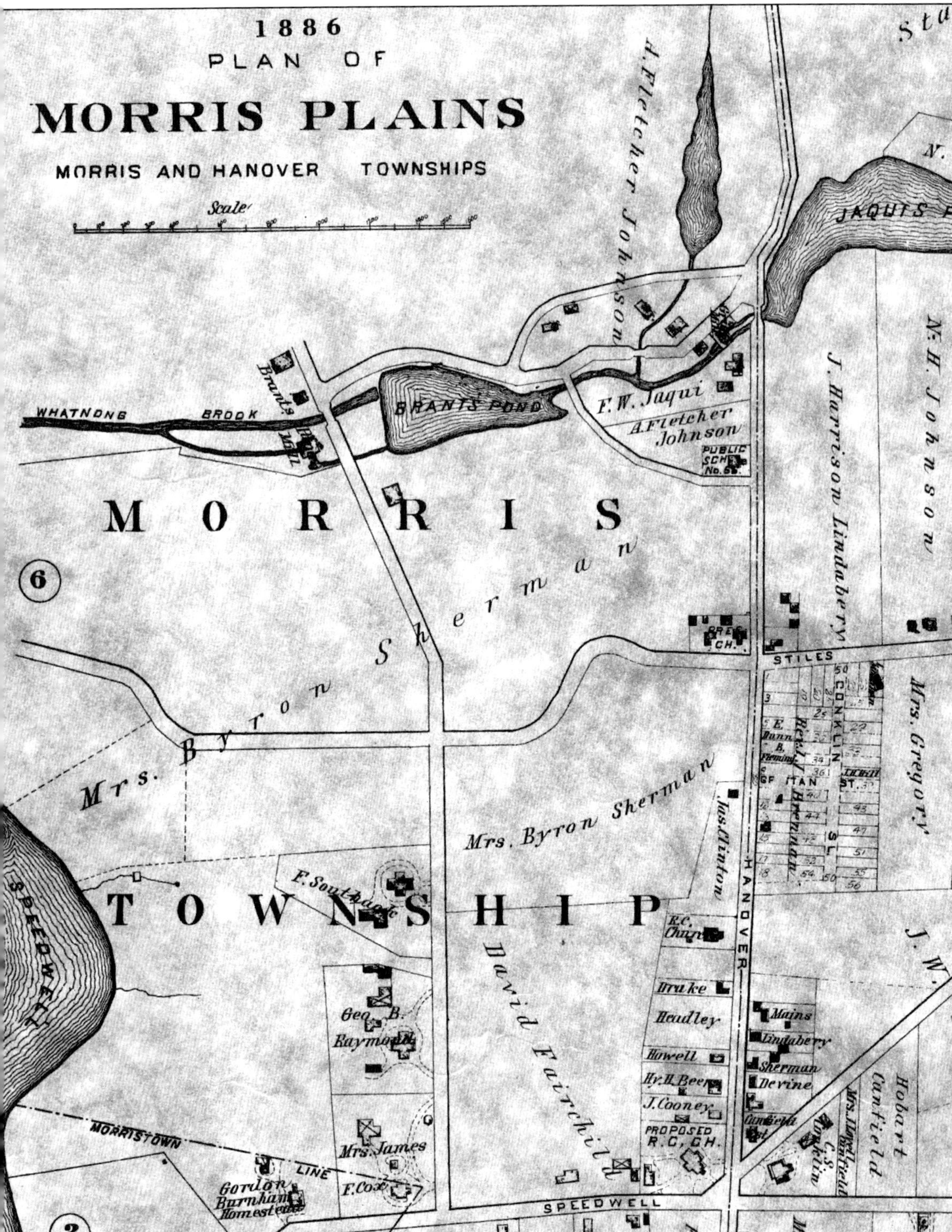

Development in 1887. This map shows the original settlement around Five Corners, the large estates and the developing commerce section and subdivisions to the north. (*E. Robinson's Atlas*

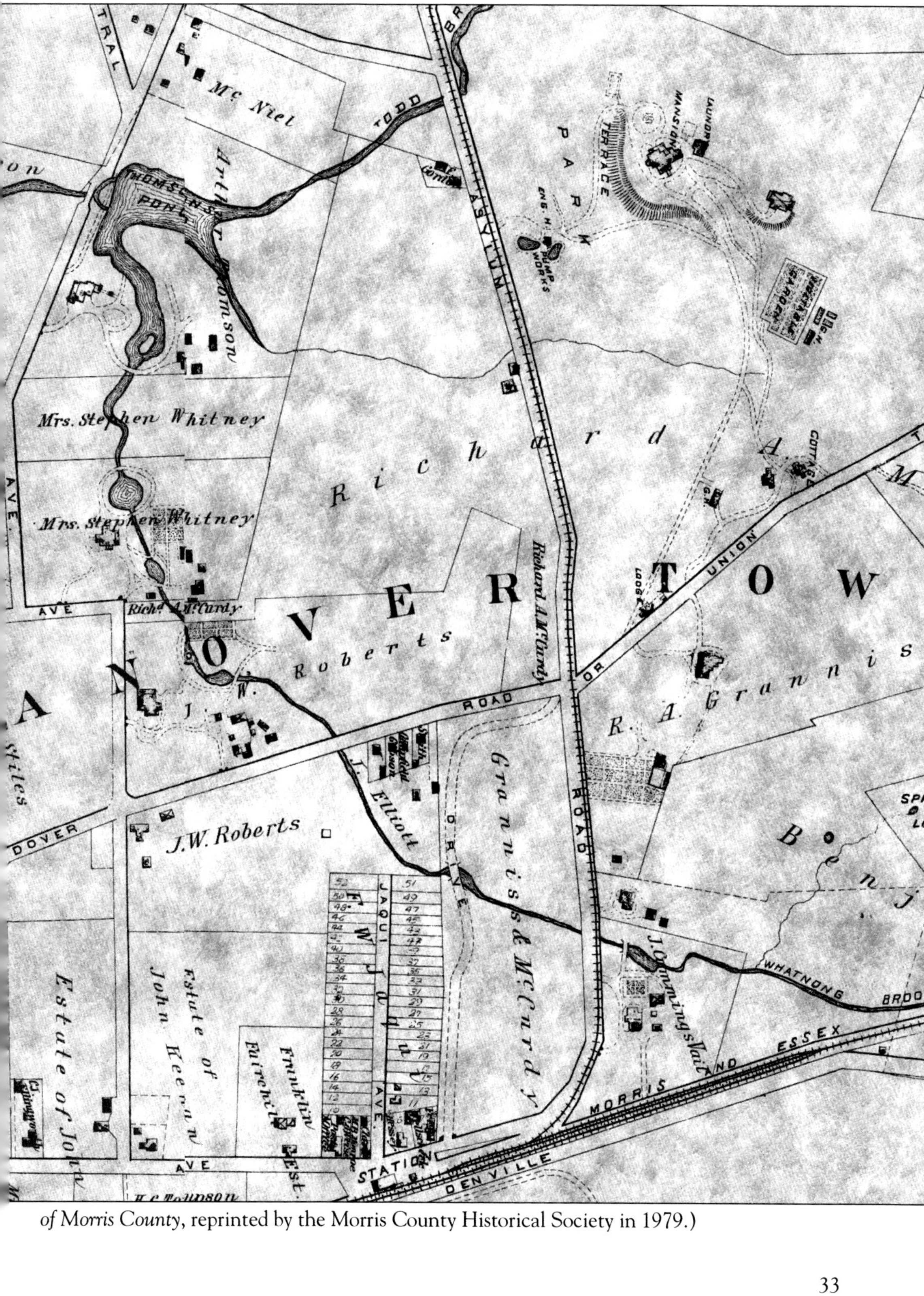

of *Morris County*, reprinted by the Morris County Historical Society in 1979.)

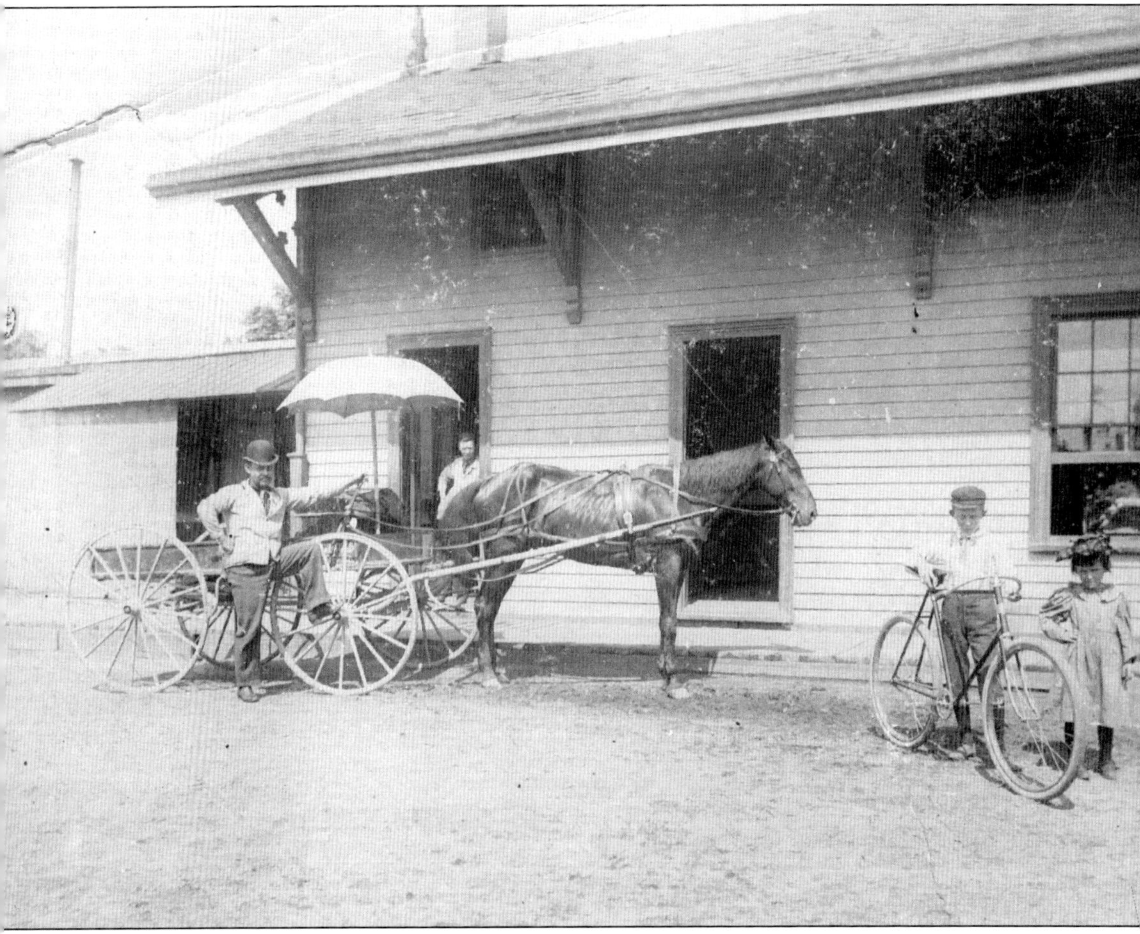

THE FRONT OF THE RAILROAD STATION, 1896. The railroad, which was extended to Morris Plains in 1848, transported everything from passengers and mail to cattle and coal. The railroad station pictured here was built in 1868 and replaced two earlier make-do structures. It must have been an exciting place to hang around, as the children in the picture appear to be doing.

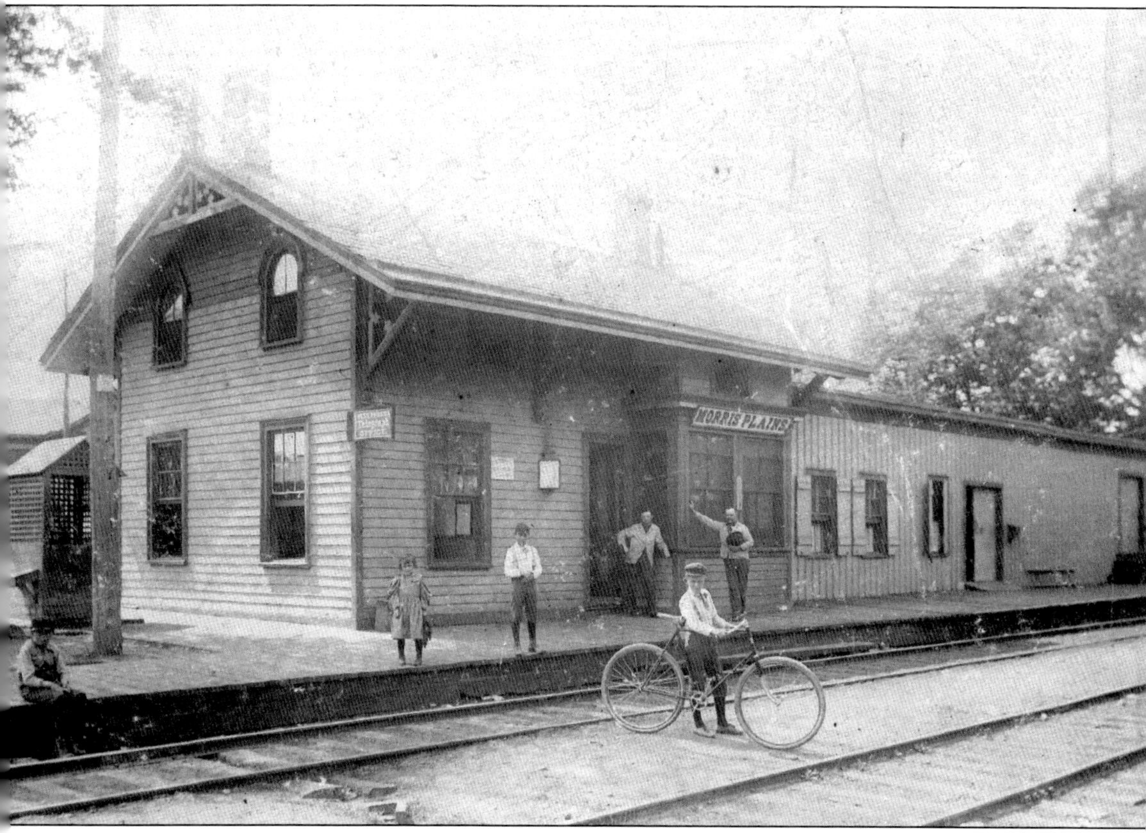

THE BACK OF THE RAILROAD STATION, 1896. The station was located approximately where the building that houses the model railroad club (the old freight building) stands today. When the new station was constructed in 1915 (on the other side of Littleton Road, after the building of the overpass), the old station was purchased by James Elliott, who moved it to 51 Jaqui Avenue and converted it to a house. There it remains today.

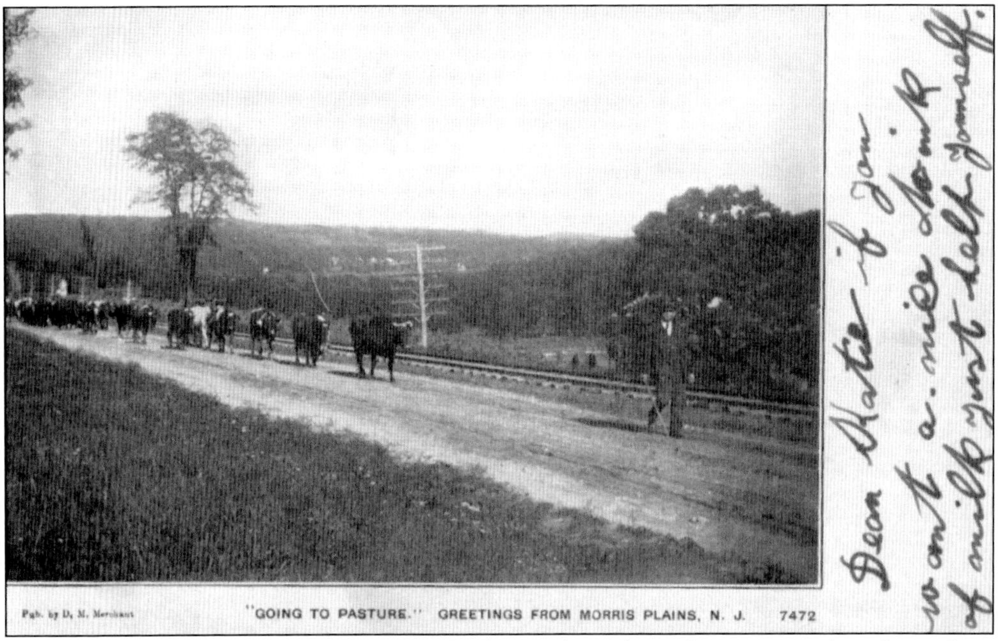

MILK ON THE HOOF. When a farmer bought livestock in those days, it was often shipped via rail. The farmer met the train and herded the cattle home. The cows would need milking after their long trip, and the farmer knew there would be neighbors waiting to do the job for the free milk.

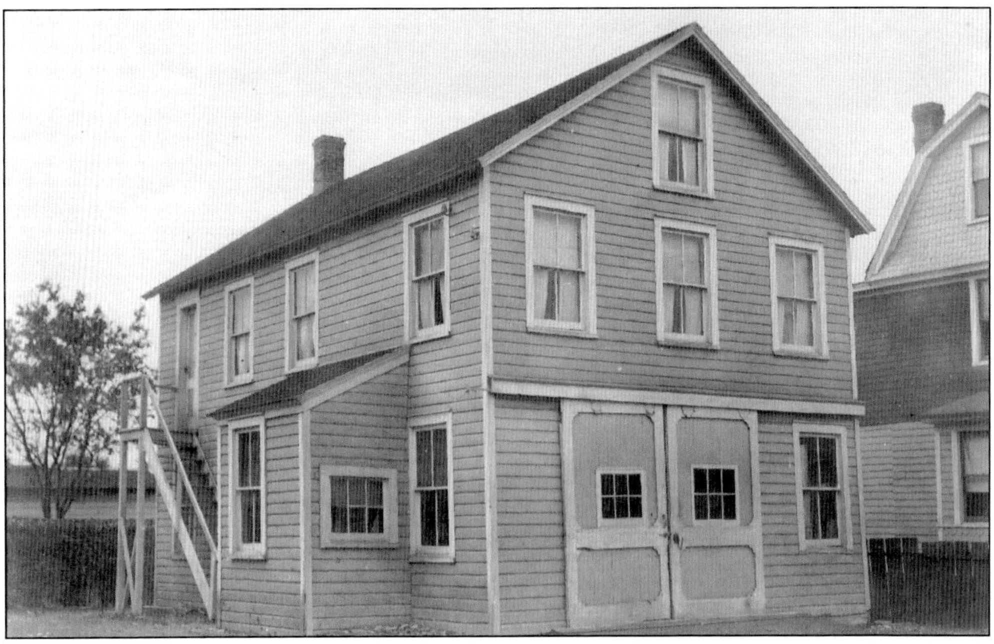

JOE TUNIS'S BLACKSMITH SHOP. Another business near the train station was Joe Tunis's blacksmith and carriage shop on the corner of Franklin Place and Speedwell Avenue. Later, as Morris Plains developed, his shop was moved farther down on Franklin so that the building now housing Arthur's Restaurant could be built. Tunis also built the small house that still stands next to Arthur's.

JOE TUNIS, THE BLACKSMITH. Joe was the son of Peter Tunis, the blacksmith at Littleton who disappeared early in the century. Joe was 90 years old when this picture was taken and lived to be 94. He admitted to being quite the horse fancier as a young man and attributed his longevity to decades of hard labor as a blacksmith.

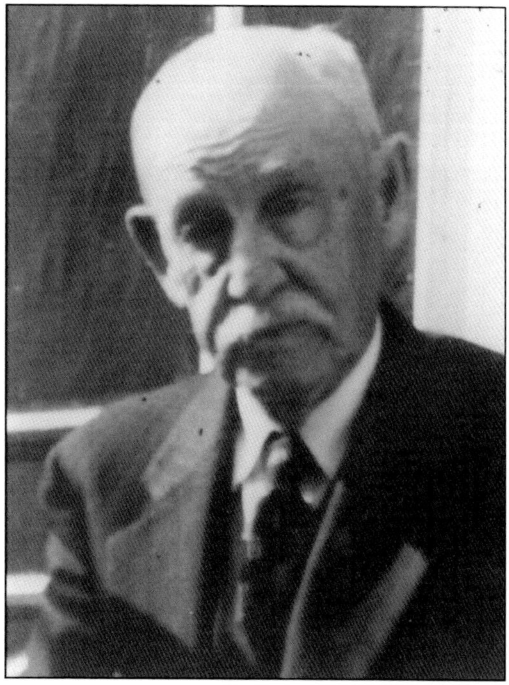

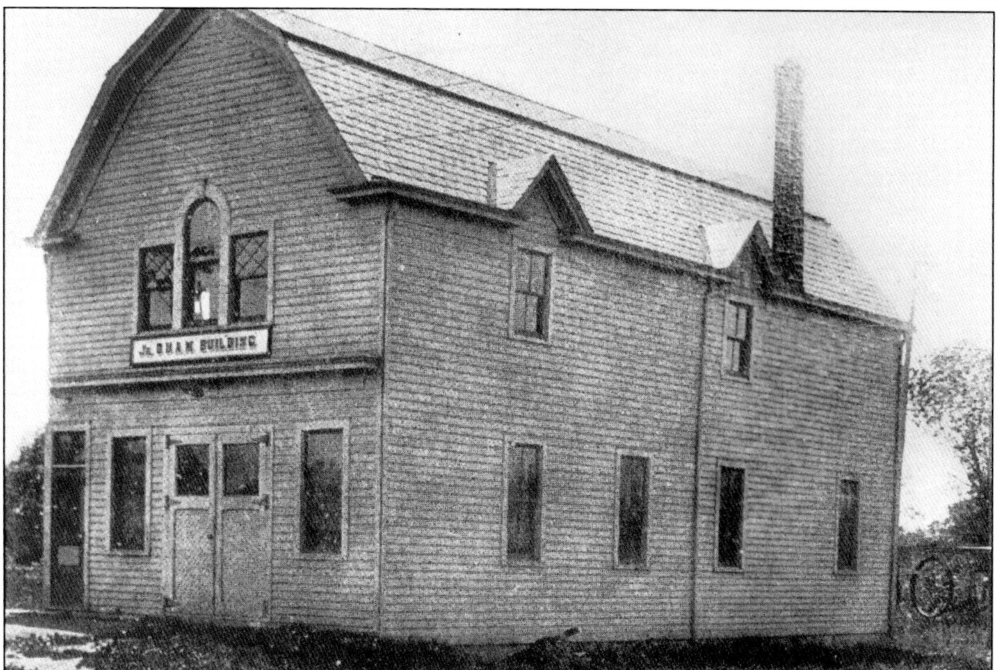

A BUILDING WITH MANY TALES TO TELL. The Junior Order of United American Mechanics (JOUAM) hall was built in the late 1800s by a group concerned about the growing influx of immigrants. In practice, its use was more inclusive. For more than 100 years, town meetings, social events and entertainments of all kinds were held there. The JOUAM building was also home to several churches in their formative years and served as the first firehouse. Note the iron ring (a railroad car wheel) on the right. The ring served as the town fire alarm.

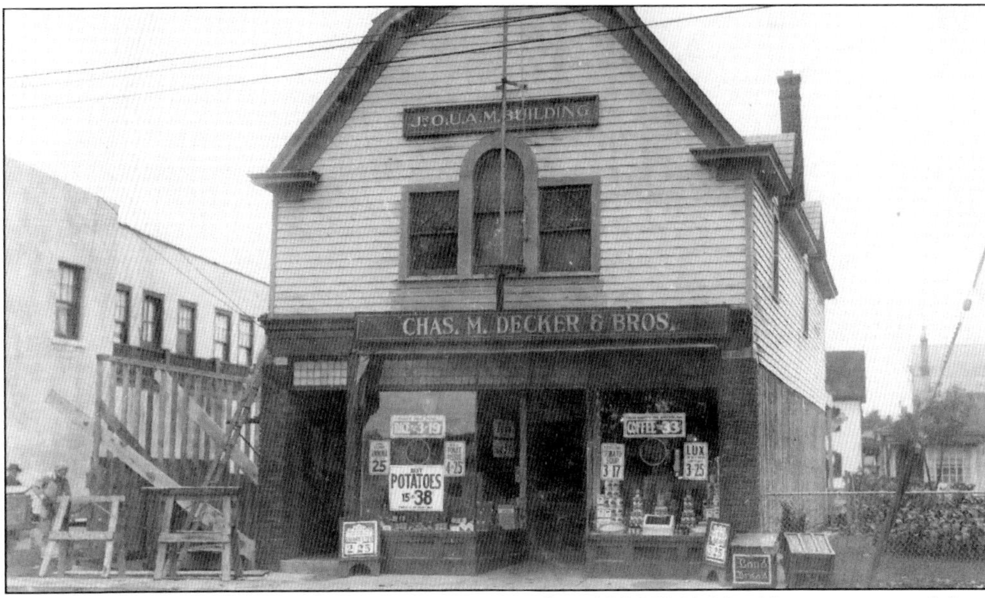

THE JOUAM IN A NEW INCARNATION. In 1920, the old JOUAM building was moved from its location on Franklin Place to 662 Speedwell Avenue. There it was enlarged and began a new life as a retail establishment, housing (at various times) Charles M. Decker & Brothers, Richard's 5 & 10¢ to $1 Store, and Pennec's Electronics. In 1994, it narrowly escaped disaster in the fire that destroyed the building next-door.

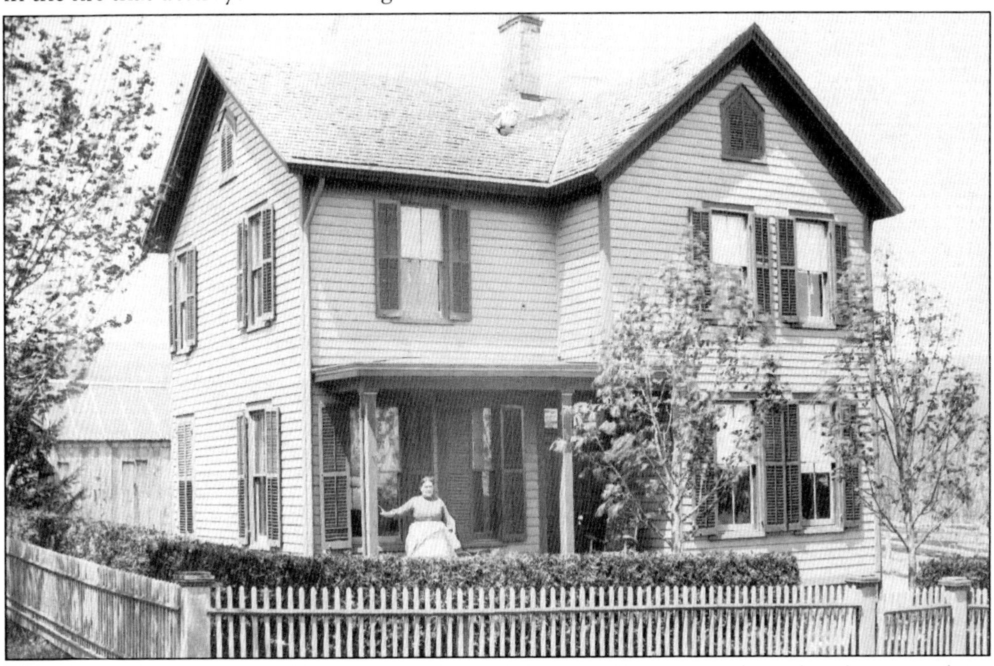

THE COFFEY HOMESTEAD, WILSONVILLE, 1907. Margaret Coffey stands on her front porch in her neat farm cottage. Wilsonville (originally Willisonville) was a small village spread along the south side of West Hanover Avenue in the late 1800s. Many of the early inhabitants were Catholic, and the local fishmonger found it worth his while to make a Friday trip out to Wilsonville, which he dubbed "Mackerelville."

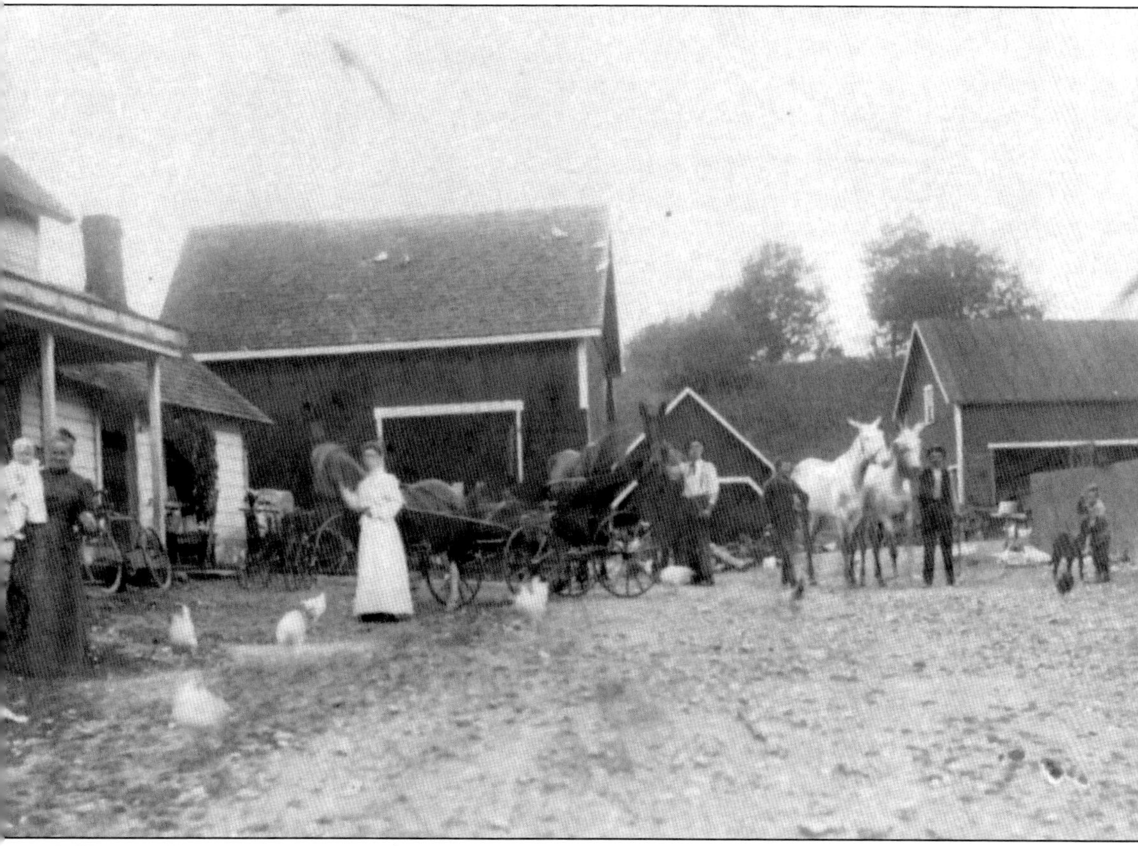

A Typical Working Farm. As the new century approached, the Morris Plains countryside was still dotted with small farms. Here at the Evans Farm on Lake Valley Road in 1905, everyone turns out to be photographed, including chickens, donkeys, and horses. Posing with the farm animals, from left to right, are Phebe Stiles Evans (holding Christine A. Evans, the daughter of Martha and Edwin), Martha Hudson Evans, Daniel Bishop Evans, Daniel Evans Jr., and his brother Edwin Merritt. The child with the goat is cousin Raymond Evans. To take a step back in time, drive (or bicycle) out Lake Valley Road. The remnants of the Evans farm still exist, with a horse at pasture and a chicken or two to greet you, just as in times past.

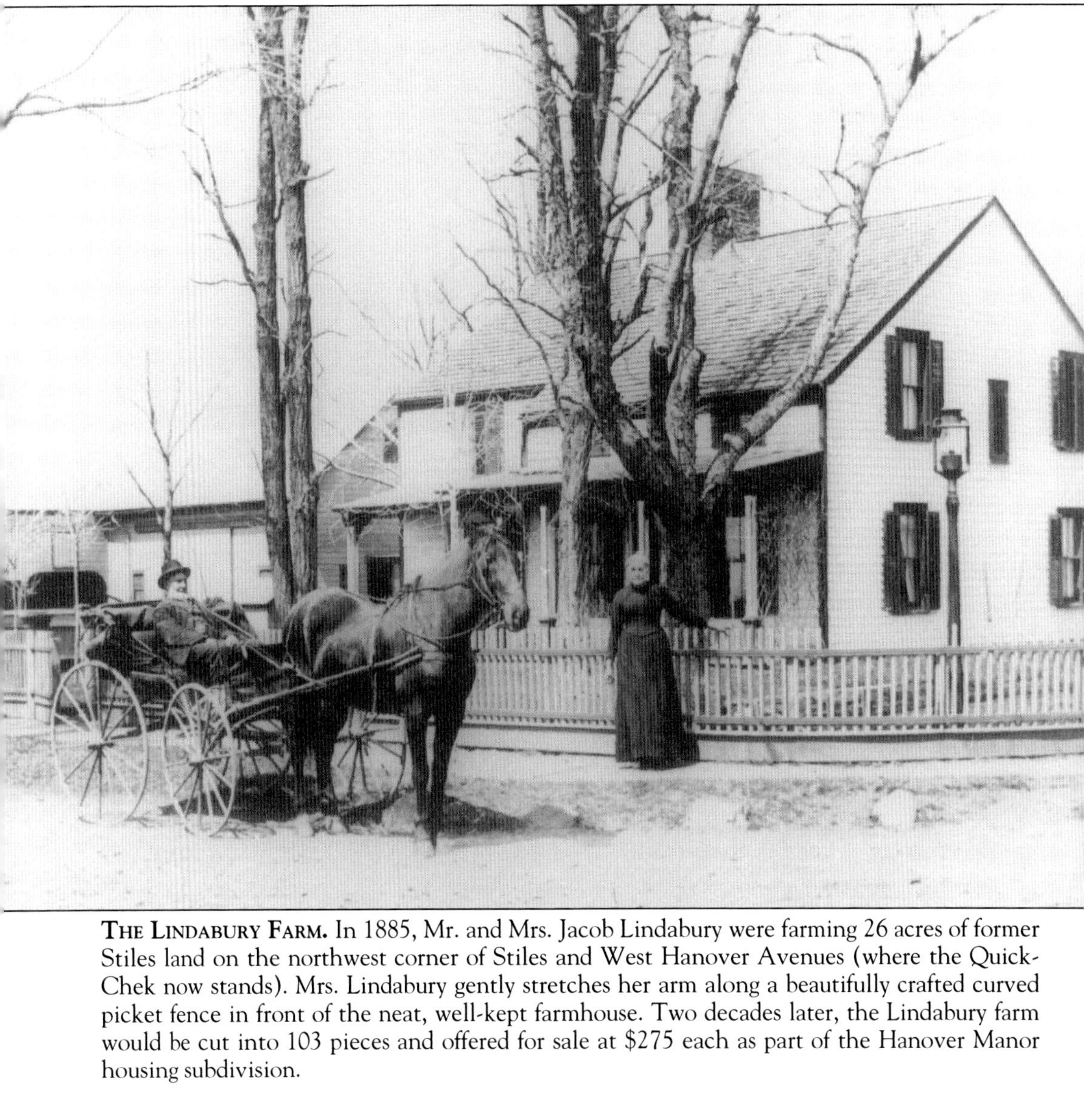

The Lindabury Farm. In 1885, Mr. and Mrs. Jacob Lindabury were farming 26 acres of former Stiles land on the northwest corner of Stiles and West Hanover Avenues (where the Quick-Chek now stands). Mrs. Lindabury gently stretches her arm along a beautifully crafted curved picket fence in front of the neat, well-kept farmhouse. Two decades later, the Lindabury farm would be cut into 103 pieces and offered for sale at $275 each as part of the Hanover Manor housing subdivision.

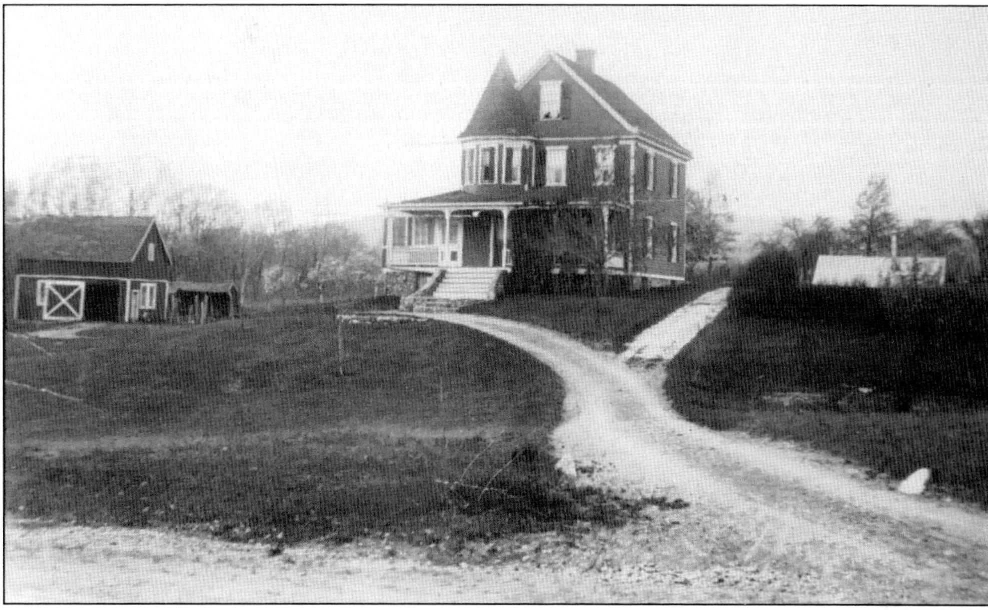

The Lindabury-Norton Home. In addition to small farms and the Five Corners settlement, there were some larger homes scattered throughout Morris Plains by the end of the 1880s. Built by George Lindabury in 1885, this handsome home (later owned by the Norton family) overlooked Jaqui's Pond.

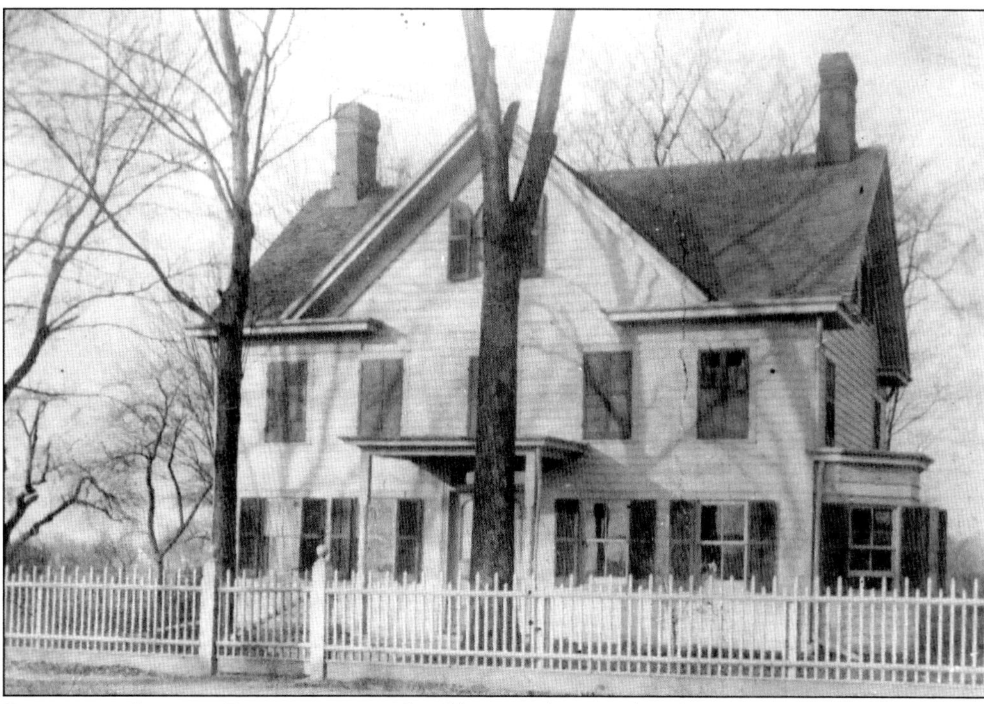

Speedwell Avenue Development. The Illingworth-Cronshey house is pictured here in the early 1900s, but it was built several decades before. Early planning meetings for the Episcopal Church were held here, and strawberry festivals were hosted in the garden to raise money to build St. Paul's Church. The house was razed in 1970 to make way for the Dayton Building.

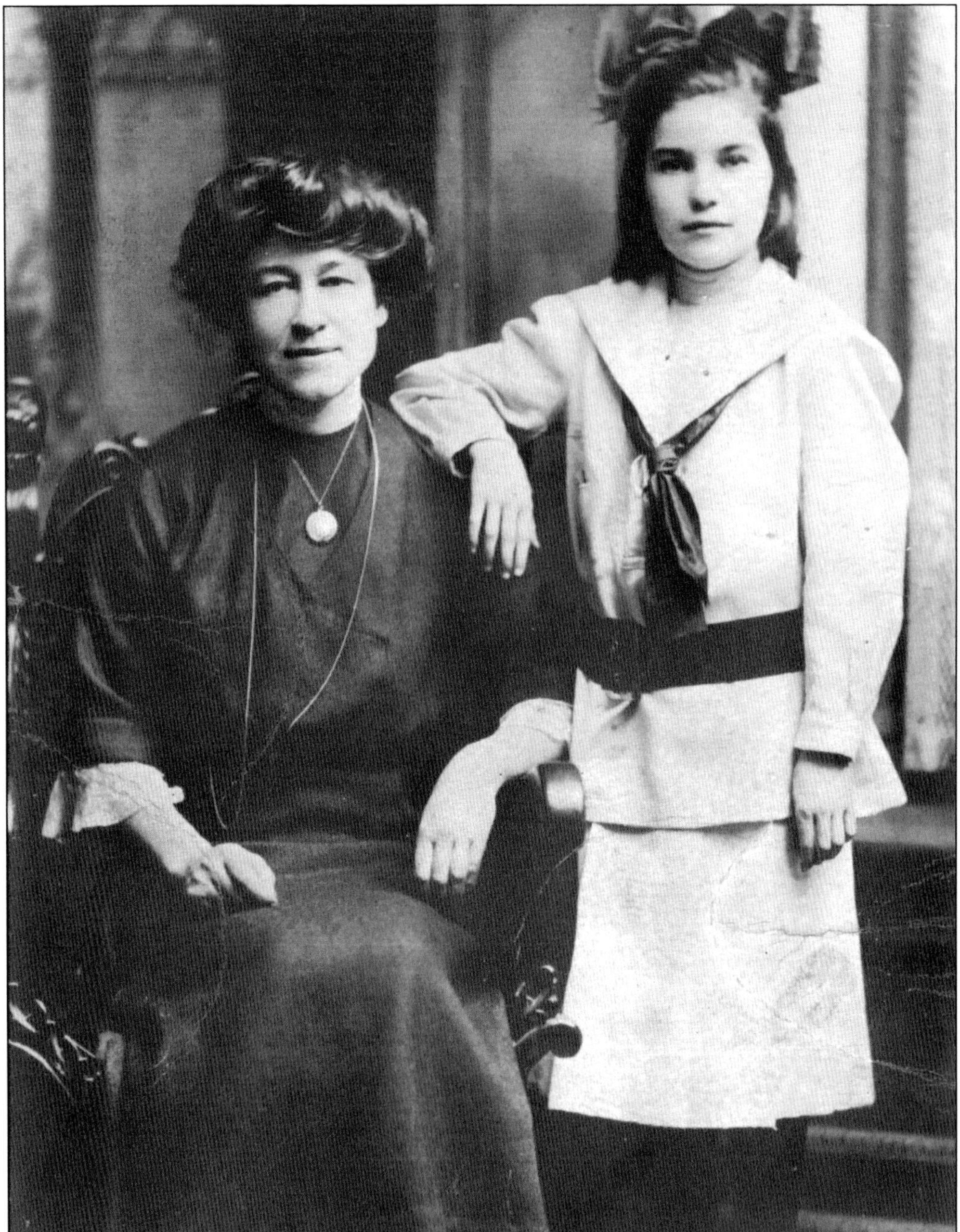

A TURN-OF-THE-CENTURY PORTRAIT. This lovely mother-daughter portrait from *c.* 1900 shows Rose Elizabeth Coleman Myers and her daughter, Sarah Myers (later Sweeney). Rose's mother and uncle came to Morris Plains from Ireland in 1850. Her mother married Patrick Coleman and settled at 61 Littleton Road. Her mother's brother was James McNeill, who had a farm on Central Avenue.

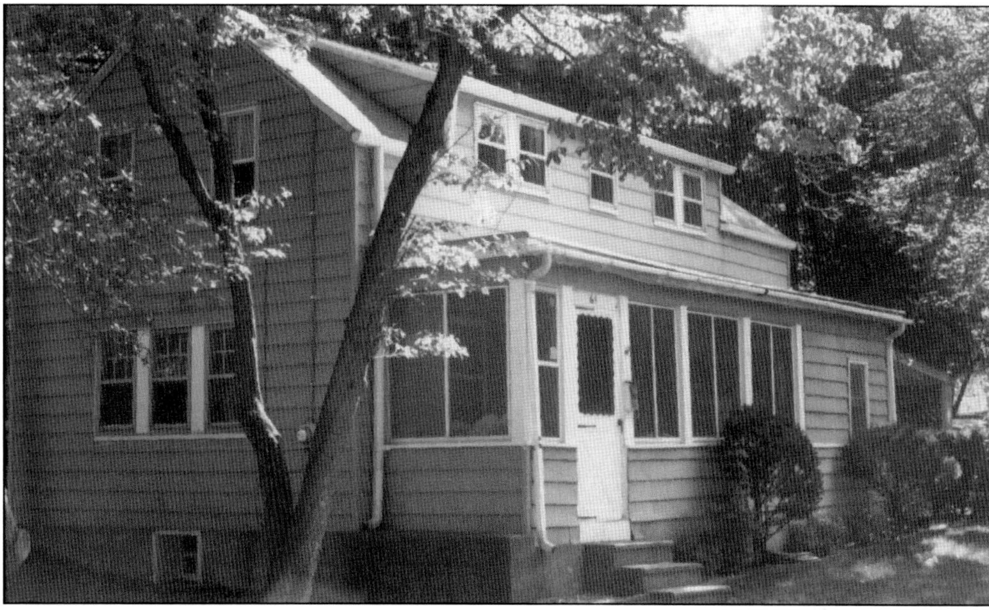

THE PATRICK COLEMAN HOUSE. This house at 61 Littleton Road, where Rose Coleman grew up, is listed on an 1853 map as "Mrs. Murphy's house." Its size and facade suggest it may have been built much earlier. It is still in use as a private home today.

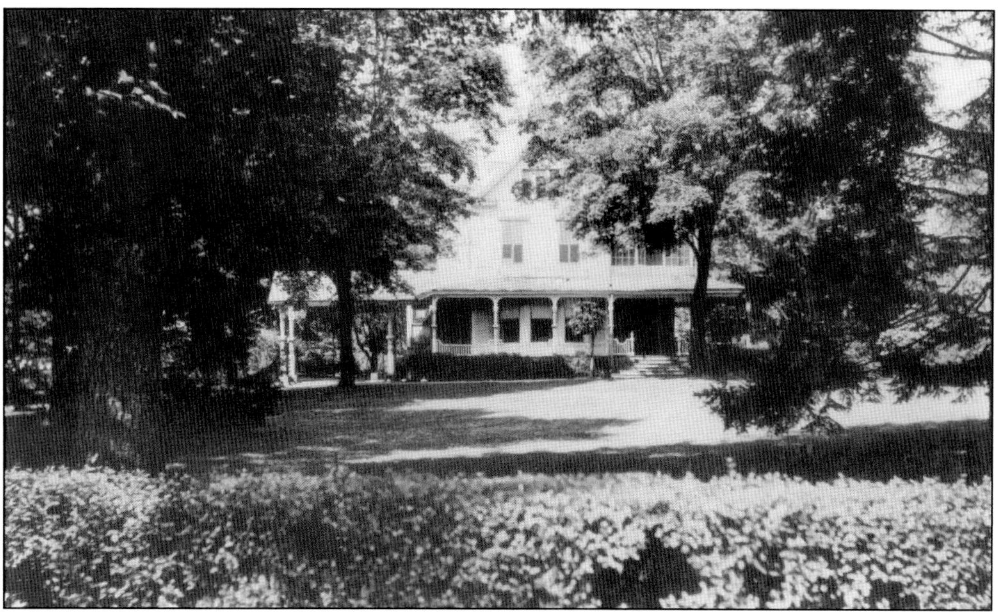

THE CONKLIN-WARD-SIMONS HOUSE. Is there anyone in Morris Plains who has not wondered about the old Queen Anne–style house sandwiched between the Texaco gas station and Peirsel's Garden Center? It was built by a New York judge, Cornelius Conklin, in 1886. The Ward family lived there during the first half of the 20th century, and then it was sold to the Simons family. Stan Simons published the *Morris News Bee* there for many years. The lovely but deteriorated house is slated for the wrecking ball.

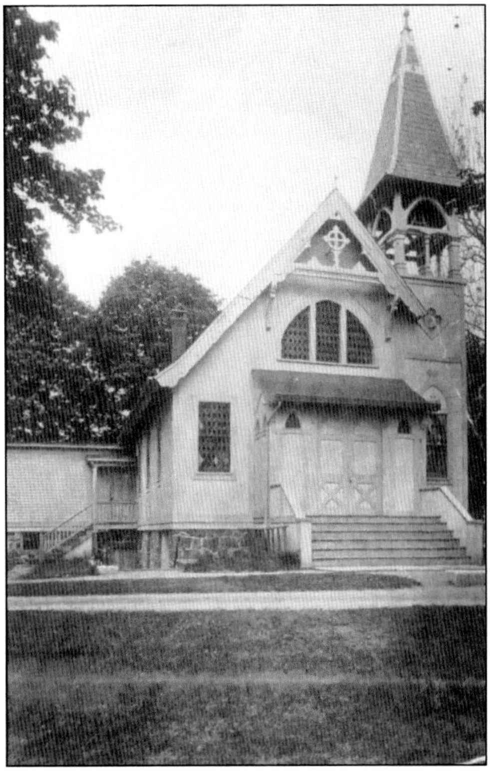

THE FIRST PRESBYTERIAN CHURCH, 1876. The Presbyterian ministry on the Plains first met in the old stone schoolhouse in the mid-1800s. This church, on the southwest corner of West Hanover Avenue and Burnham Road, was built and decorated entirely by its small congregation.

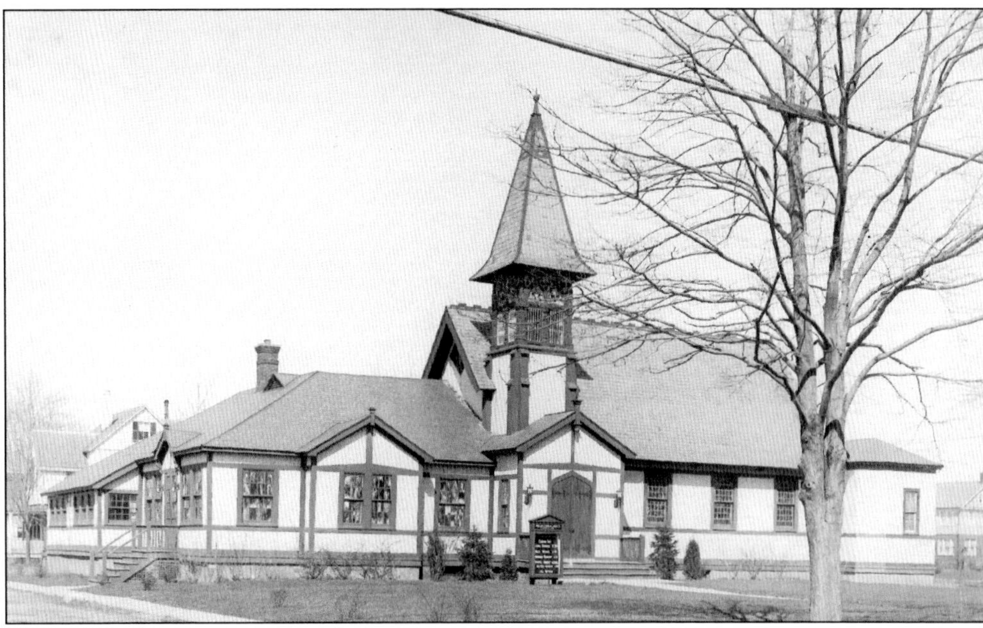

THE PRESBYTERIAN CHURCH MOVES. In 1912, the congregation decided to move their church closer to town. Logs were placed under the church, and it was hitched up to a horse-powered windlass. The horses pulled the church over the logs, which were continually "greased" with soap. The move through fields and lanes took two weeks. The old church, pictured here in the 1920s, was replaced by today's modern structure in 1954.

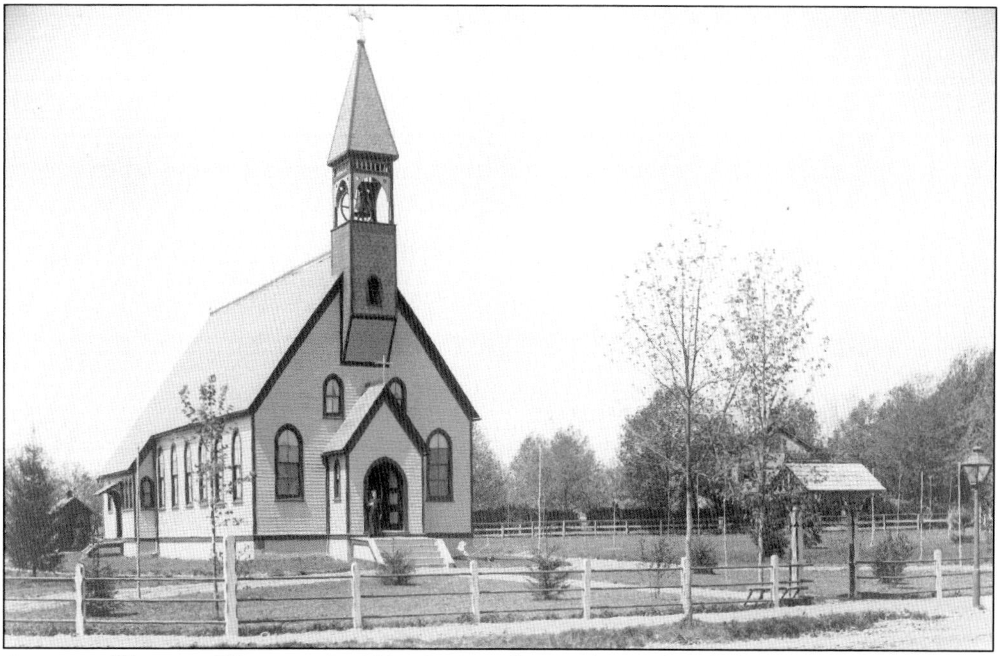

ANOTHER VOICE OF WORSHIP. In 1881, St. Virgil's Parish was founded in the home of Andrew Murphy in Wilsonville. The next year, a church was built at 48 West Hanover Avenue. Six years later, this church was moved to the southwest corner of West Hanover at Five Corners. This picture was taken in 1890. Fr. James Brennan is standing in the doorway. The present-day church was erected at the corner of Hanover and Speedwell Avenues in 1957.

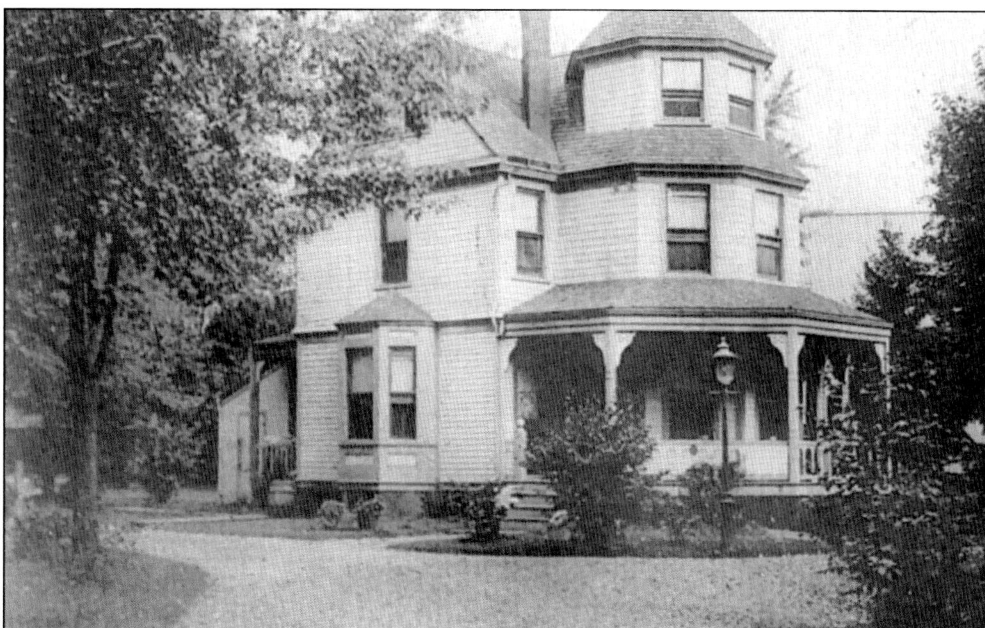

THE OLD RECTORY. In 1895, St. Virgil's rectory was built with a graceful round porch and Victorian "gingerbread" details. It was razed in 1936, and a new rectory was constructed.

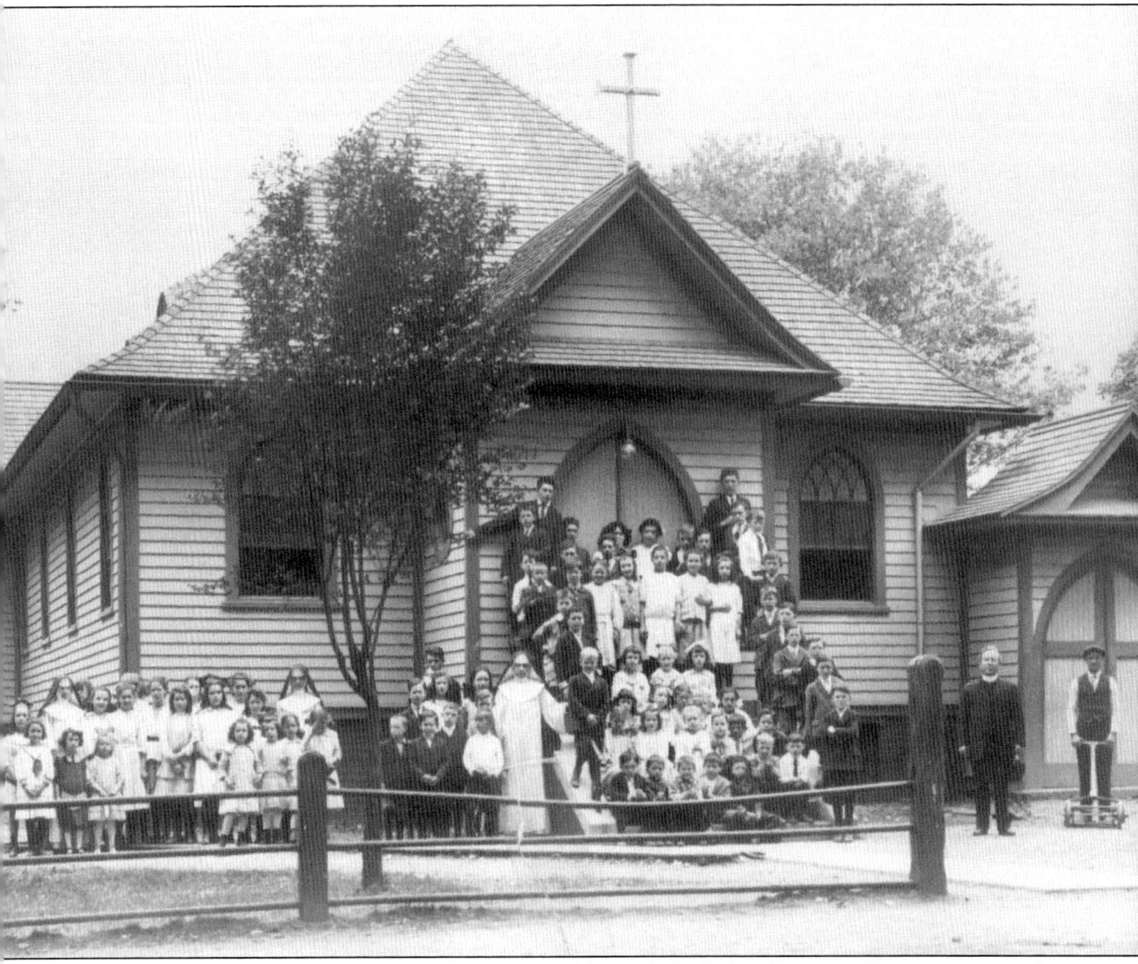

St. Virgil's School, 1916. In 1910, the old parish hall (built in 1895) was converted to a four-room school. The principal was Sister Clementine. In the picture, the Reverend Michael J. Glennon stands on the right near the school groundskeeper and janitor.

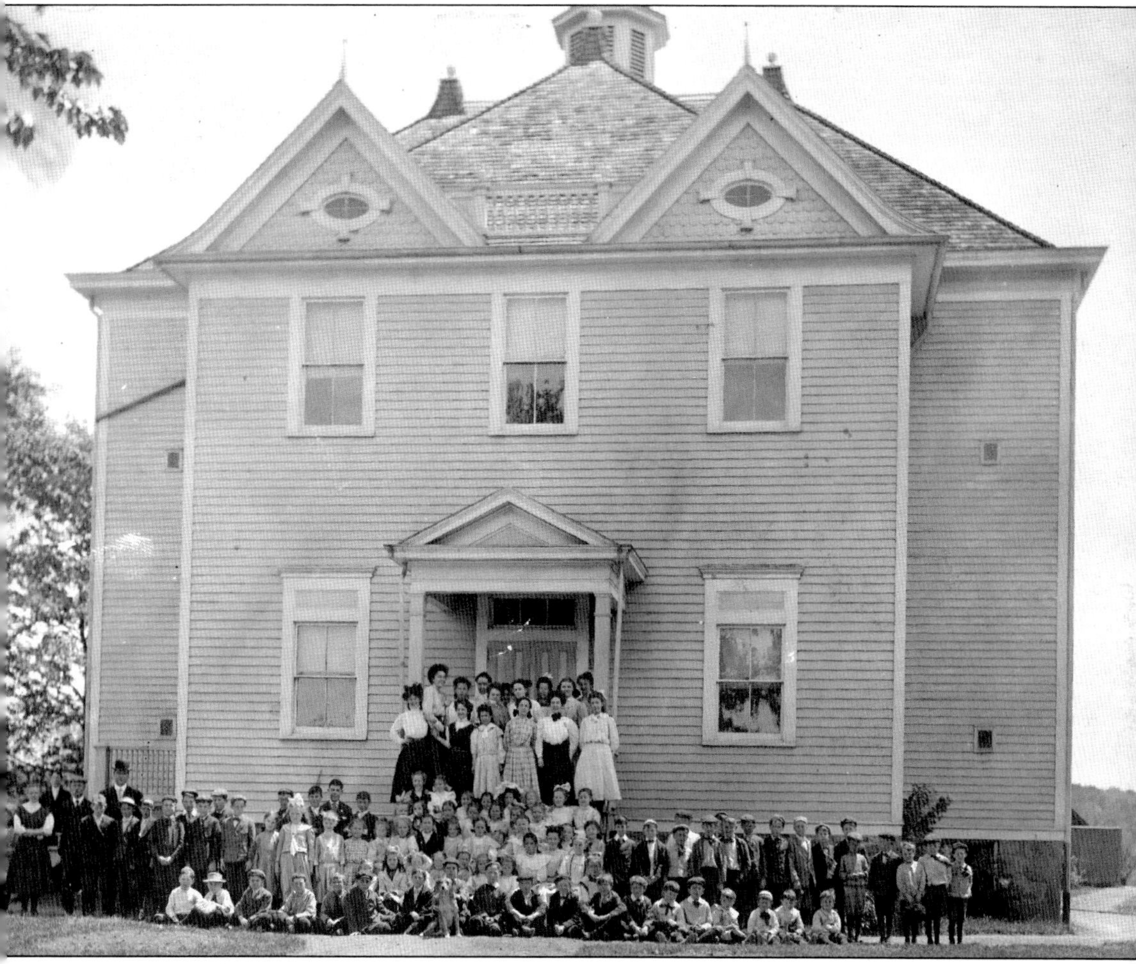

A New Public Schoolhouse. In 1908, a new school was erected closer to the center of town, replacing the 1866 frame schoolhouse on West Hanover Avenue. The new school was located where the municipal building now stands, at Speedwell Avenue and Academy Road. In this 1908 picture, Andrew Coffey and his dog, Buster, stand out in front row center.

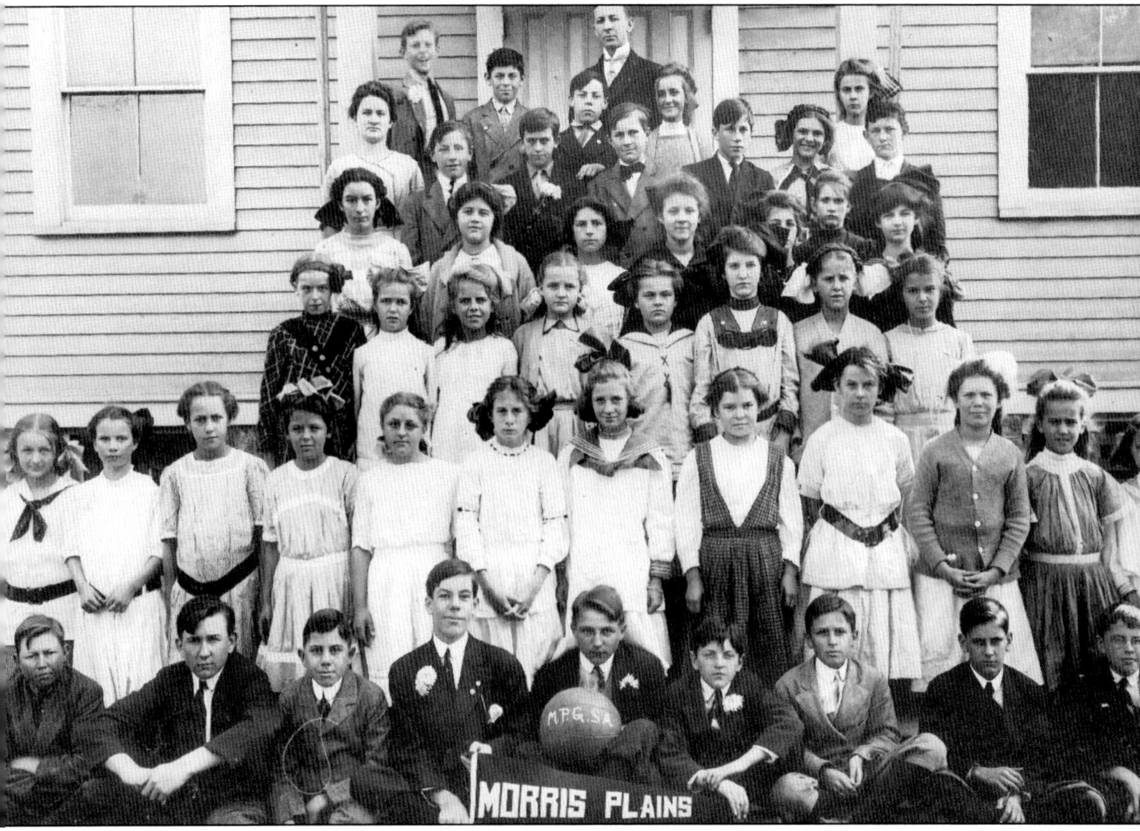

SCHOOL DAYS PAST. Another class poses in front of the Hanover School, *c.* 1914. The students, from left to right, are as follows: (first row) R. Willerer, N. Toohey, W. Conquest, G. Coursen (future mayor), S. Ayers, R. Totten, one unidentified student, J. Boyd, and R. Parker; (second row) one unidentified student, F. Heslin, G. Lyons, M. Laurie, A. Timan, A. Cronshey, one unidentified student, H. Baldwin, one unidentified student, M. Mains, D. Lyons, and ? Conquest; (third row) M. Ammerman, Elisa Lindstrom, one unidentified student, ? Florin, one unidentified student, R. Patterson, and R. Beers; (fourth row) H. Parsons, E. Housel, one unidentified student, Edith Olin, Annabelle Tunis, C. Gordon, and Louise Evans; (fifth row) J. Bossert, L. Skillman, C. Clausen, Maurice Skillman, Alan Betts, one unidentified student, and J. Titman; (sixth row) E. Fisher, C. Hodges, A. Lindabury, Alice Rule, Edward Levick, M. Willouby, and T. Spargo.

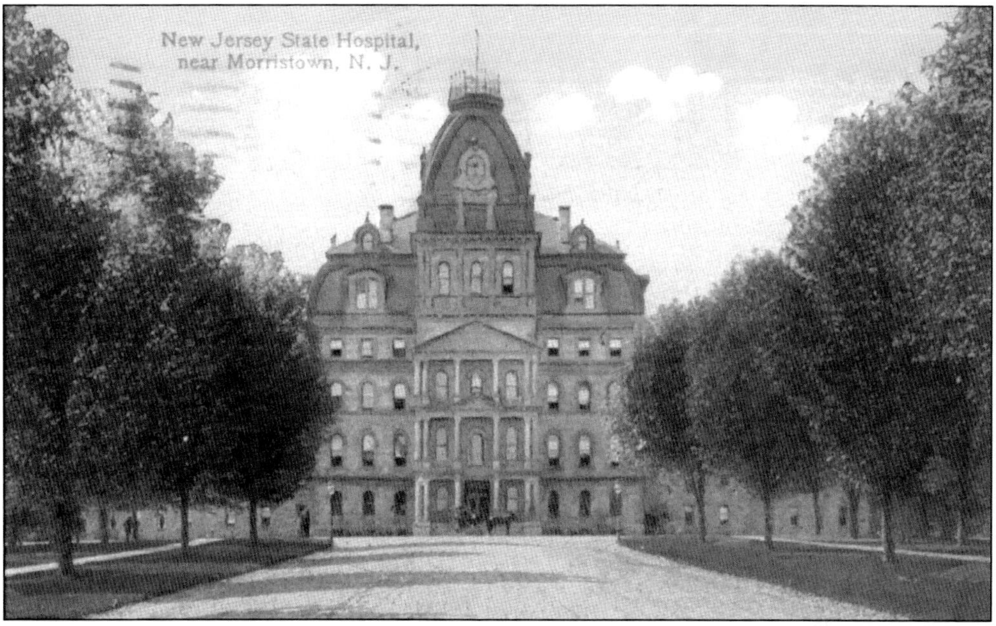

A MAJOR IMPACT ON THE PLAINS. In the spring of 1871, a state commission was formed to decide where to build a new insane asylum. Judge George Vail of Morris Plains was on that commission, but he resigned in June. In August, Morris Plains was chosen, and 400 acres were purchased from local farmers (over 250 acres were Judge Vail's). Five years later, the doors of the hospital opened to the first 292 patients. The asylum soon became known as Greystone for the color of the local gneiss of which it was built.

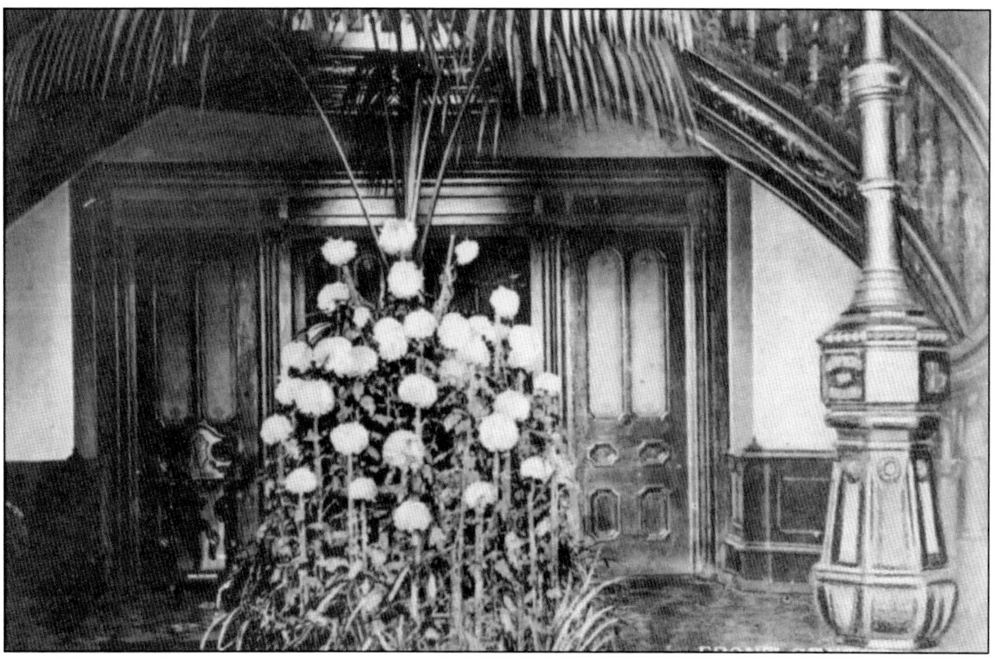

AN INTERIOR VIEW OF GREYSTONE. Greystone was designed by Dr. Thomas Kirkbride, who espoused uncrowded conditions, fresh air, and treating patients ass if they had a curable illness, all progressive notions in the Victorian age.

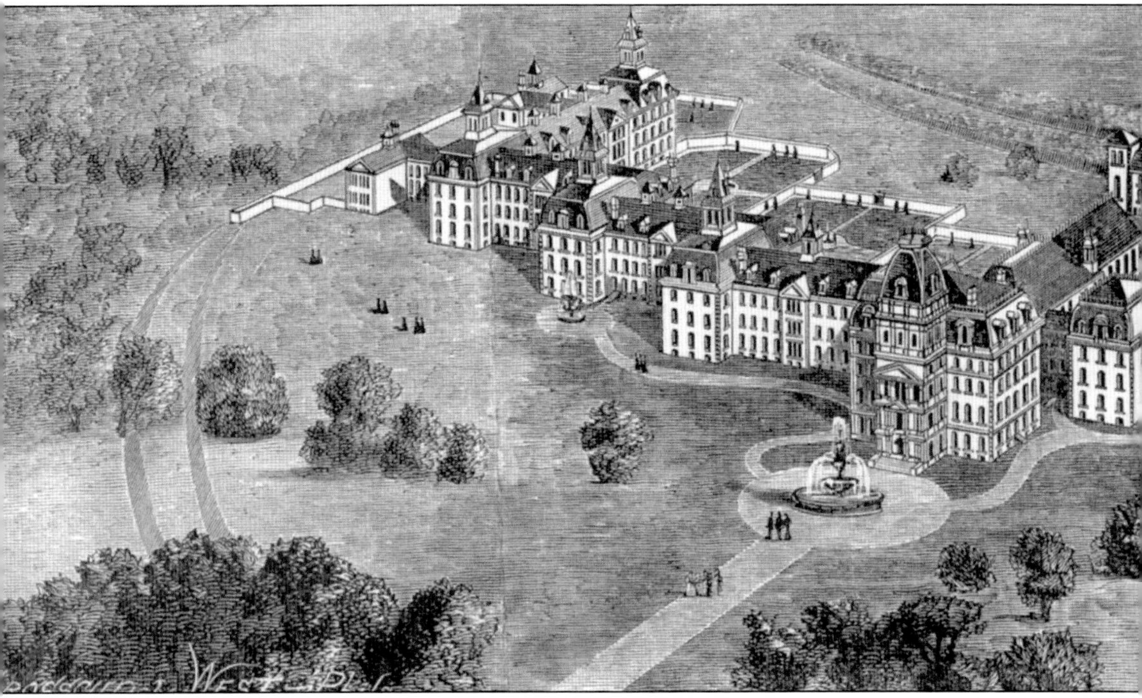

Greystone, 1882. The asylum was a huge enterprise, almost the creation of a self-sufficient small town. The basement of Greystone, with its internal rail system, boasted the largest continuous foundation in the country until the Pentagon was built. Greystone's patient capacity when first opened was 600 beds, but in the 1960s it housed 7,847 patients. Today, due

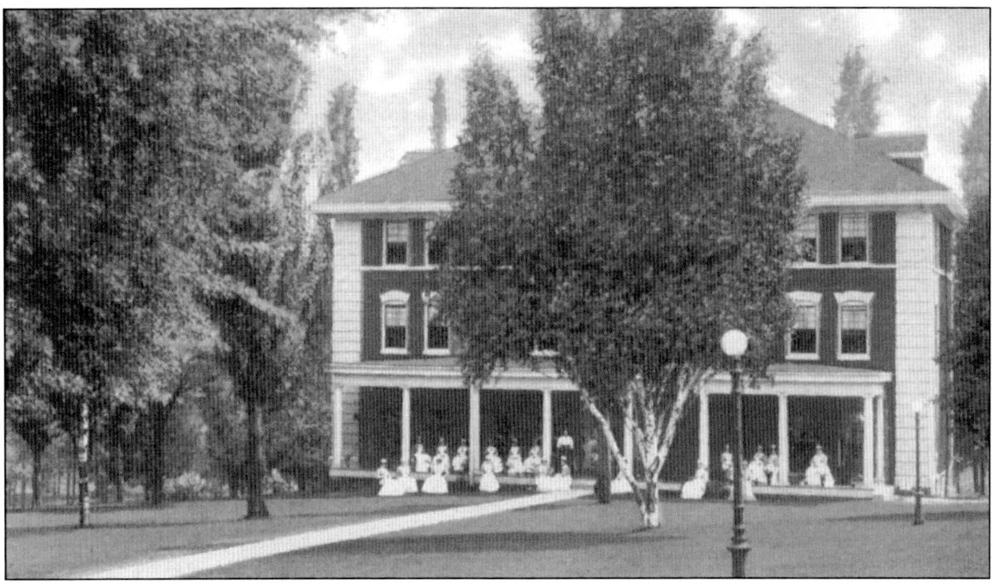

The Cottage for Female Attendants. This "cottage" was only one of innumerable outbuildings on the hospital grounds, including barns, carriagehouses, stables, boiler rooms, coal towers, kitchens, pantries, bakeries, icehouses, slaughterhouses and residences for medical and farm personnel. There were 8 miles of pipes, 2,000 doors, 2,500 windows and 13 miles of baseboards.

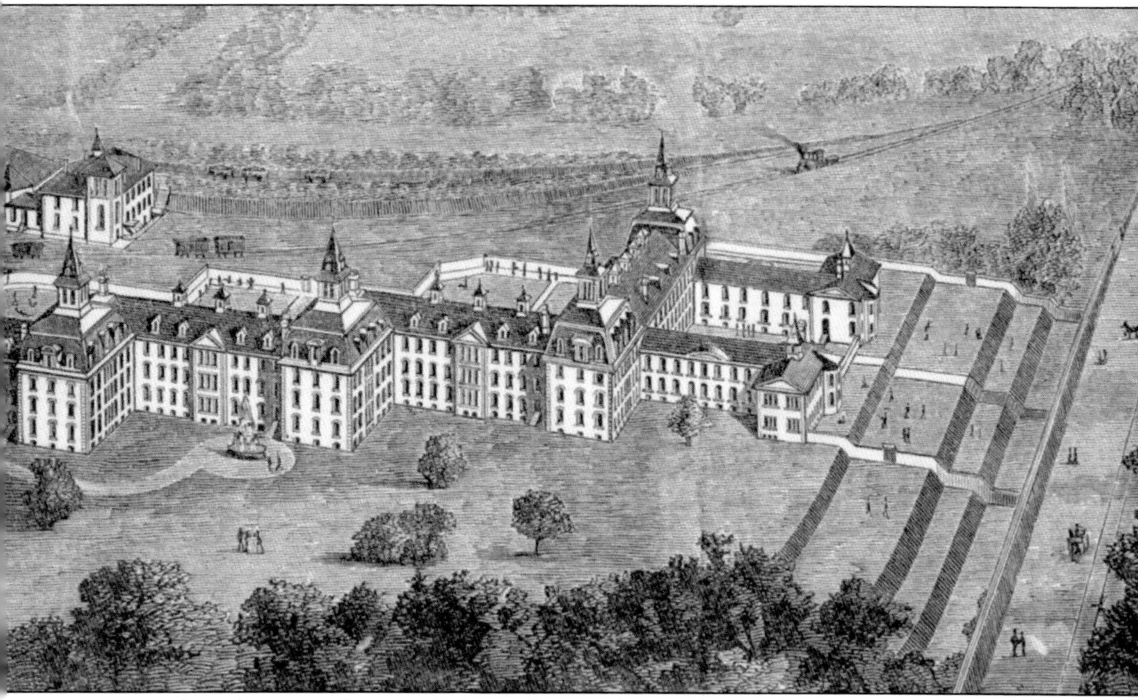

to the use of psychotropic drugs and changed societal attitudes, much of Greystone is empty and disintegrating. Governor Whitman has announced the final closing of the old asylum three years hence.

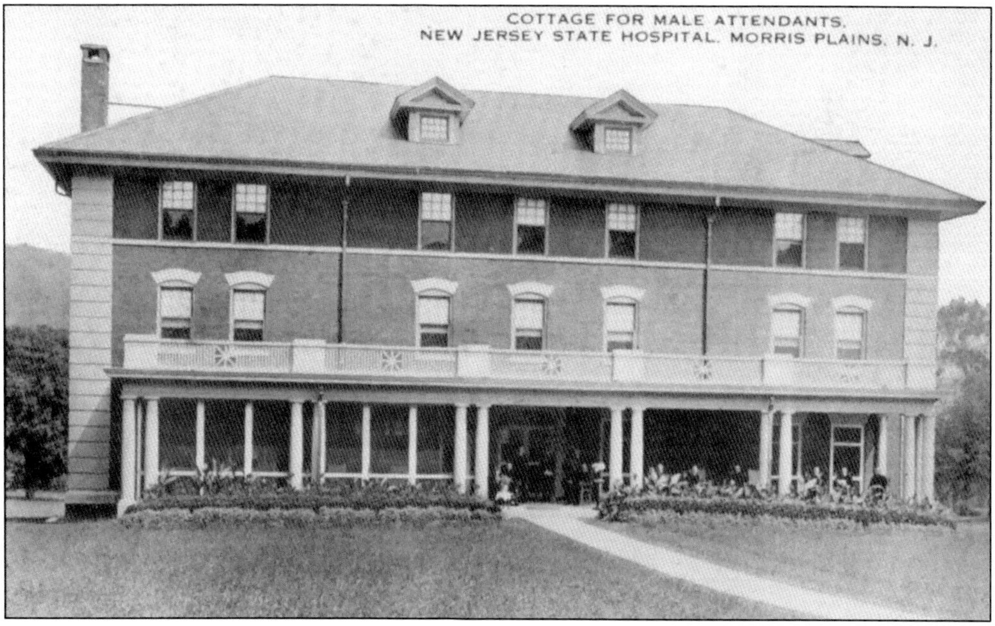

THE COTTAGE FOR MALE ATTENDANTS. During the five years of Greystone's construction, some of the workers became a local problem, drinking and carousing after paydays. Special police had to be hired. Historian Julia Beers calls that period Morris Plains's "reign of terror."

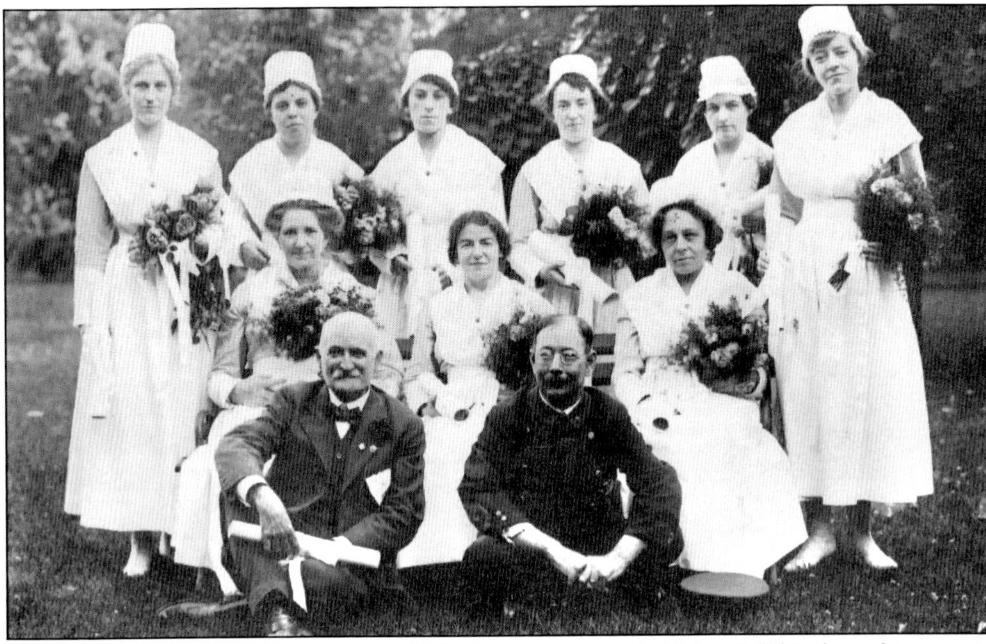

A GROUP OF NURSES AT GREYSTONE, 1900. Greystone provided jobs of all kinds, and it was said that you could not find a young person in Morris Plains who had not taken a "graduate course" at the asylum. Shown, from left to right, are the following: (first row) J.K.R. Hewitt, and J.F. Burns (father of George Burns); (second row) Mrs. Smith, Miss Currie, and Miss Matthews; (third row) Miss Luz, Miss Lloyd, Miss House, Miss Phelan, Mrs. Babington, and Miss Simonsen.

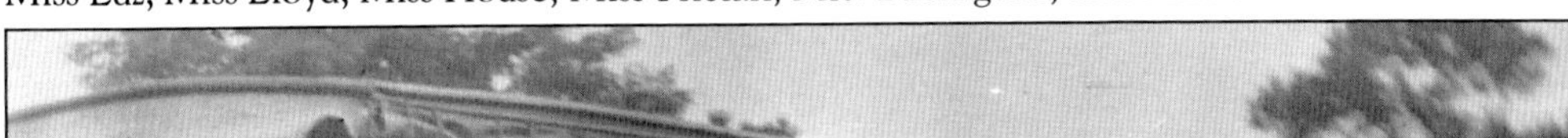

GOING TO GREYSTONE, 1905. A railroad spur and a road (Granniss Avenue was originally called Asylum Road) were built to carry people and supplies to Greystone. The total cost to build Greystone was $2,250,000—including its dozens of outbuildings, kitchens, engines, boilers, machinery, furniture, 430 acres of land, miles of railroad track, gas works, three reservoirs, water works, and roadways.

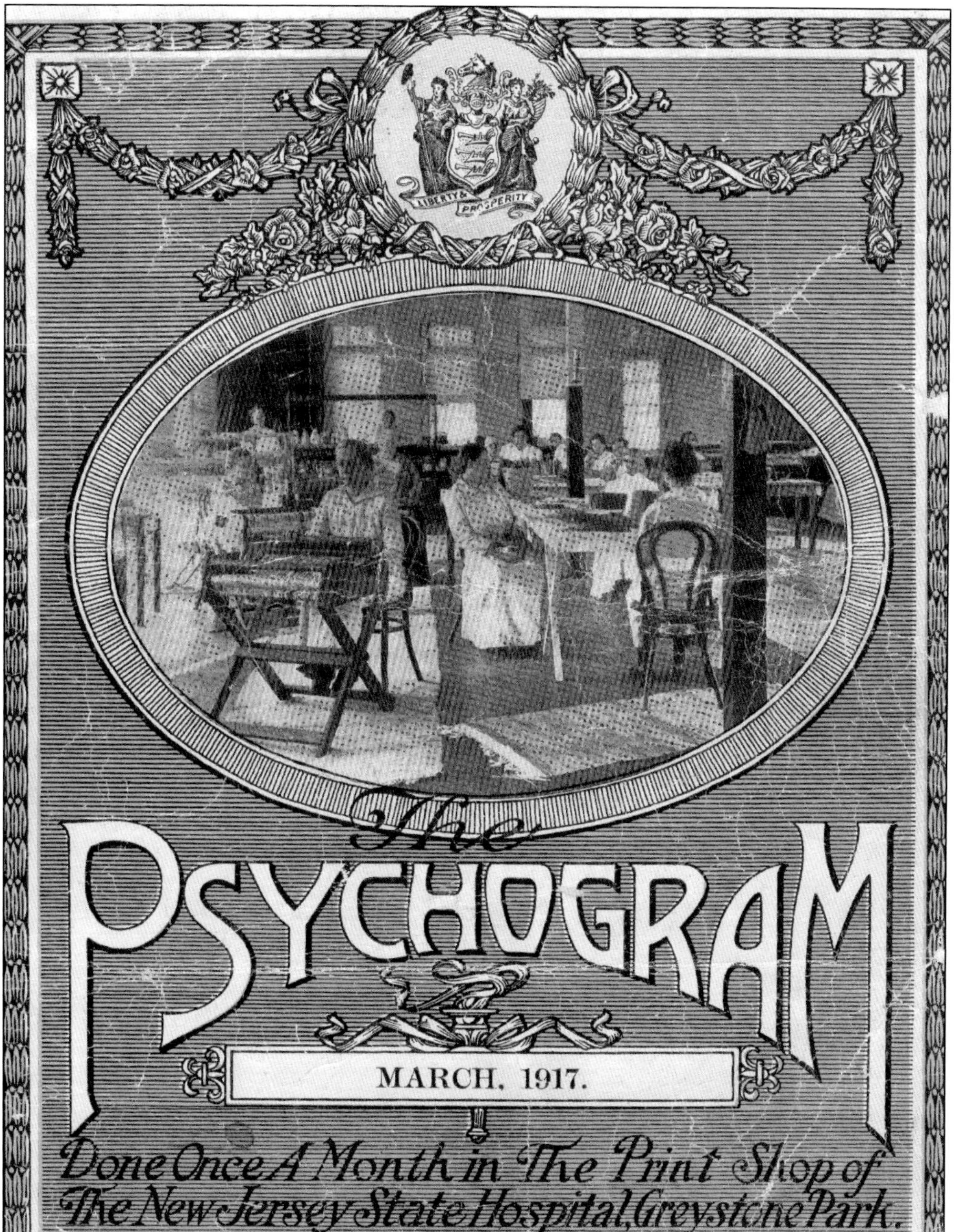

THE "PSYCHOGRAM." Part of the treatment philosophy at Greystone was to involve patients in arts and crafts or other worthwhile pursuits. This interesting newsletter was written and produced by the patients at Greystone. The cover picture shows women patients weaving and conversing, appearing far from "insane." Another surviving literary effort by a Greystone patient is a book of poetry called *Rhymes of a Raver*.

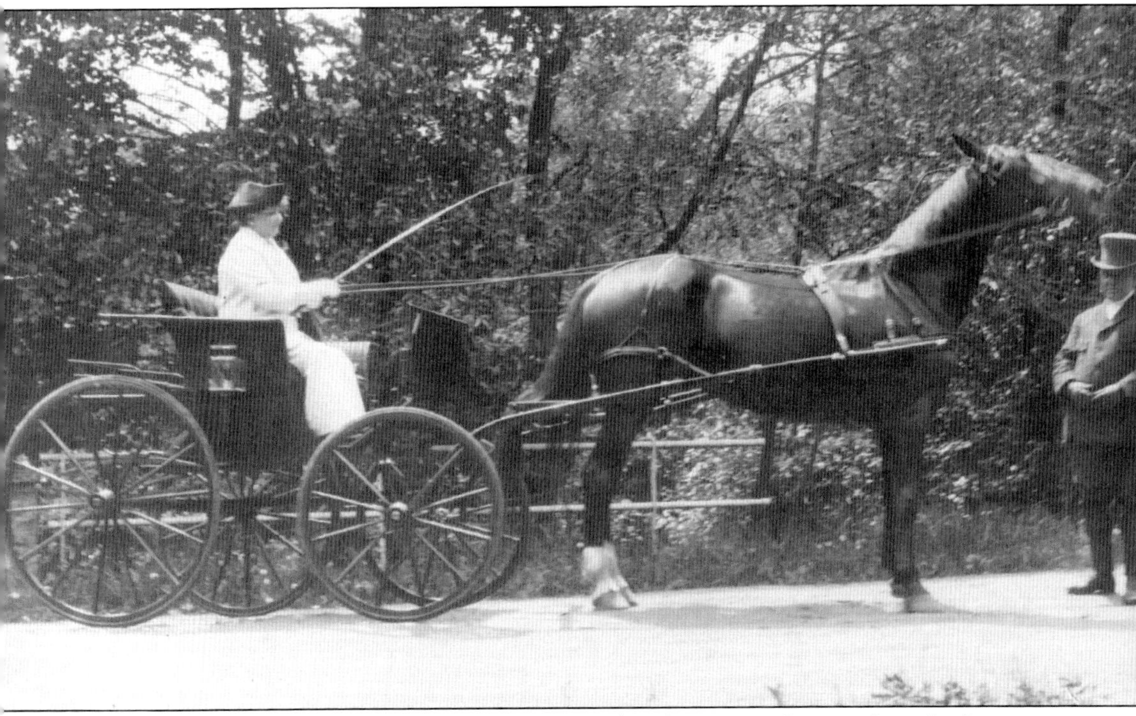

The Doctor's Wife. Dr. Britton Evans was the doctor in charge of medical matters at Greystone. Mrs. Evans is shown in her buggy on Central Avenue, the main road to the hospital. The coachman is John Cavanaugh. The Evanses lived in Moses Stiles's old house on Glenbrook Road, which was razed in the 1960s to make way for the Totten housing development.

Four

FIRE!

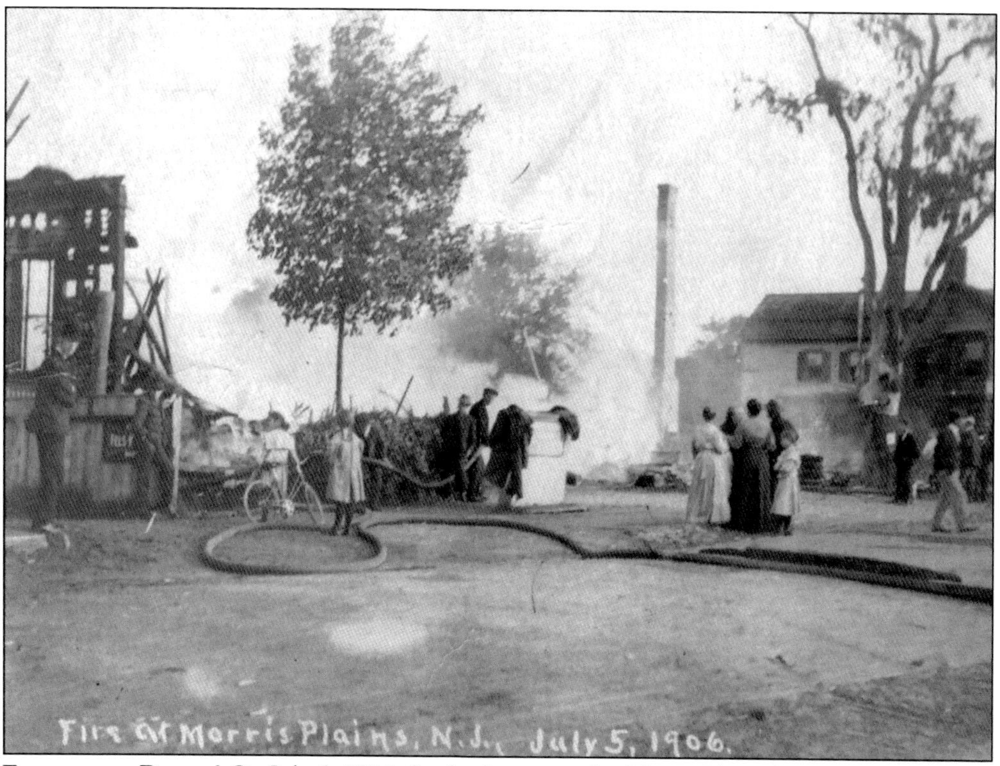

FIRE ON THE PLAINS! On July 5, 1906, fire broke out in the Morris Plains business section. The railroad gate keeper gave the alarm. The fire began in the Wiese Hotel or, by other accounts, the candy store next-door. Whatever the origin of that errant spark, a hastily assembled bucket brigade proved useless. This picture shows a single hose trained on a blackened gap south of the old Clark grocery store, which was then owned by Daniel Merchant.

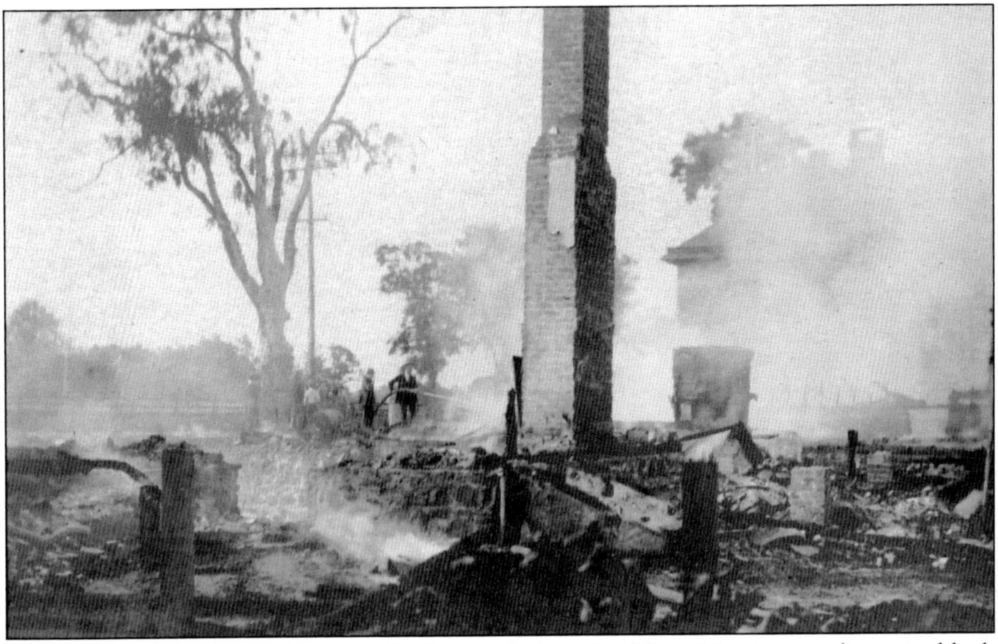

The Business Block is Destroyed. By the time help arrived from Morristown, the entire block had burned, sparing only the Clark building. The chimney is all that remained of the Wiese Hotel. Among the few articles saved were a piano and a cash register belonging to butcher Joe Layer. It was obvious that dependence upon fire protection from nearby towns was not sufficient.

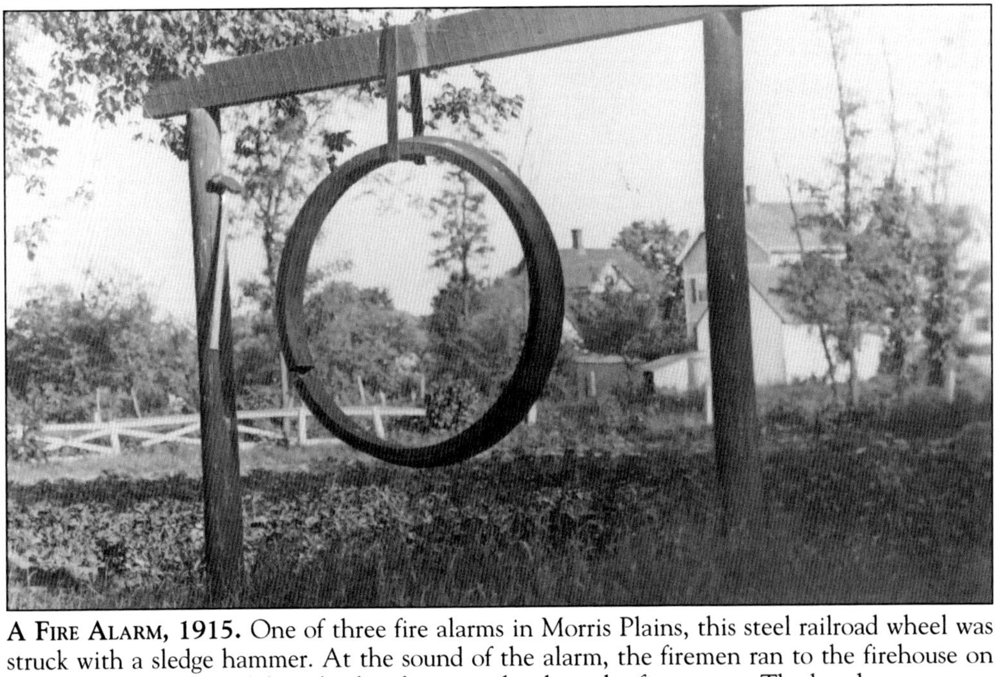

A Fire Alarm, 1915. One of three fire alarms in Morris Plains, this steel railroad wheel was struck with a sledge hammer. At the sound of the alarm, the firemen ran to the firehouse on Franklin Place, some of them leading horses to hitch to the fire wagon. The hand pumper was pulled over dirt roads by the firemen themselves. It took eight men pumping furiously to raise a stream of water to 30 pounds pressure. (Courtesy JFPLMMT.)

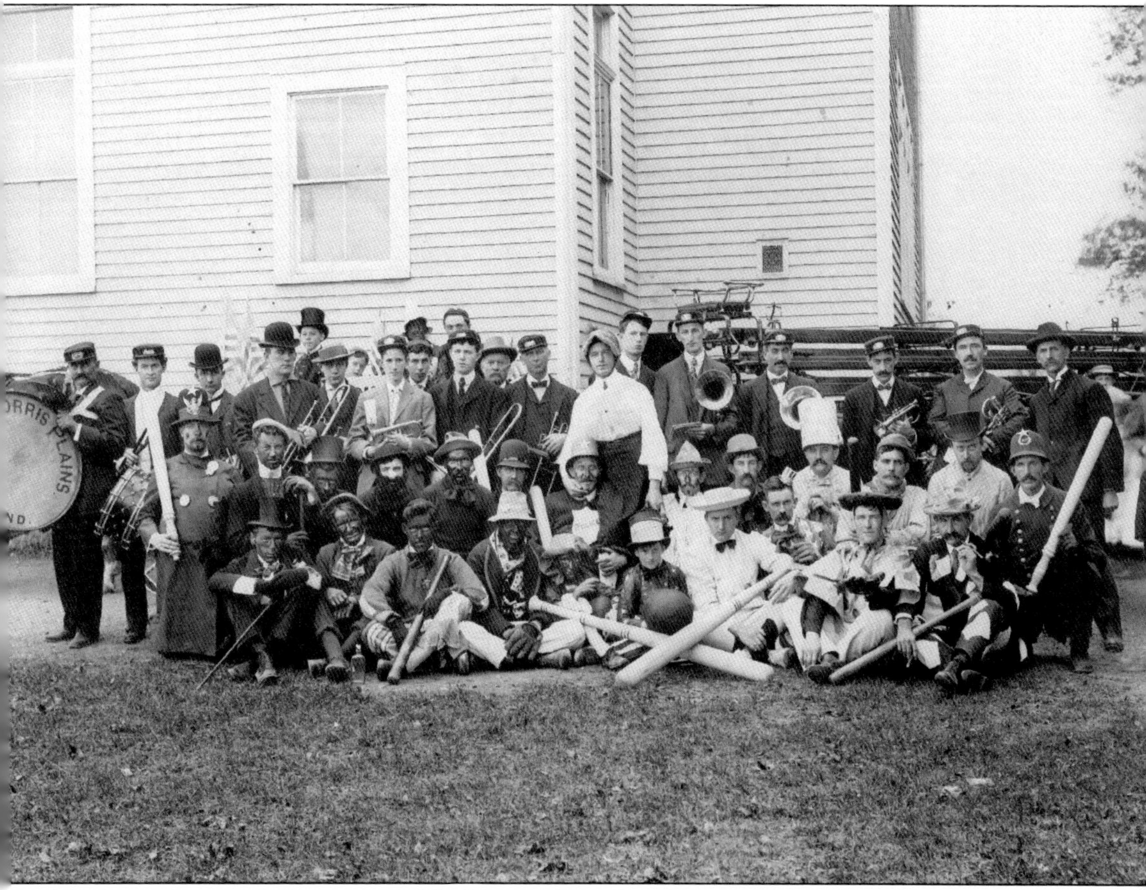

THE FIRST FIREMEN'S FAIR, 1907. The Morris Plains Fire Association was formed within a year after the great town fire. To raise money for uniforms, the new firemen organized a fair featuring music and costumes. Revelers at the fair include, from left to right, the following: (first row) Frank Burns, Will Layer, Tom Madden, Bill McGuinness, Charles Kelsch, Joe Layer as Uncle Sam holding the ball, Bob Granniss as Buster Brown, John Cronshey as Happy Hooligan, Frank Maines holding glove, and Andrew Chamberlain; (second row) Henry Elzerman in military dress with the bat, Ollie Hill, Bob Beers in the top hat, Bob Chamberlain, Walter Kelsch, Joe Tunis in the helmet, Albert Lindstrom, Clarence Beddow as Mrs. Katzenjammer, Albert Williams in the Mexican hat, Ed Hill, Ed Housel as Fluffy Ruffles, Stan Lyon, one unidentified person, and Gates Parsons as a cop; (third row) George Morris with the drum, Jack Maher, one unidentified person, Marvin Hart, Arch Covert, Jack Fraser, Bill Nunn, two unidentified persons, Charles Kelsch, Farquhar Fraser, John Monahan, George Myers, Larry Monahan Sr., and Al Bartron.

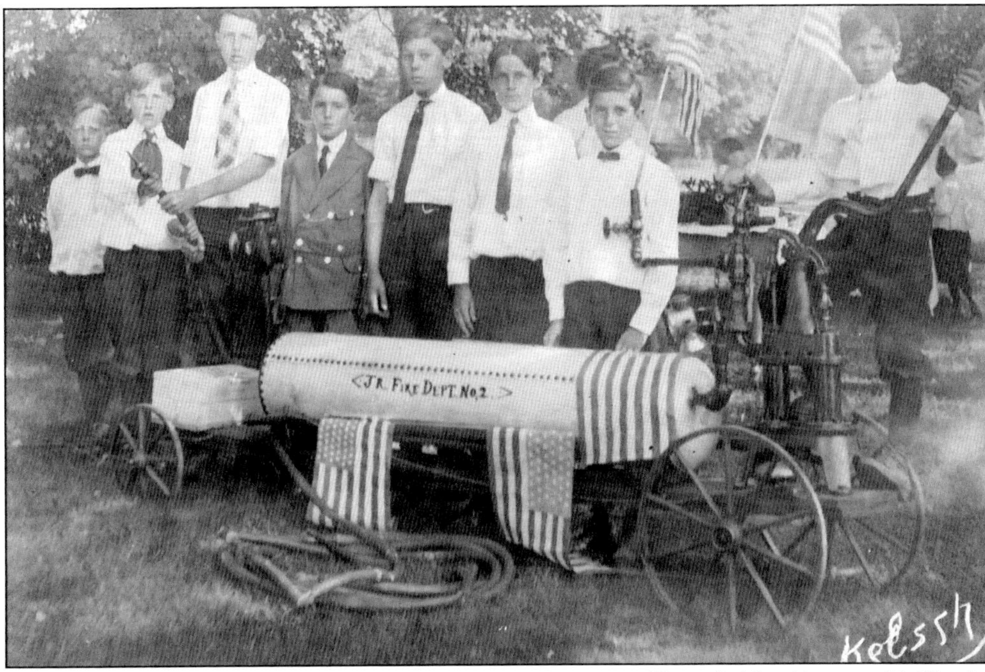

Morris Plains Junior Fire Department, 1908. A group of boys led by 11-year-old Charles Thompson cobbled together this small pump and a garden hose that successfully threw a stream as high as a single-story house. Hopefully the boys were kept out of harm's way when fire struck. The boys, from left to right, are Charlie Thompson, Charles Bartron, Salvador Marra, Art Olin, Henry Parsons, James Patterson, and Irving Barton.

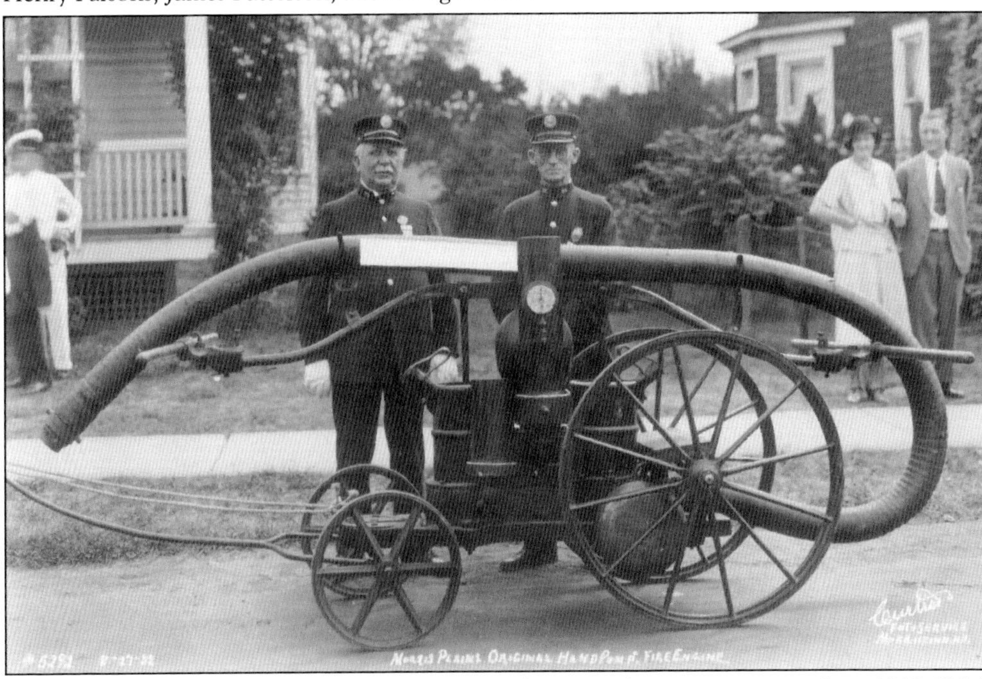

The First Apparatus. Shown is the original hand pumper from 1908, on parade in 1932. D.M. Merchant, the first assistant fire chief, and John Cronshey, veteran fireman, stand by its side.

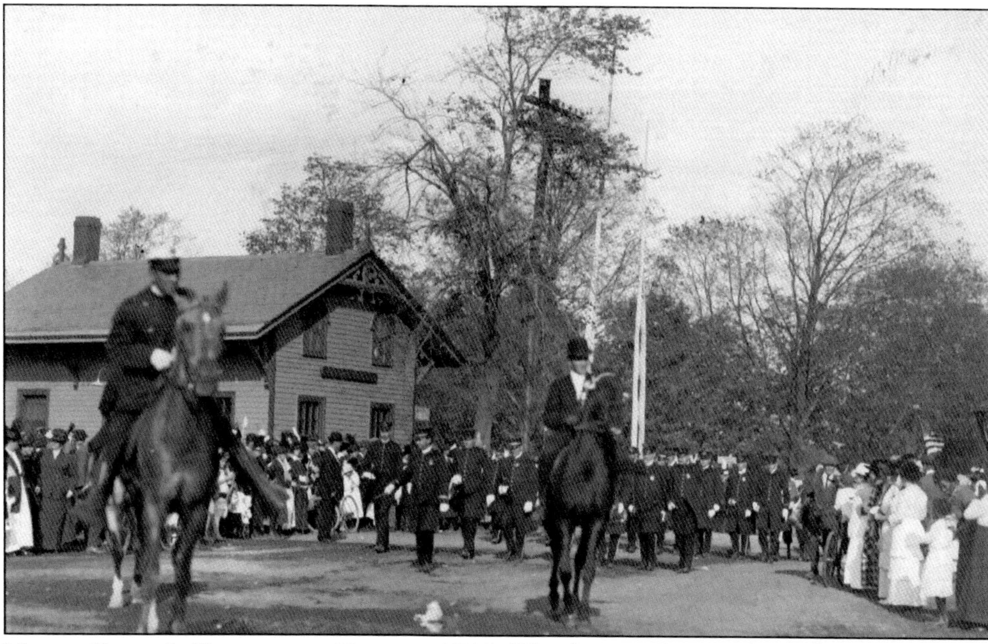

MORRIS PLAINS'S BRAVEST ON PARADE, 1912. The firemen form ranks and parade over the tracks by the railroad station. The crowd watches in all its finery, the women in dresses and hats and the men in suits and proper bowlers—a glorious, long-ago day of patriotism and high spirits.

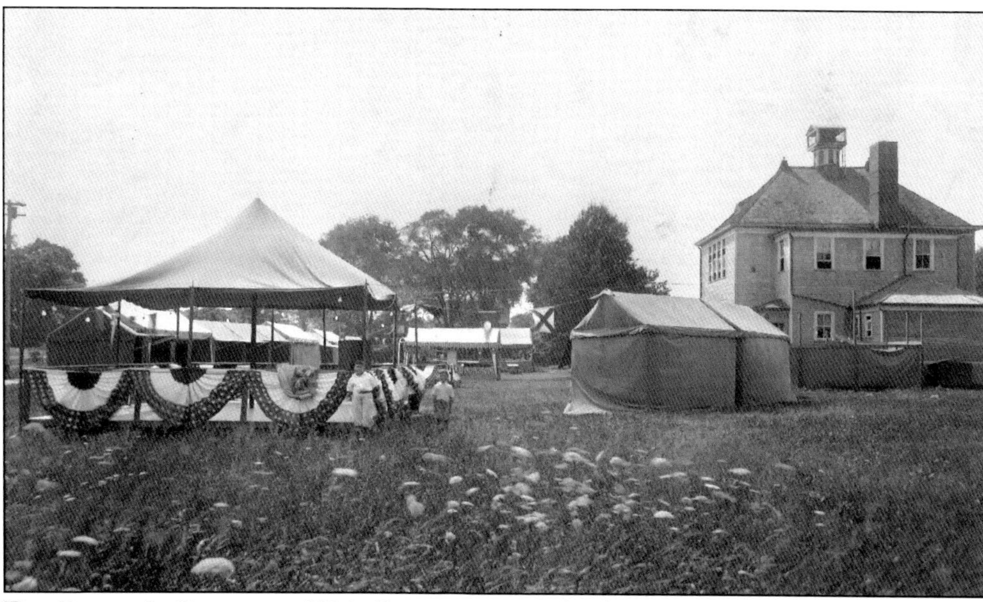

THE FIREMEN'S CARNIVAL, 1931. For many years, the firemen organized a carnival to raise funds for equipment. This picture shows the carnival set up in a field south of the fire station. The Ladies Auxiliary, formed in the early 1920s, ran the food booth. (Courtesy JFPLMMT.)

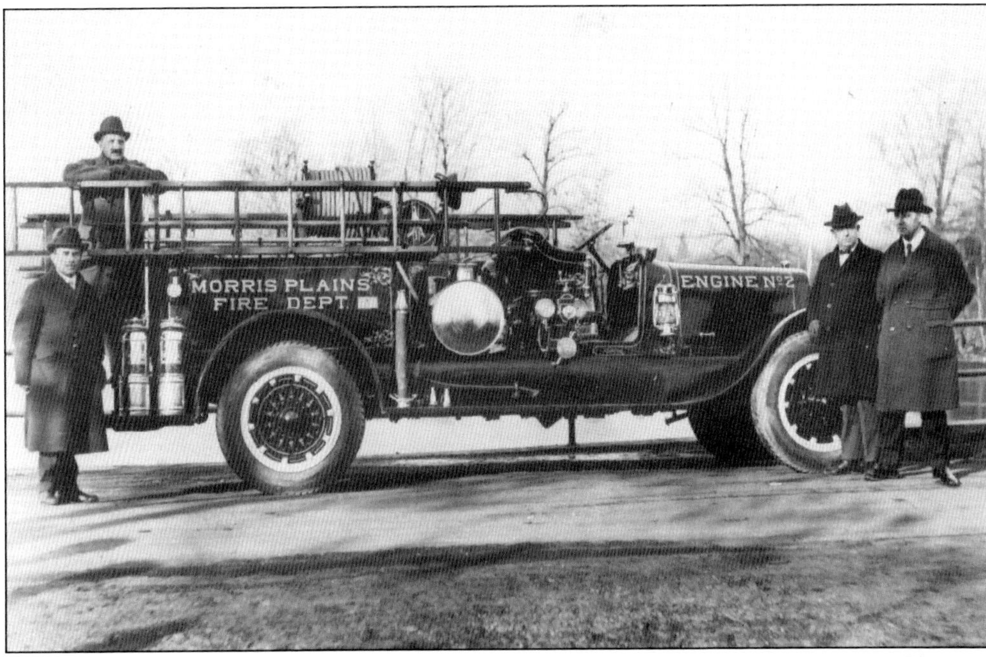

WATEROUS ENGINE PURCHASED IN 1923. Alexander Rennie, Dr. R.V.D. Totten, Clarence Beddow, and Carlton Dobbins inspect the new Waterous fire truck. The town had purchased its first mechanized apparatus, a Howe pumper on a Model T car chassis, in 1917. Unfortunately, the Howe was sitting in a boxcar waiting to be uncrated when fire destroyed half the business section in 1917.

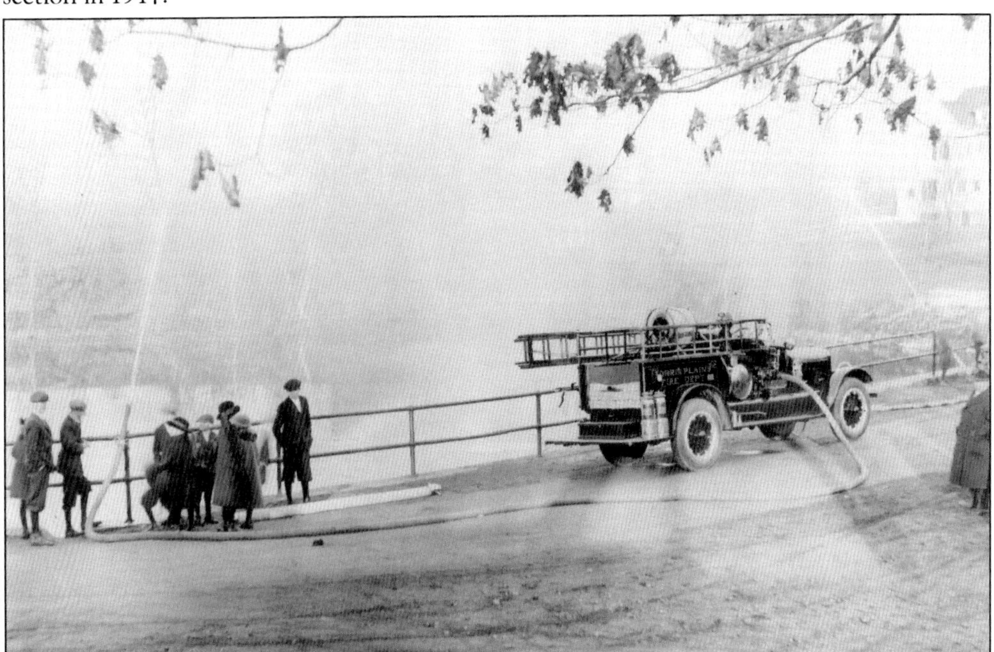

TESTING THE NEW WATEROUS HOOK AND LADDER, 1924. The new fire truck, a far cry from the old hand pumper, is tested at Jaqui Pond on a cold December day. (Courtesy JFPLMMT.)

THE NEW QUARTERS FOR THE FIRE STATION. In 1923, the new borough school was built, and the old schoolhouse at Academy Road and Speedwell was sold to the Fire Association. The Franklin Place firehouse was abandoned and the school redesigned to fit the needs of the fire company.

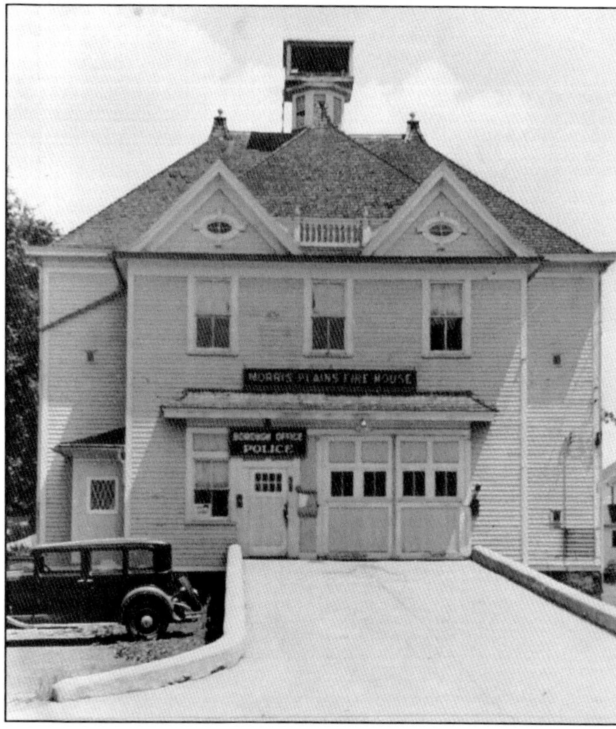

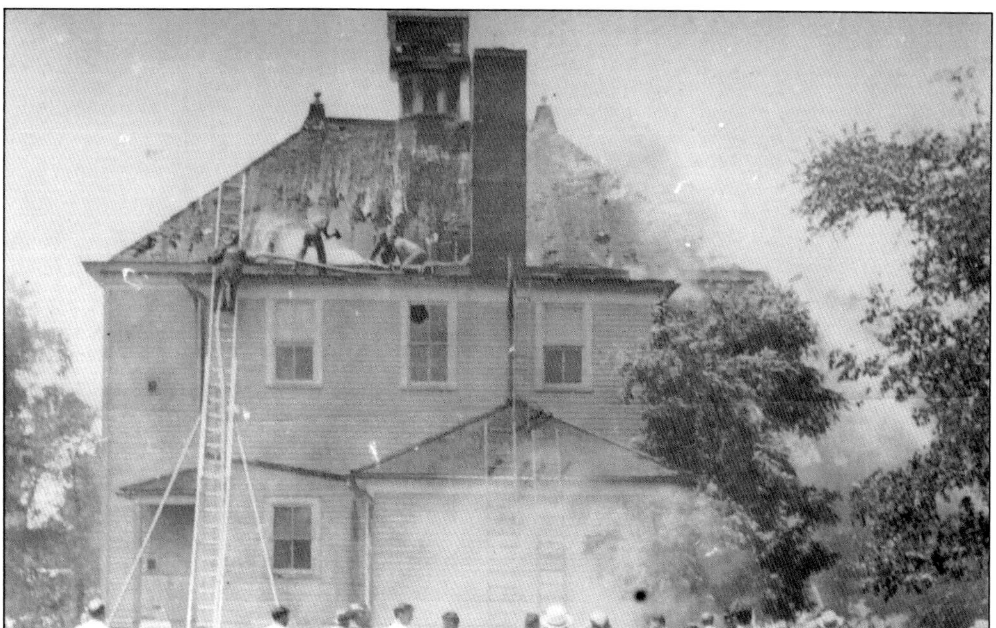

THE FIRE STATION BURNS, 1940. On August 2, burning paper from a trash fire wafted upward and caught under the eaves of the fire station. Several men risked their lives climbing to the roof in an attempt to get to the fire's source, but the station was damaged beyond repair. Fireman J. Edgar Bartron lost an eye. Later that year, the Fire Association sold the land to the Borough for $1, and a new municipal building was built to house both firemen and town government.

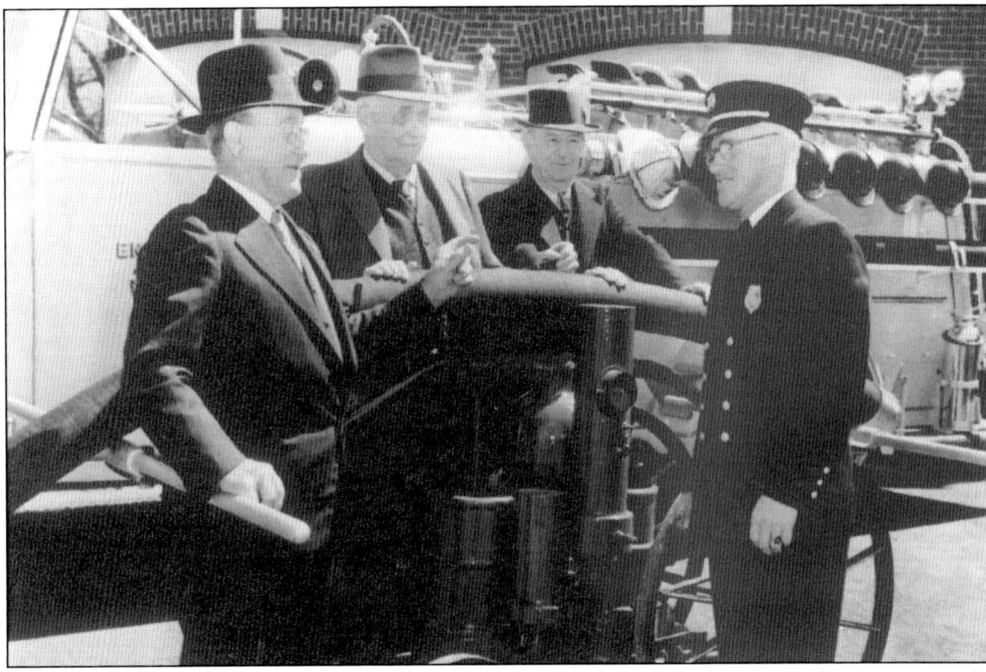

The Original Hand Pumper on Parade, 1957. At the 50th anniversary firemen's parade, three former firemen chat with Chief Gordon Parsons. The men, from left to right, are Albert Lindstrom, Stanley Lyon, Frank Gilligan, and Chief Parsons.

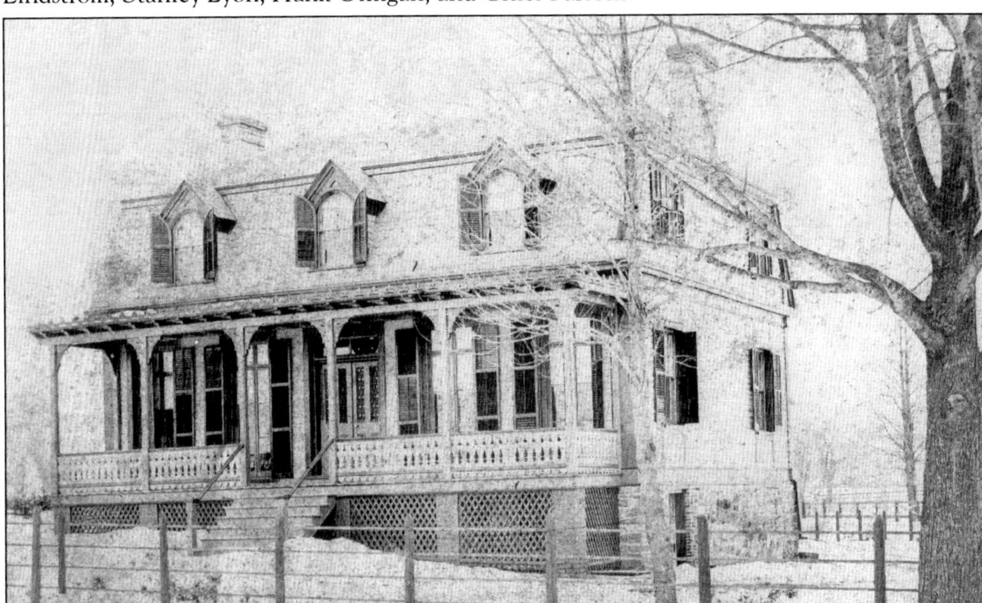

The Canfield-Ferris House. This beautiful mansion was located about where the Acme market is today. It caught fire during a card party in 1915. A 21-year-old man, Eugene Coffey Jr., was killed when the chimney fell on his legs while he was attempting to save canned goods in the basement. At that time, most buildings were doomed if the fire had a good start. In that case, the firemen's job was to save the household contents. Thus, on this terrible day, Mrs. deKanstein's rosewood furniture was saved, but Gene Coffey died for the sake of a few pickles.

Five

Progress on the Plains

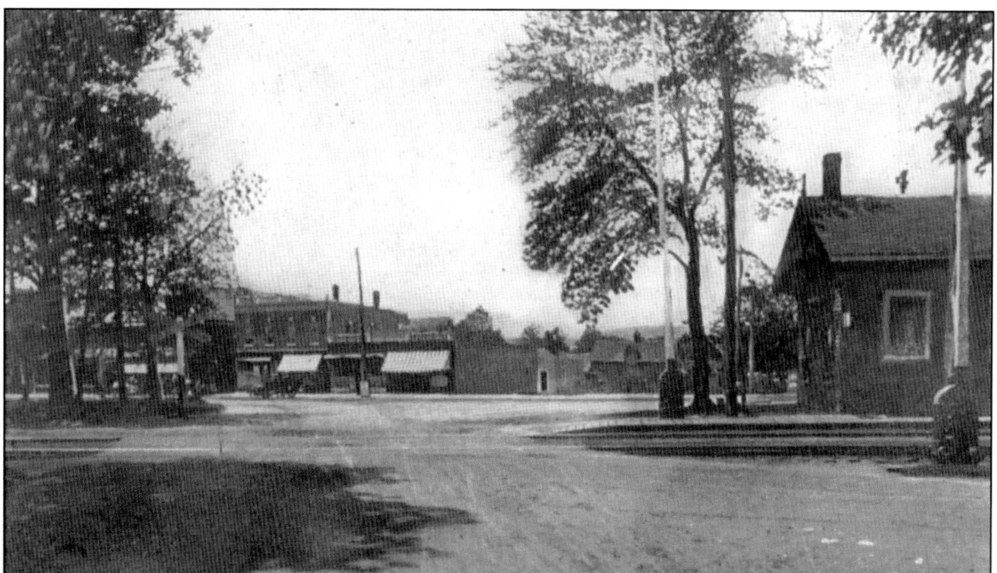

Before the Railroad Overpass. Until 1915, the Delaware, Lackawanna & Western Railroad intersected Littleton Road, necessitating a gate keeper. The station is at the right. A new station would be built on the other side of Littleton Road after the overpass was completed. (Littleton Road met the Speedwell Extension business block several hundred yards to the north of Franklin Place in those days.)

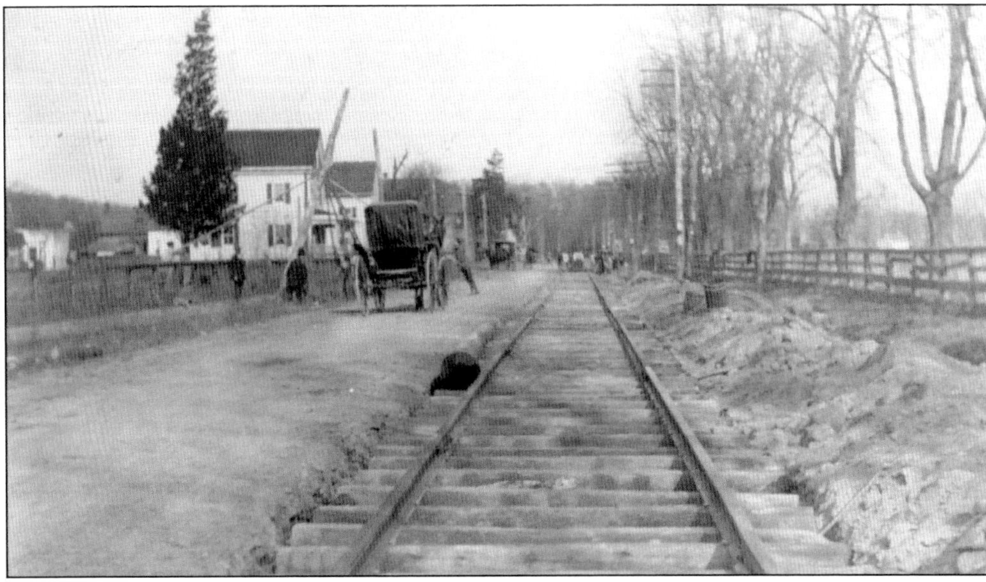

THE TROLLEY COMES TO MORRIS PLAINS, 1909. A power pole is hoisted into place beside the trolley tracks on Speedwell Avenue, north of Glenbrook Avenue. On August 27, 1909, officials of the Morris County Traction Company initiated the new trolley service by traveling from the Morristown Green to Five Corners by horse and then returning to Morristown by trolley.

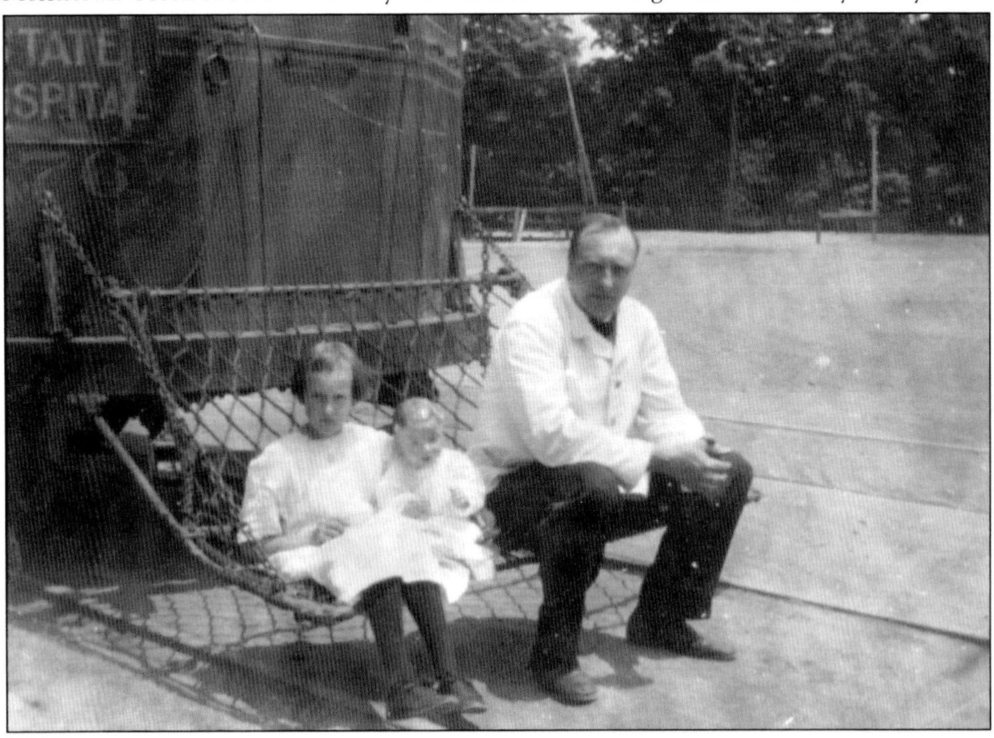

MARY ELZERMAN AND HER FATHER. The trolley line was extended to the north end of town in 1910. The trolley station was in Hendrik Elzerman's restaurant on the south corner of Jaqui, which he was leasing from Dan Merchant. In this picture, Elzerman and his daughter, Mary, sit in the "cow catcher" of a trolley.

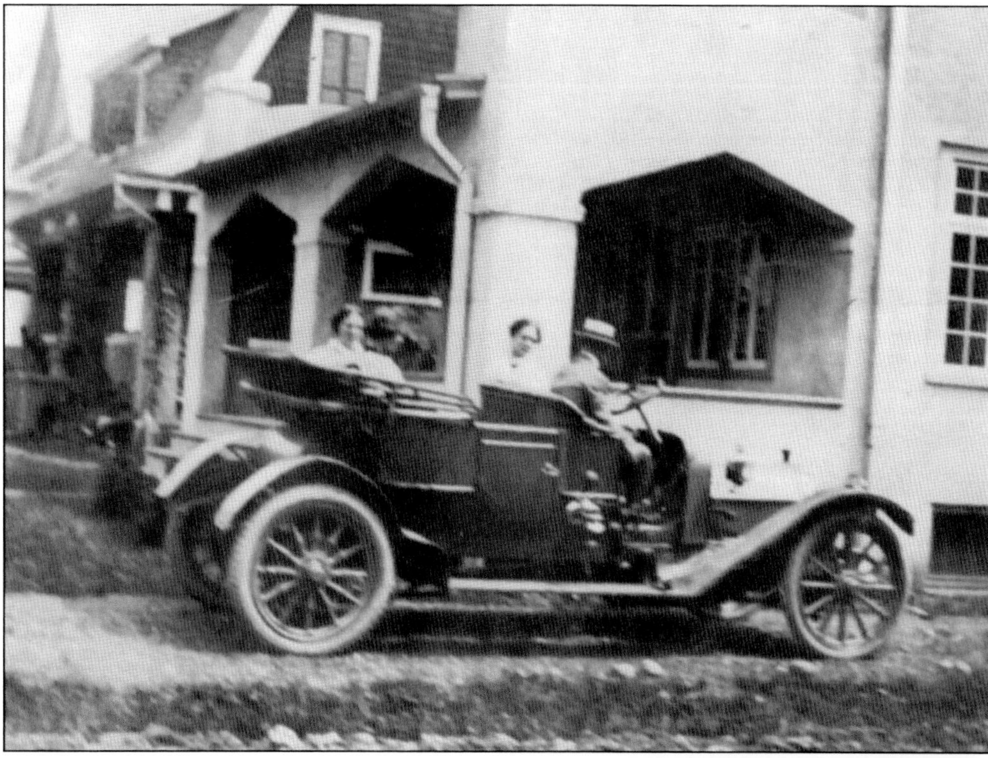

Dr. Dobbins at the Wheel, 1914. By this time, the automobile had transformed the way people lived and worked. Dr. Carlton Dobbins's automobile is parked at his 28 Glenbrook Road home. Dobbins was a dentist in Morristown.

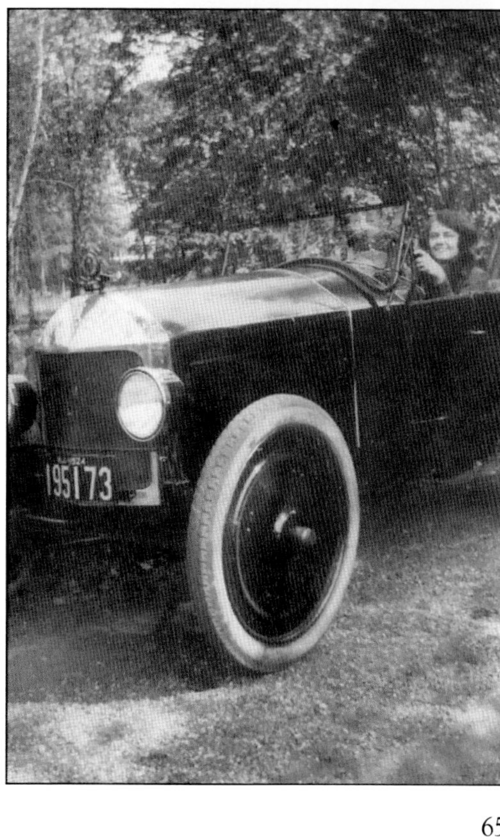

The Romance of the Automobile. This is Alan Florin's Aunt Josephine in a car that her brother, Robert, put together with parts of many cars. The Florin gas station was on Speedwell Avenue, where the Rub-a-Dub Laundry stands today.

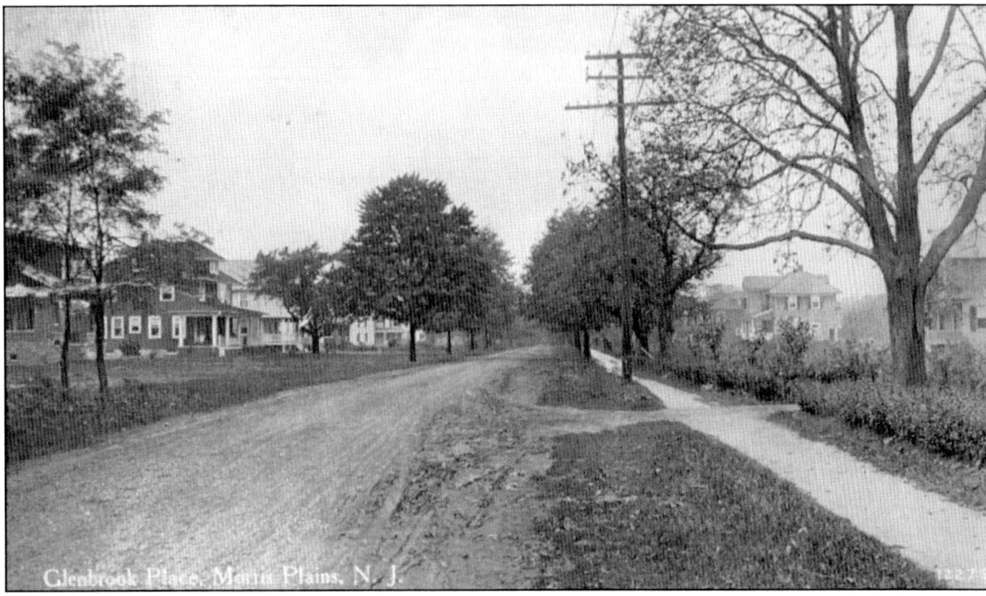

GLENBROOK ROAD, 1912. As the little town of Morris Plains developed, so did its civic pride. Dan Merchant, whose various businesses grew with the town, published a series of postcards displaying the charms of turn-of-the-century Morris Plains. Shown is Glenbrook Road looking west toward the library.

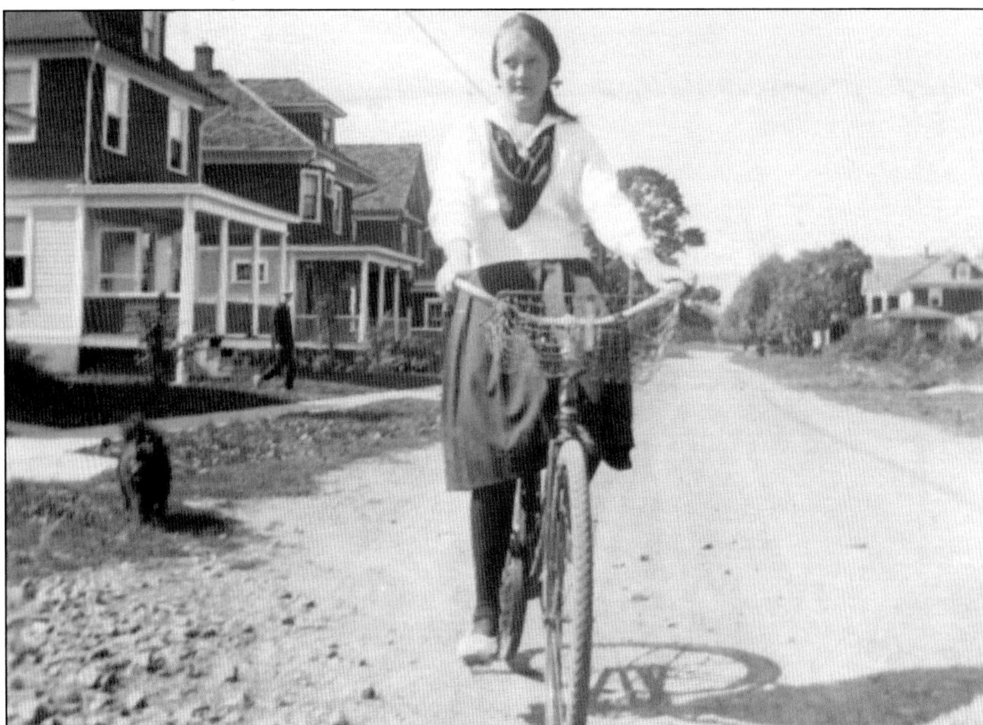

FRANKLIN PLACE, C. 1918. Mary Elzerman Whitehead rides her bike. When this picture was taken, Franklin Place was already built up with many houses that are still standing. One street north, in F.W. Jaqui's subdivision, new homes lined both sides of Jaqui Avenue.

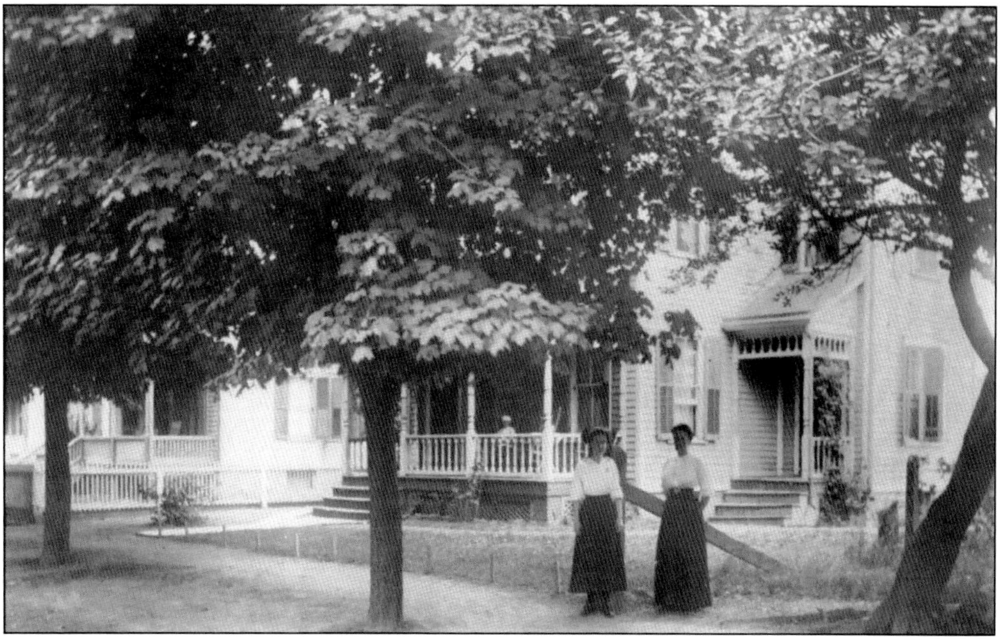

The House at 85 West Hanover Avenue, 1915. The old Five Corners section of Morris Plains was still a vibrant residential neighborhood in the early part of the 20th century. In this photograph, Mary Coss Blaine and her sister, Margurite Coss Creede, pose under the trees while Walter Coss, their father, sits on the porch.

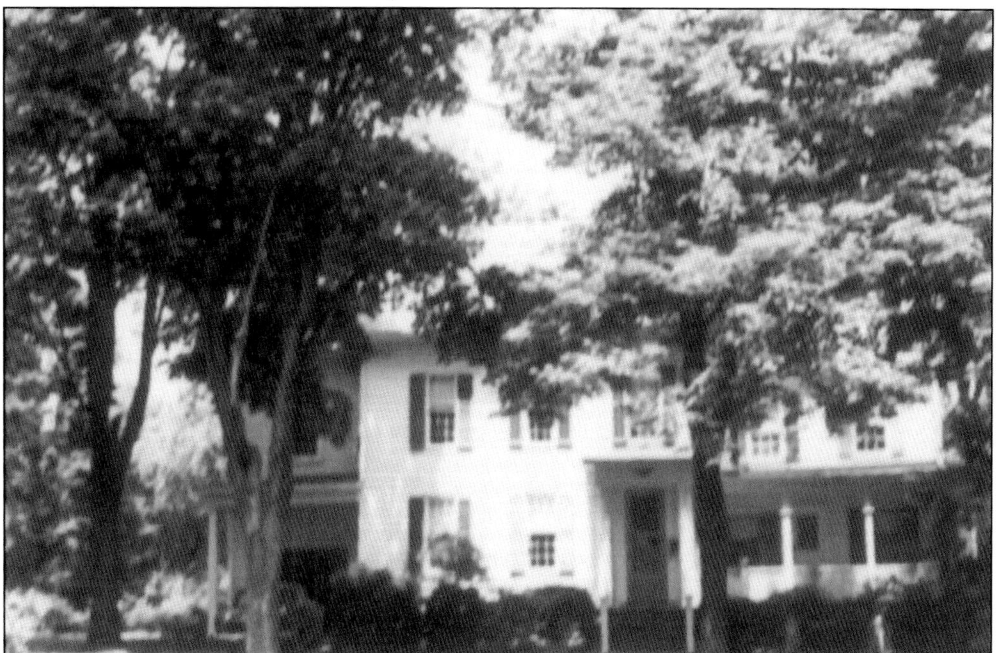

A Gracious Speedwell Avenue Home, Saved. Today known as Bretton Woods, the old Ferris-Laudig house has found new life as a premier reception and party venue. It was built in 1915 to replace the Canfield home that had been destroyed by fire. In 1940, the house was sold to Dr. and Mrs. Guy Laudig. It was transformed into Bretton Woods by Earl Freeman in 1982.

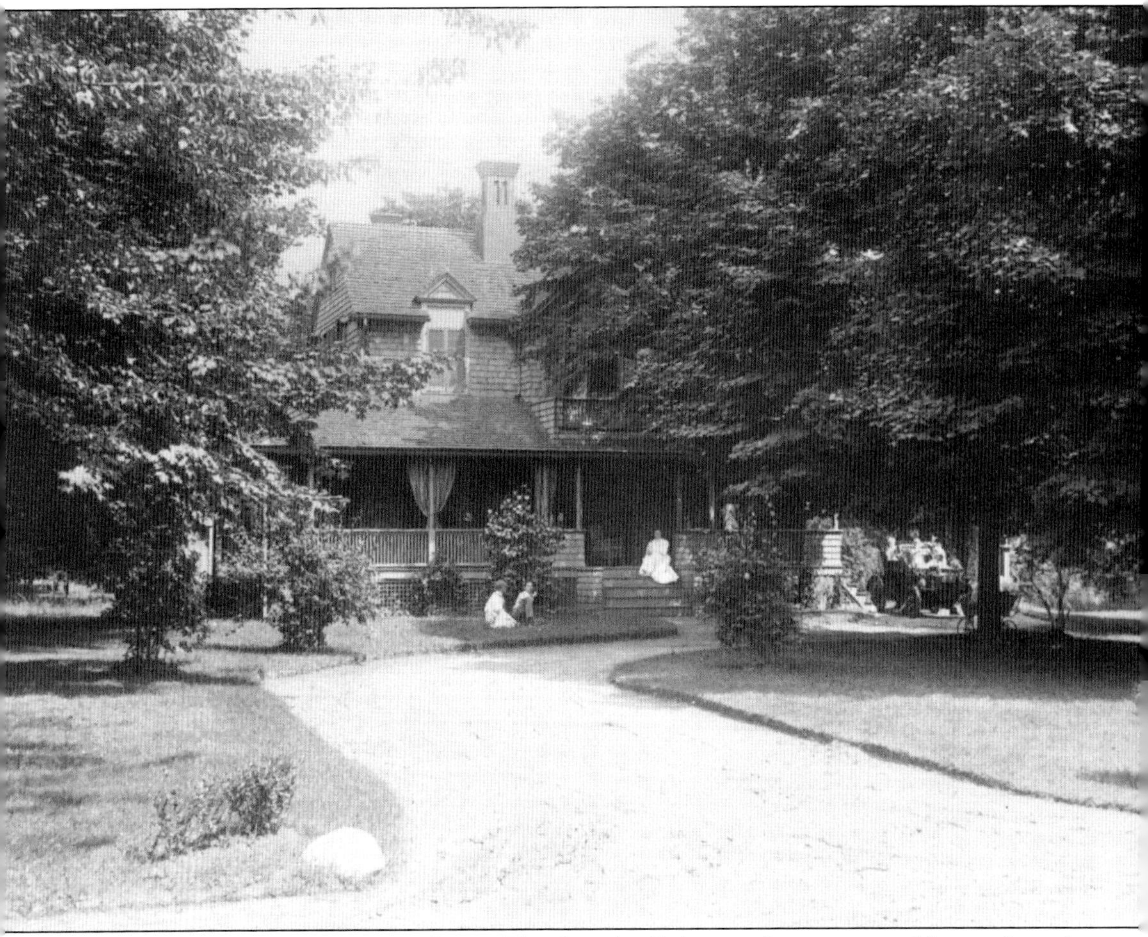

A Speedwell Avenue Home, Gone. This Speedwell Avenue home is a world away from the simple farmhouses of only 20 years earlier. The Parker-Thompson house, shown in 1915, boasts a graceful front porch and beautiful plantings. A baby carriage is in the shade near the open car. On this site today is the Dunkin' Donuts mall.

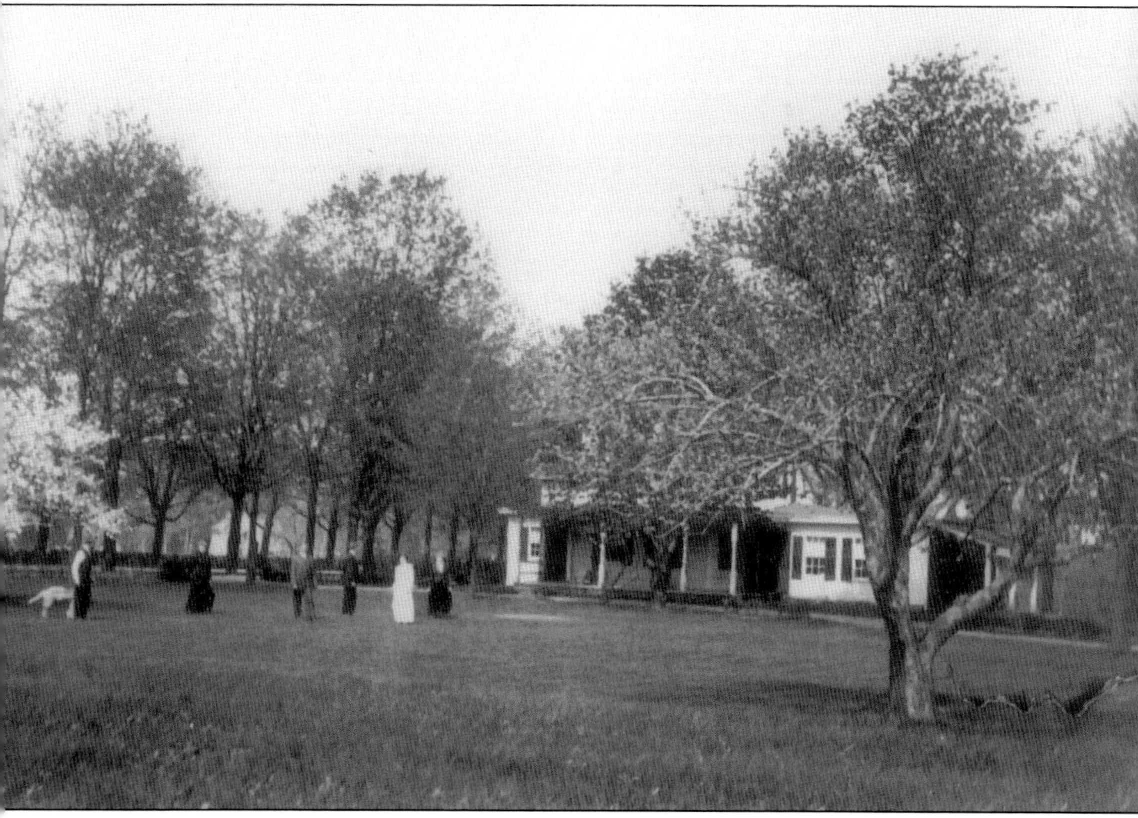

THE McGUINNESS HOMESTEAD. The old home at One Littleton Road, originally built by the Fairchild family, has survived intact from at least 1830. In 1884, the house became the McGuinness homestead. This panorama shows members of the McGuinness family enjoying a spring day on the sweeping front lawn. Some years later, the lawn was radically shortened as the railroad claimed land to build the overpass and parking areas for the new station. Shown, from left to right, are William McGuinness with his dog, Dearie, and his wife, Elizabeth McGuinness; an unidentified family friend; William McGuinness Jr. and his wife, Clara McGuinness; Mary Alice McGuinness (Alice), the daughter of William Sr. and Elizabeth.

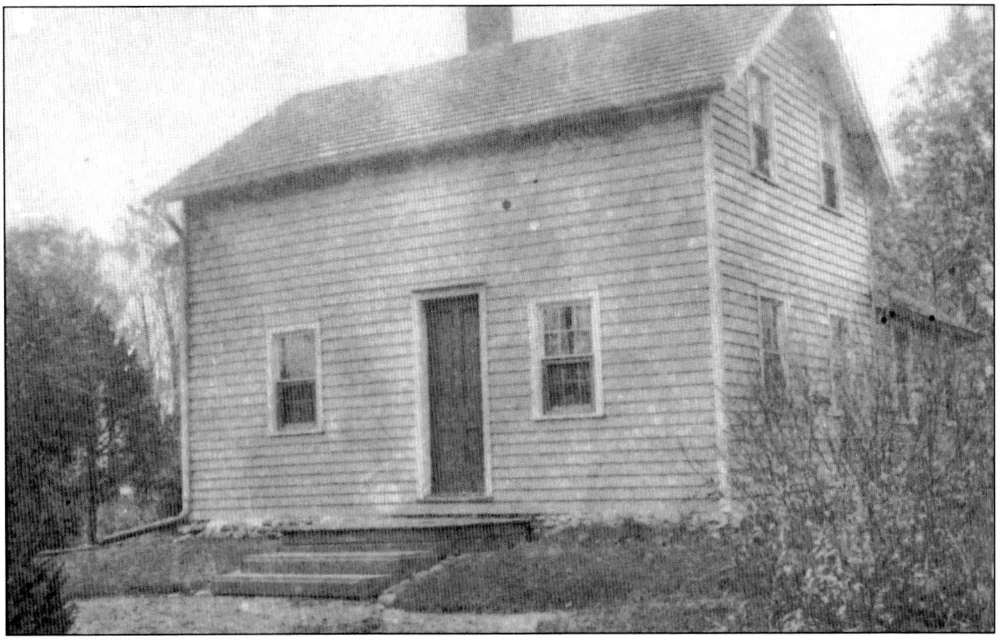

Grandpa Elliott's House. James Elliott arrived in Morris Plains from Ireland in 1856 to "pick stone" for paving the streets of Newark. He was later to become the railroad gate keeper at the Littleton Road crossing. He built a plain little cottage near the site of the future Trinity Lutheran Church for his wife and children.

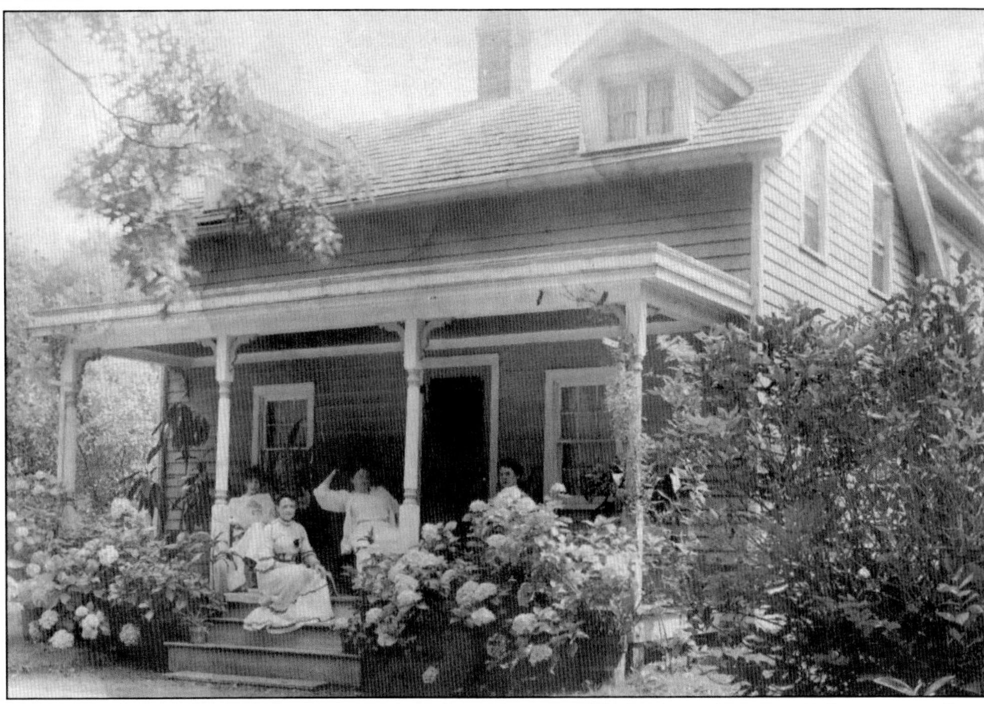

Grandpa Elliott's House, the Next Generation. With the addition of dormers, a front porch and beautiful landscaping, Grandpa Elliott's old house is fancy enough to be a picture postcard setting for these latter-day Elliott women.

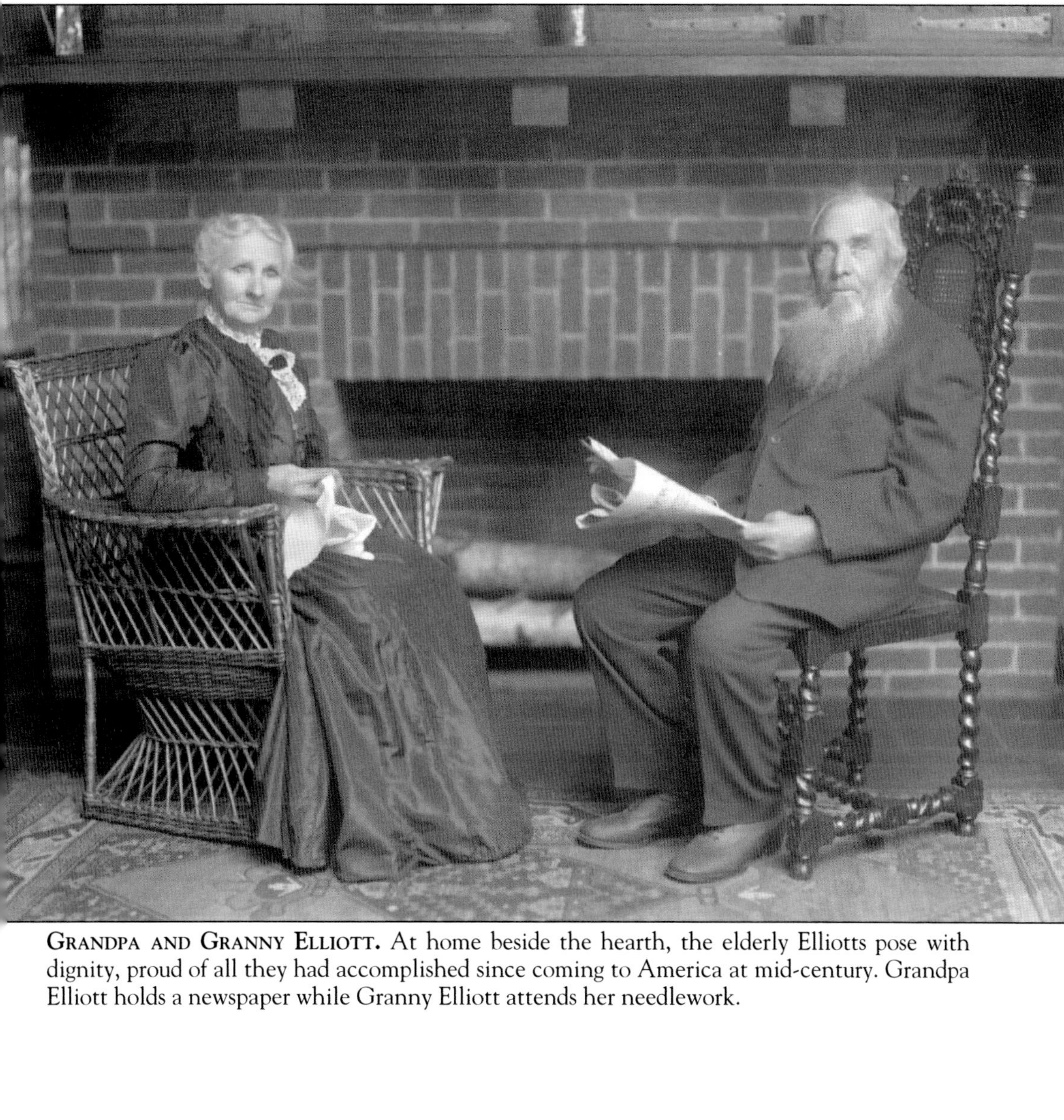

GRANDPA AND GRANNY ELLIOTT. At home beside the hearth, the elderly Elliotts pose with dignity, proud of all they had accomplished since coming to America at mid-century. Grandpa Elliott holds a newspaper while Granny Elliott attends her needlework.

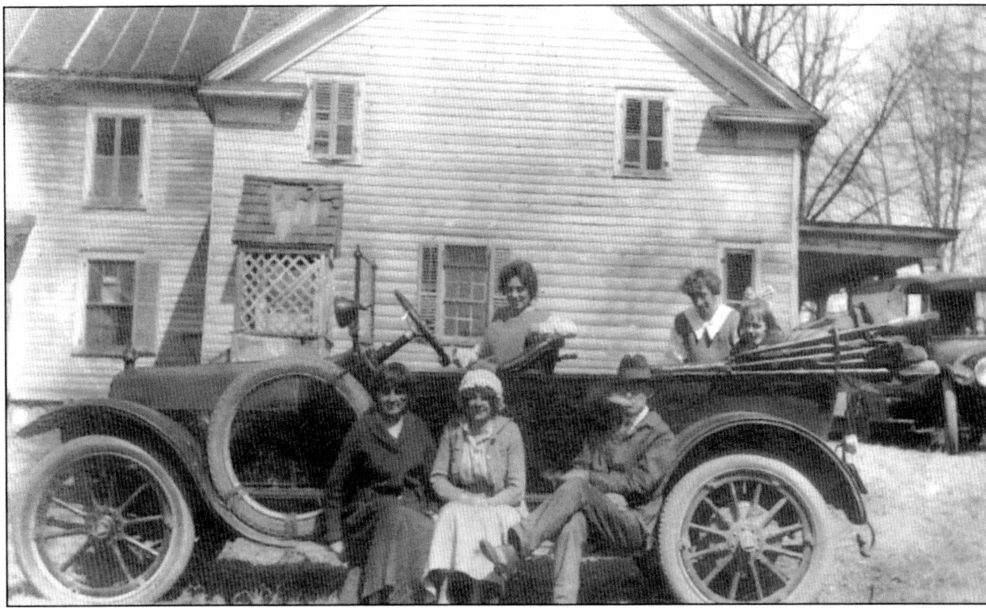

Lynoaks, an Early 20th-Century Farm. Helen Hildebrant Schnack's grandfather, William Moore, first saw the old farm from his bicycle on a day's outing from New York City. In this 1920 picture, a family friend is seated on the running board next to Hannah and William Moore. Their daughter, Cora Moore (Helen Schnack's mother), sits with friends in the car. The Moore-Hildebrant farm is still there, opposite the new recycling center in the triangle between Route 10 and Tabor Road.

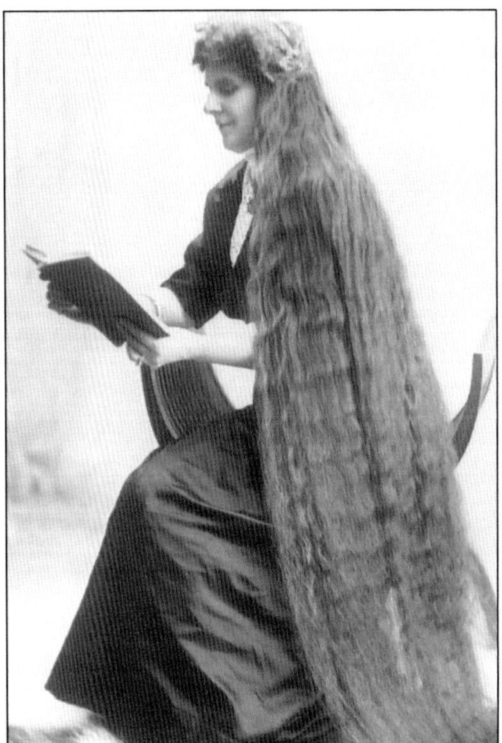

Hannah Moore in 1890. Helen Hildebrant Schnack's grandmother was an early beauty representative for a firm called Seven Sutherland Sisters. At age 18, she was paid to travel across America displaying her luxuriant 8-foot-long hair as proof of the efficacy of Sutherland's Hair Grower and Scalp Cleaner. Gazing upon these magnificent tresses, few could resist rushing to purchase last century's version of "hope in a bottle."

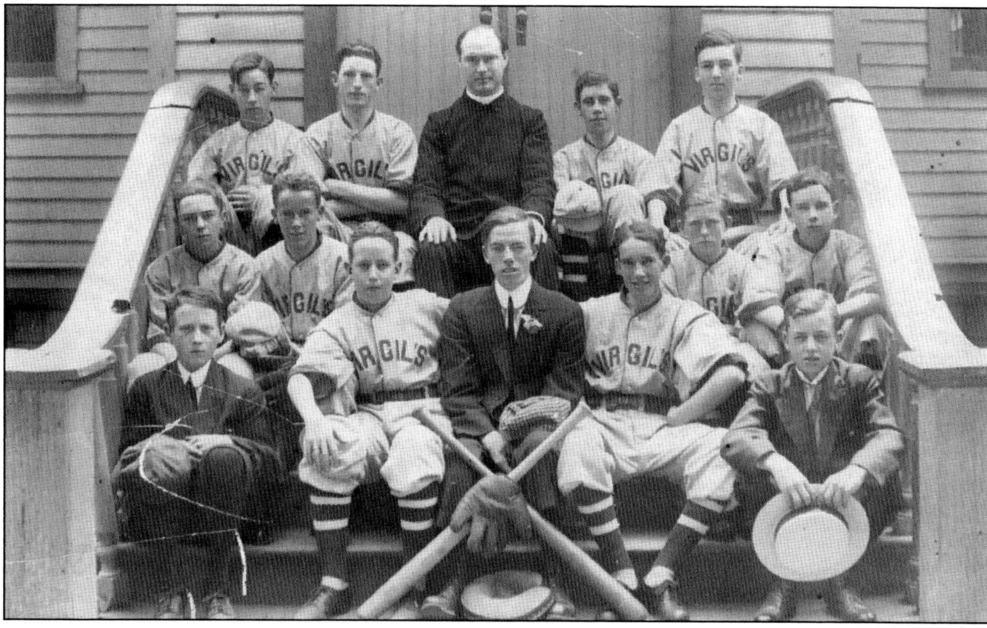

St. Virgil's Baseball Team, 1912. What did boys do before automobiles and television? They played ball. Shown, from left to right, are the following: (front row) Harry Rogers, team manager Joe Gilligan, Eugene Coffey, and John Grady; (middle row) Bill Levick, Bill Coffey, Madison Drake, and Jimmy Connell; (back row) Ed Murphy, Dick Noonan, Father O'Neill, Andrew Coffey, and Larry Monahan. Young Gene Coffey was to die three years later fighting the Canfield house fire.

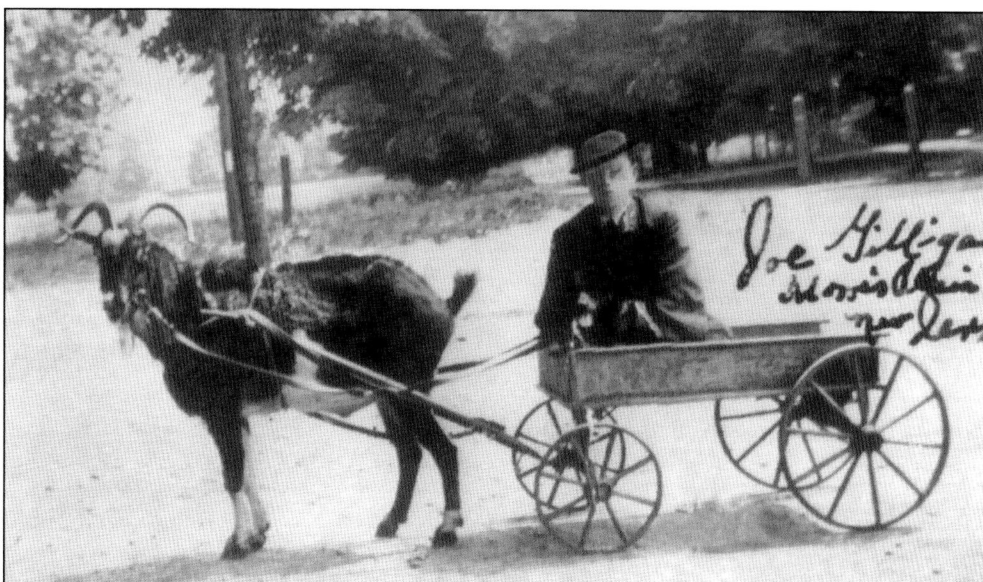

Joe Gilligan, Hero. As a child, Joe Gilligan lost both legs, an arm, and all but two fingers when he fell in front of a streetcar in Brooklyn. Yet he lived an amazingly full life. As a boy, he traveled all over in this goat cart and was manager of St. Virgil's baseball team. In 1908, he won widespread acclaim for saving the lives of three drowning boys at the sandpit pond. He was a musician, businessman, and a popular guest at parties and entertainments.

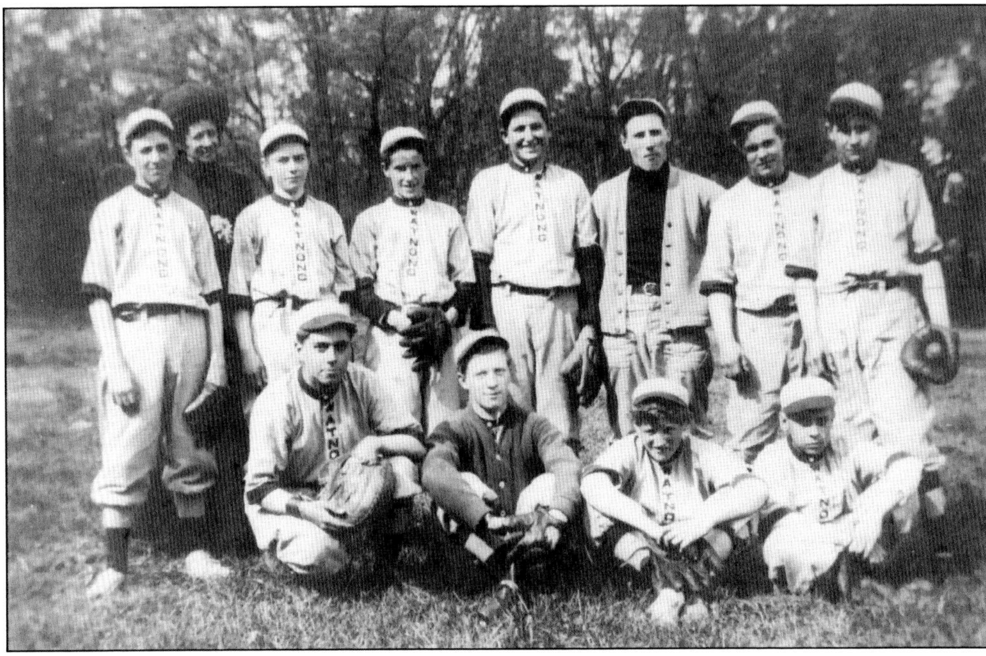

THE WATNONG BASEBALL TEAM, 1911. These boys also partook of the great American pastime. Mr. and Mrs. Herbert Tunis provided the equipment and uniforms in memory of their deceased son. The players, from left to right, are as follows: (front row) Bob Fulford, Bill Stewart, Joe Layer, and Biff Lindstrom; (back row) Kylie Myers, Billy Levick, Billy Coffey, Punk Laurie, Howard Miller, Howard Osborne, and C. Osborne. Mrs. Tunis is at the back on the left.

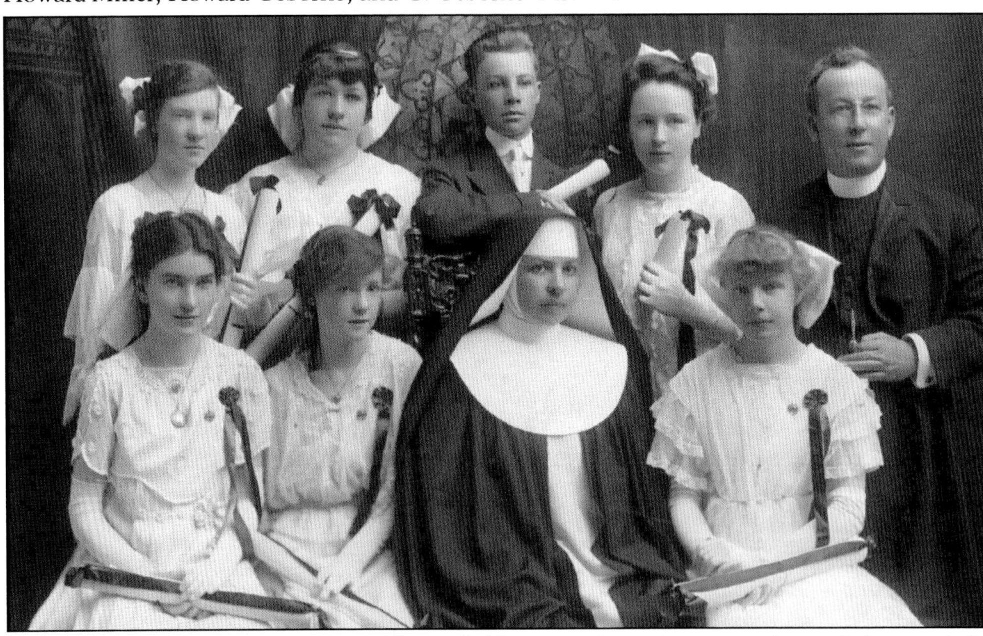

ST. VIRGIL'S 1916 GRADUATION. These children are dressed exquisitely, and their eighth-grade graduation must have been a very special day for them. Shown, from left to right, are the following: (front row) Mary Myers, Grace Arnold, Sister Clementine, and Helen Byrnes; (back row) Esther Arnold, Ann Murphy, Edgar Miller, Mary Cook, and Father Glennon.

Six

MAY WE SERVE YOU?

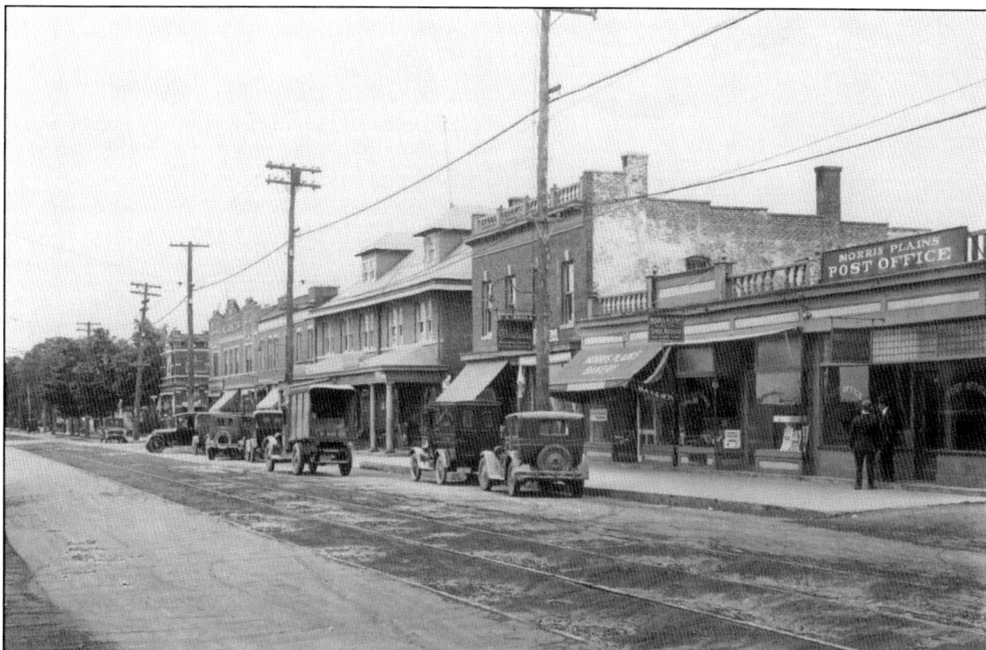

THE GROWTH OF COMMERCE. As the new century progressed, profound change came to the Plains. Nowhere was this change more evident than in the small town's business section. In this 1920 streetscape, we see Merchant's expanded store in the center of town, the Morris Plains Bakery, Morris Plains Shoe Repair, Zecca's Ice Cream, Elzerman's new restaurant (at far left), and other thriving businesses. The post office now had its own building, although home delivery would not come for another 16 years.

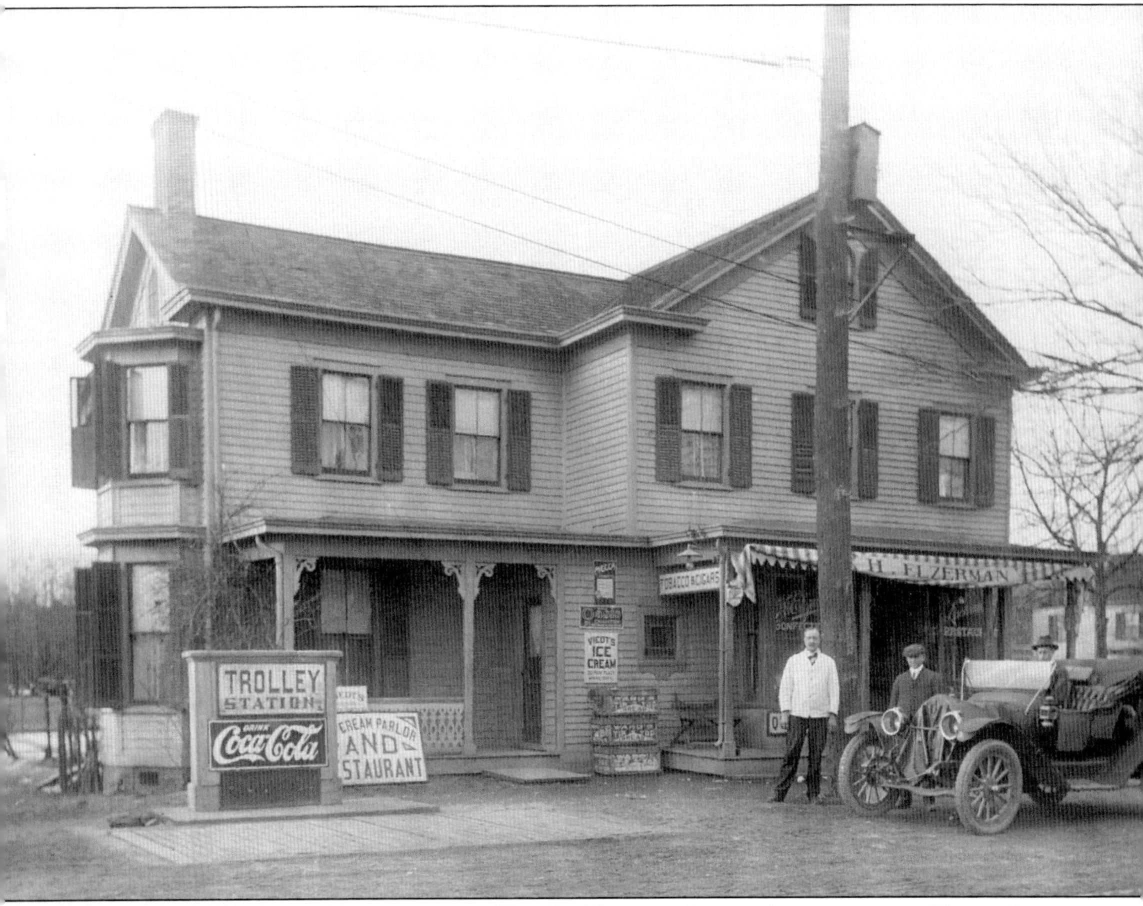

The Store at the Corner, 1915. This building, at the southwest corner of Jaqui Avenue, symbolizes the early establishment and endurance of commerce in Morris Plains. In the mid-1700s, it was Jacob Young's provisions store. A century later, Isaac Clark was storekeeper. In 1887, Clark's young clerk, Dan Merchant, bought the business. The small store would become the cornerstone of Merchant's many mercantile enterprises. At the time of this picture, Merchant was leasing the store to Hendrik Elzerman, who had a restaurant and ice-cream parlor there. The building was also serving as the trolley station. After 250 years, the venerable old building is still there, although apartments have taken the place of the aisles of merchandise.

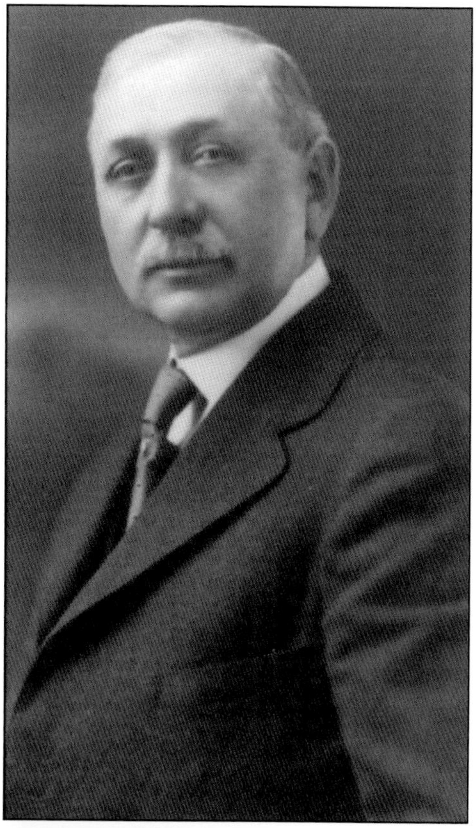

"THE WORLD CONTRIBUTES, MERCHANT'S DISTRIBUTES." This was the motto of Daniel Manning Merchant, "Mr. Morris Plains." From humble beginnings working 18-hour days for Isaac Clark, Merchant had built a small-town retail empire by the turn of the 20th century. Merchant served his town as everything from postmaster to fire chief and, by unanimous acclaim, was elected the first mayor of Morris Plains when it was incorporated in 1926.

EMPLOYEES IN FRONT OF MERCHANT BUILDING, LATE 1920S. In 1901, Dan Merchant erected a two-story department store where he sold groceries, hardware, clothing, shoes, cement, livestock feed, tin, hay, straw, paint, coal, home furnishings, insurance, real estate, and more. An ardent modernist, Merchant had the first telephone and the first electricity in town; he was also the first to offer "frosted" (frozen) foods to the public. Shown, from left to right, are the following: (front row) ? Rogers, William Morgan, and ? West; (back row) Dan Merchant, Ned Merchant, Ed Hill, one unidentified person, Theodore Stiff, and D.L. Gibbs. The last three employees are unidentified. (Courtesy JFPLMMT.)

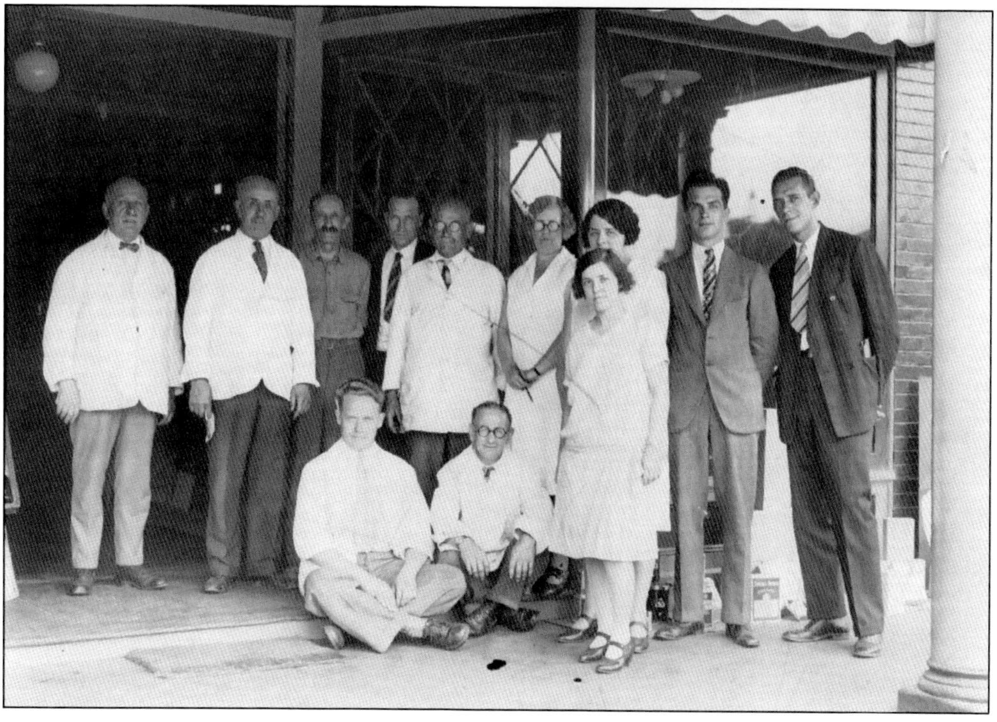

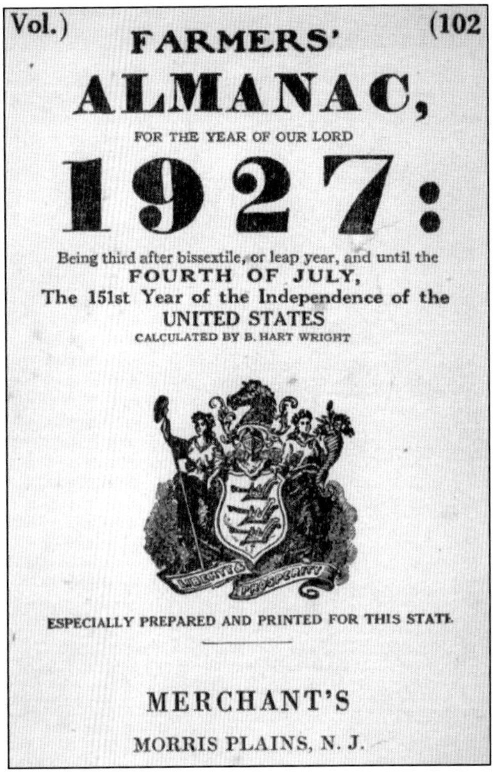
Vol.) (102

FARMERS'

ALMANAC,

FOR THE YEAR OF OUR LORD

1927:

Being third after bissextile, or leap year, and until the
FOURTH OF JULY,
The 151st Year of the Independence of the
UNITED STATES
CALCULATED BY B. HART WRIGHT

ESPECIALLY PREPARED AND PRINTED FOR THIS STATE

MERCHANT'S

MORRIS PLAINS, N. J.

FARMERS' ALMANAC, COMPLIMENTS OF DAN MERCHANT. In addition to his other enterprises, Dan Merchant, along with four partners, owned the publishing rights to the *Farmers' Almanac* from 1907 to 1933.

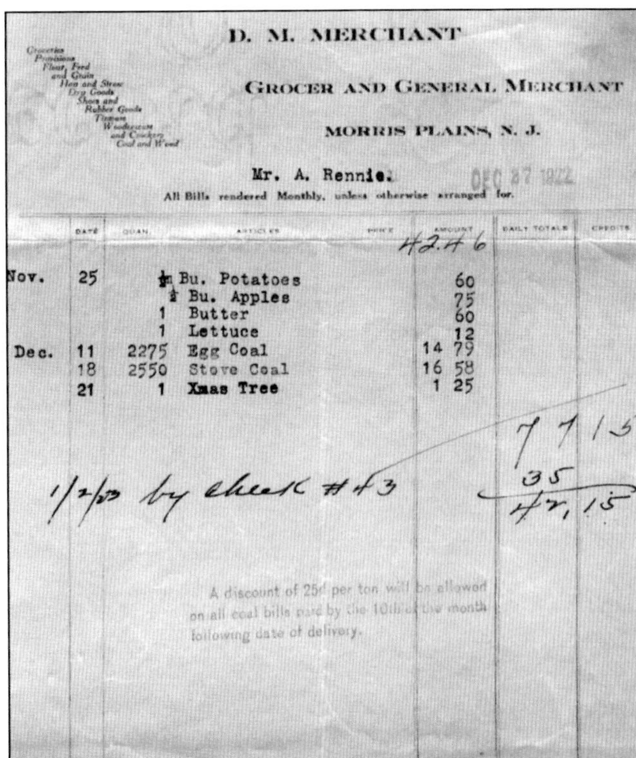
Groceries
Provisions
Flour, Feed and Grain
Hay and Straw
Dry Goods
Shoes and Rubber Goods
Tinware
Woodenware and Crockery
Coal and Wood

D. M. MERCHANT

GROCER AND GENERAL MERCHANT

MORRIS PLAINS, N. J.

Mr. A. Rennie. DEC 27 1922

All Bills rendered Monthly, unless otherwise arranged for.

	DATE	QUAN.	ARTICLES	PRICE	AMOUNT	DAILY TOTALS	CREDITS
					42.46		
Nov.	25	1/2	Bu. Potatoes		60		
		1/2	Bu. Apples		75		
		1	Butter		60		
		1	Lettuce		12		
Dec.	11	2275	Egg Coal		14 79		
	18	2550	Stove Coal		16 58		
	21	1	Xmas Tree		1 25		
						77 15	
						35	
1/2/23 by check #43						77.15	

A discount of 25¢ per ton will be allowed on all coal bills paid by the 10th of the month following date of delivery.

A STATEMENT FROM MERCHANT'S, 1922.
Mr. Rennie bought everything from apples and butter to coal and a Christmas tree at Merchant's. The tree was $1.25. After Merchant's new store was built, Merchant created the "Good Luck Cash and Carry" store in the Young-Clark building. Today, the Merchant Building houses Duffield's Hardware.

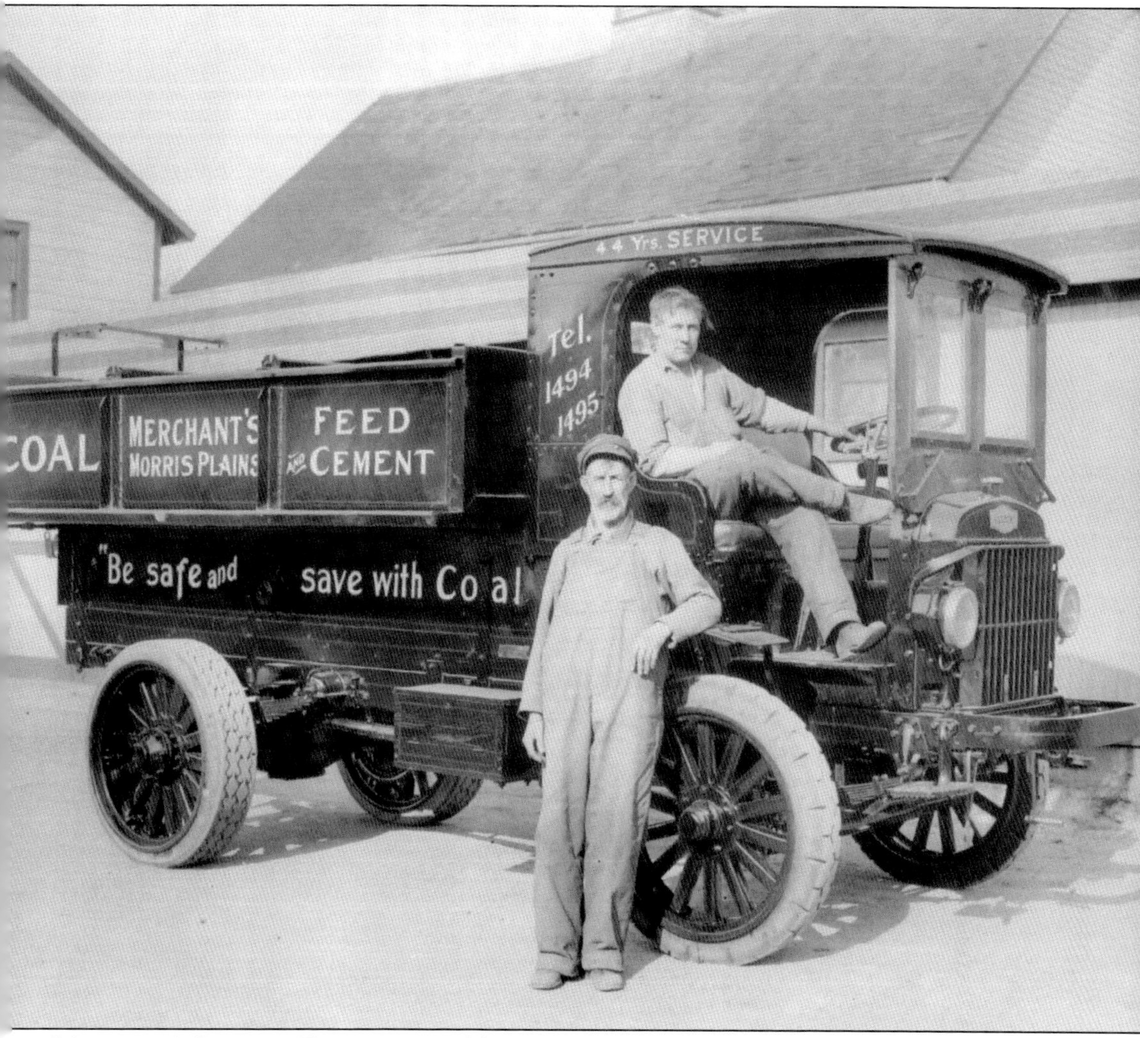

MERCHANT'S DELIVERY TRUCK, 1930. After 43 years in business, Merchant's motto was, "If you need it, Merchant's has it." Merchant's business acumen was matched only by his compassion. Early historian Julia Beers wrote of him, "There are children in Morris Plains who would have gone hungry but for Mr. Merchant's generous spirit, but that is unwritten history that he would not want divulged."

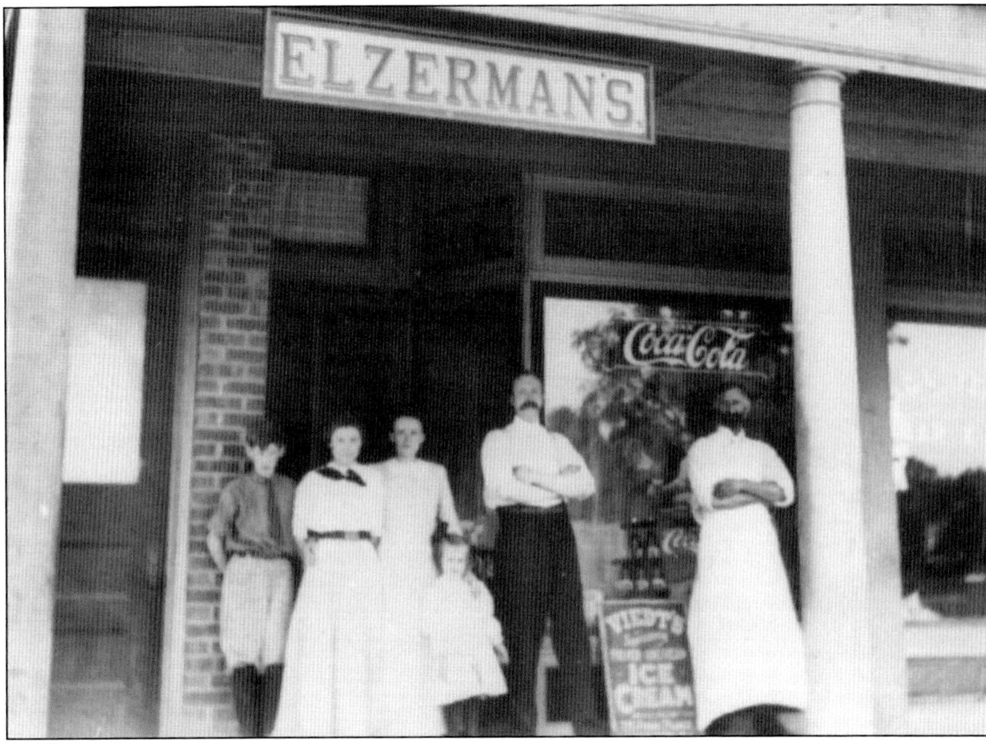

HEINRICH ELZERMAN'S FIRST RESTAURANT. As the prosperity of the 20th century took hold, people became more accustomed to eating out. Heinrich Elzerman was just the man to serve them. He arrived in Morris Plains as a pastry chef at Greystone after cooking on the high seas for the Holland America Lines. He is shown in this 1908 photograph standing in front of his first restaurant, which was in the Layer building on the business block. Pictured, from left to right, are Joe Layer Jr., Louise Layer, Mrs. Elzerman, Mary Elzerman, Heinrich Elzerman, and Joseph Layer Sr.

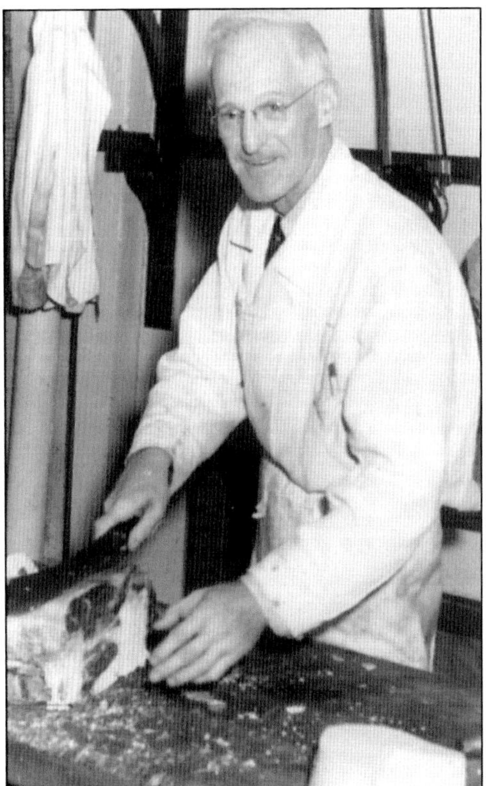

JOE LAYER JR., 1941. For 67 years, there was a Joseph Layer Butcher Shop in Morris Plains, despite being burned out twice. The younger Layer closed the store for the last time in 1962. Joe Layer Jr. and his wife, Adelaide, were extremely civic-minded, serving their town in many capacities through the years.

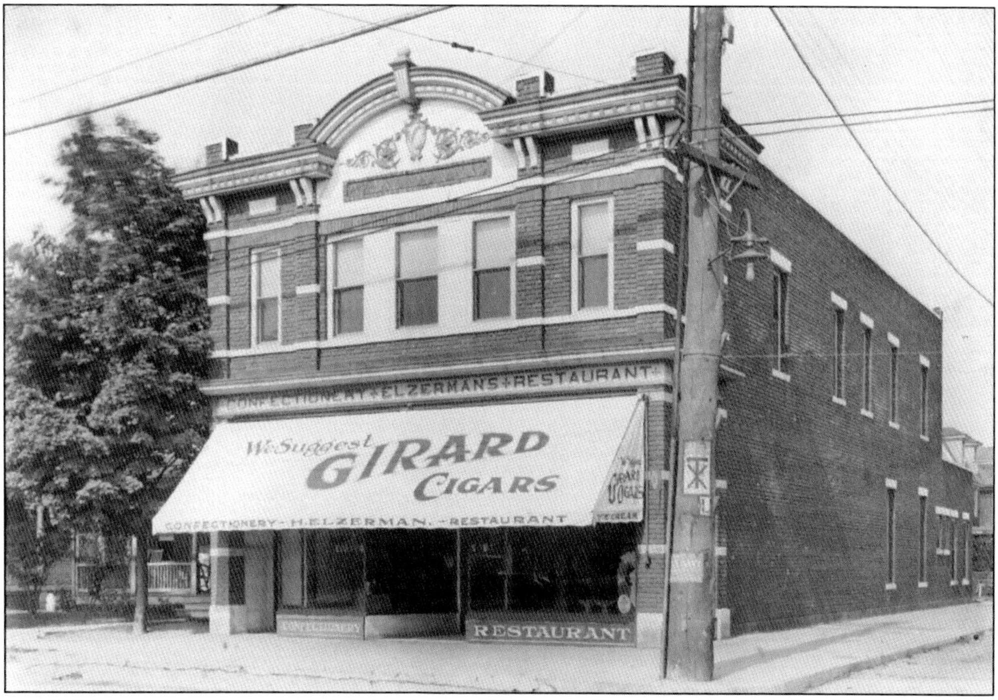

A Restaurant of His Own. In 1917, Heinrich Elzerman built a restaurant on the southwest corner of Franklin Place. Today, the graceful building is painted an elegant black and white. It houses Arthur's Tavern. Before Arthur's Tavern, longtime residents remember the Brook Tavern. "The Brook" first introduced Arthur's time-tested menu of steak (and lots of it), sauteed potatoes, and big bowls of pickled green tomatoes and peppers. Below, Heinrich Elzerman stands proudly behind the ice-cream counter.

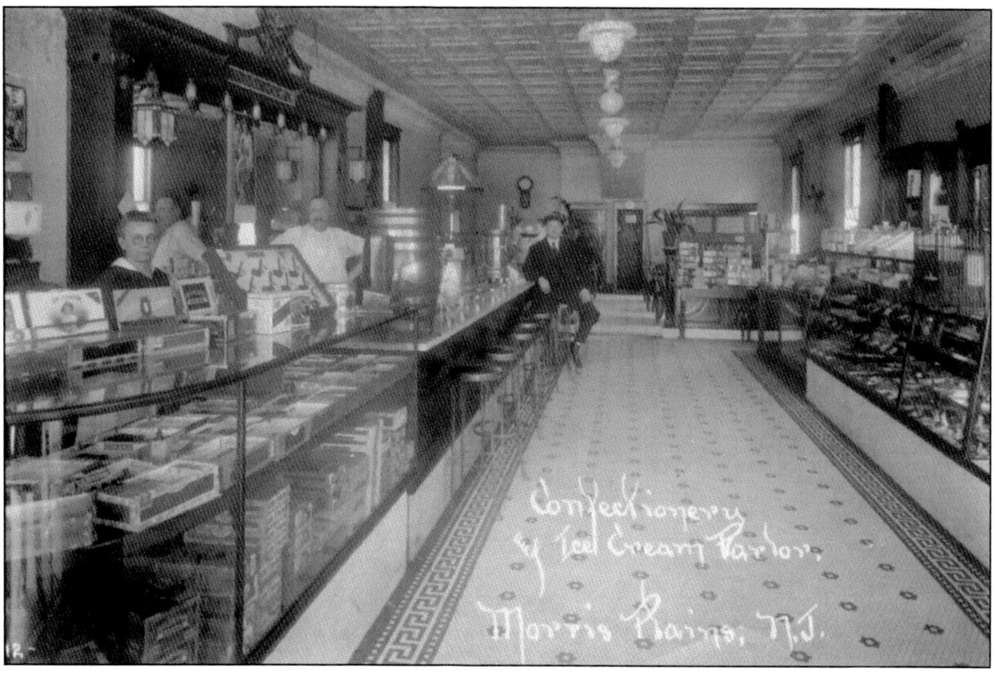

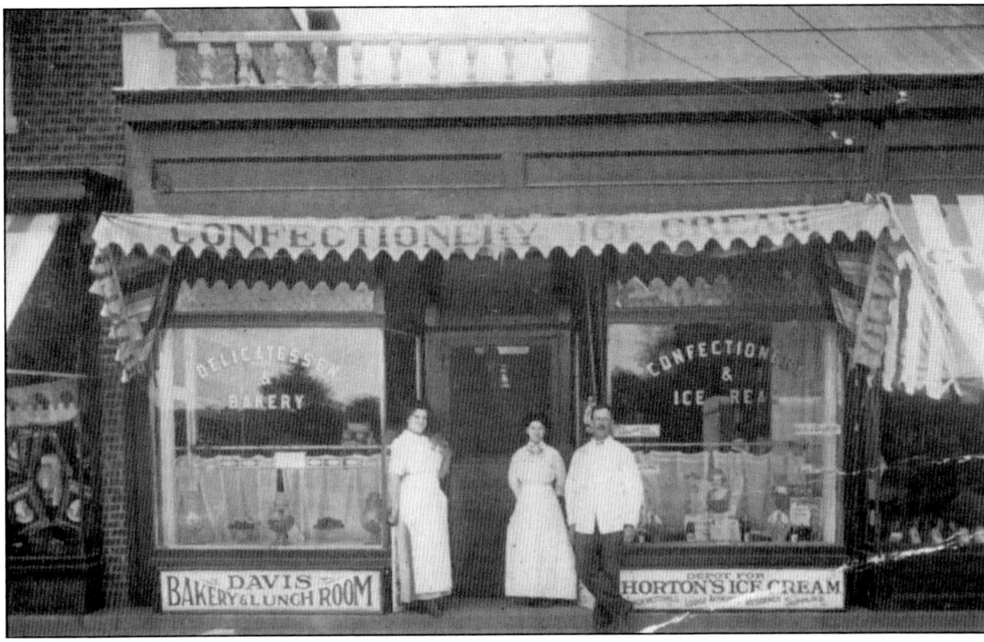

The Davis Bakery, 1915. The Davis Bakery and Lunch Room was on the site of today's Plaza Diner. In 1920, it was the Morris Plains Bakery.

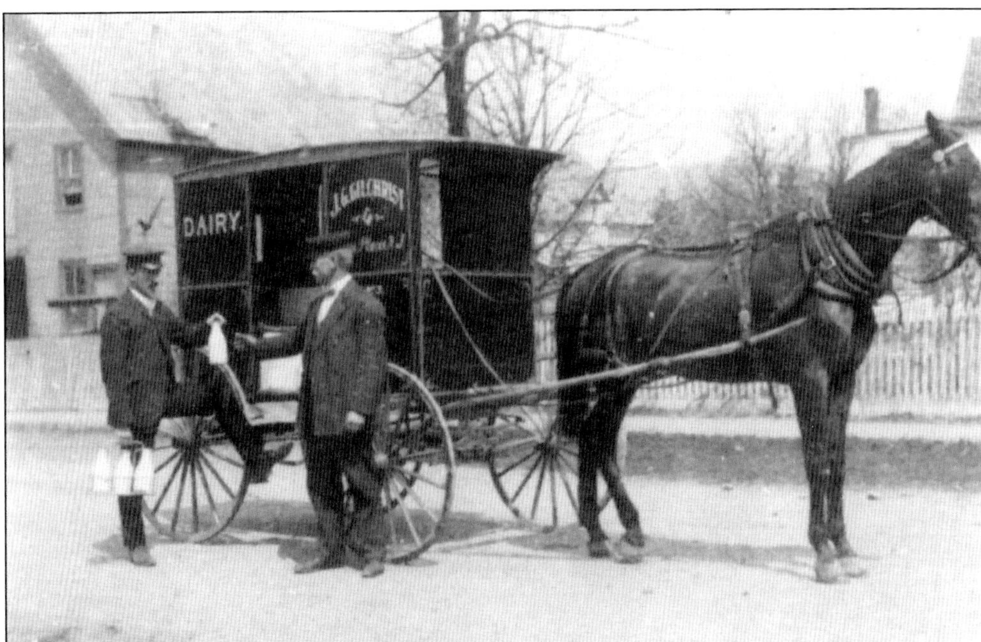

Mr. Gilchrist, Milkman. By 1912, milk was delivered to houses by Mr. Gilchrist, who used a horse and buggy to make his daily rounds, starting from his home at 18 Mountain Way.

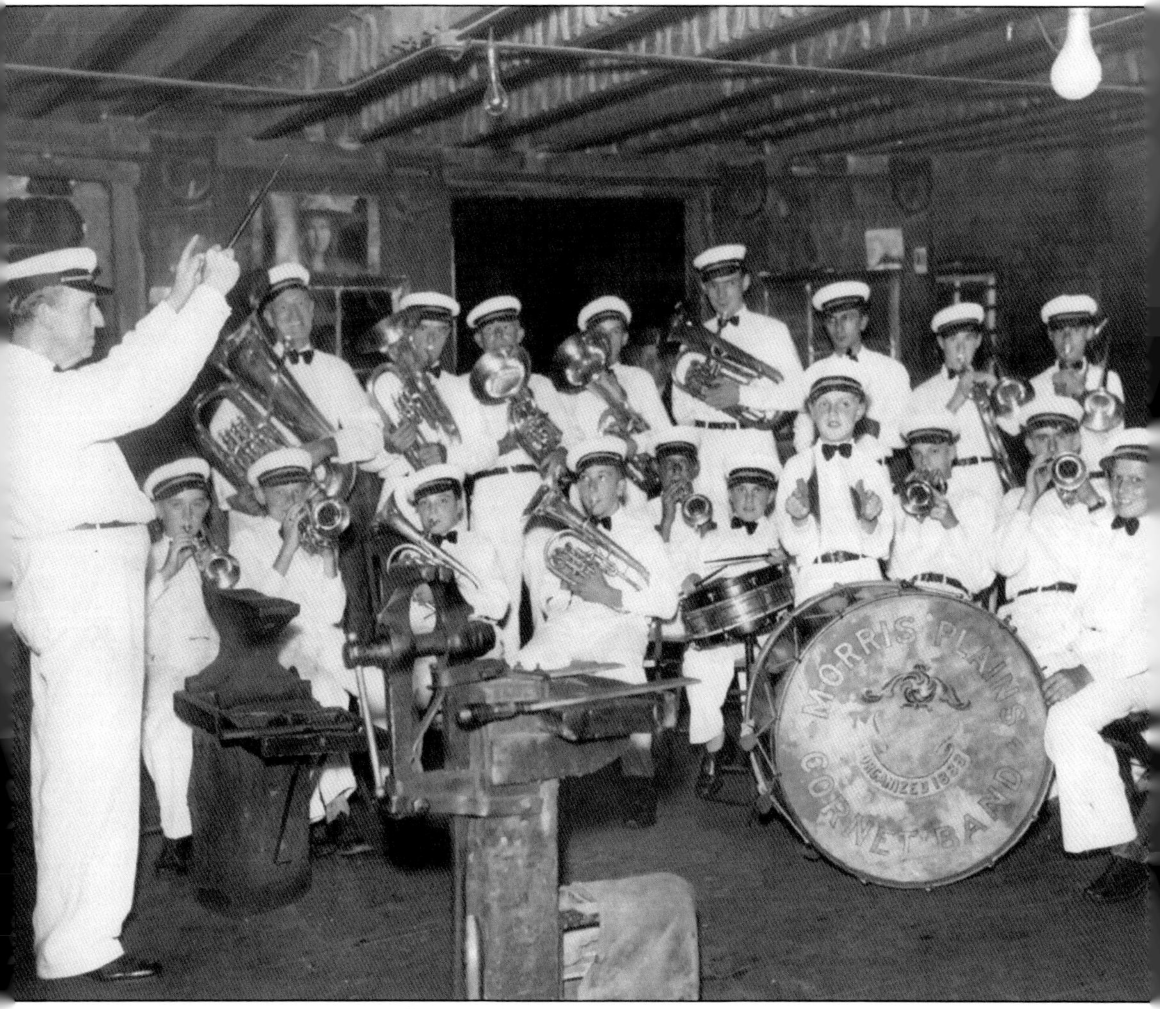

MORRIS PLAINS'S MUSIC MAN. The remarkable Lawrence "Larry" Monahan Jr., blacksmith by trade but musician at heart, found a way to share his life-long love of music with thousands of people. Starting in 1888, amidst anvils, hammers, and horseshoes, Monahan taught the boys of Morris Plains how to play marching music. Among the Morris Plains families represented by band members in this 1930s photograph are Monahan, Fraser, Young, Miller, Barry, Gilligan, Menshin, Murdician, Mills, Walsh, and Martin.

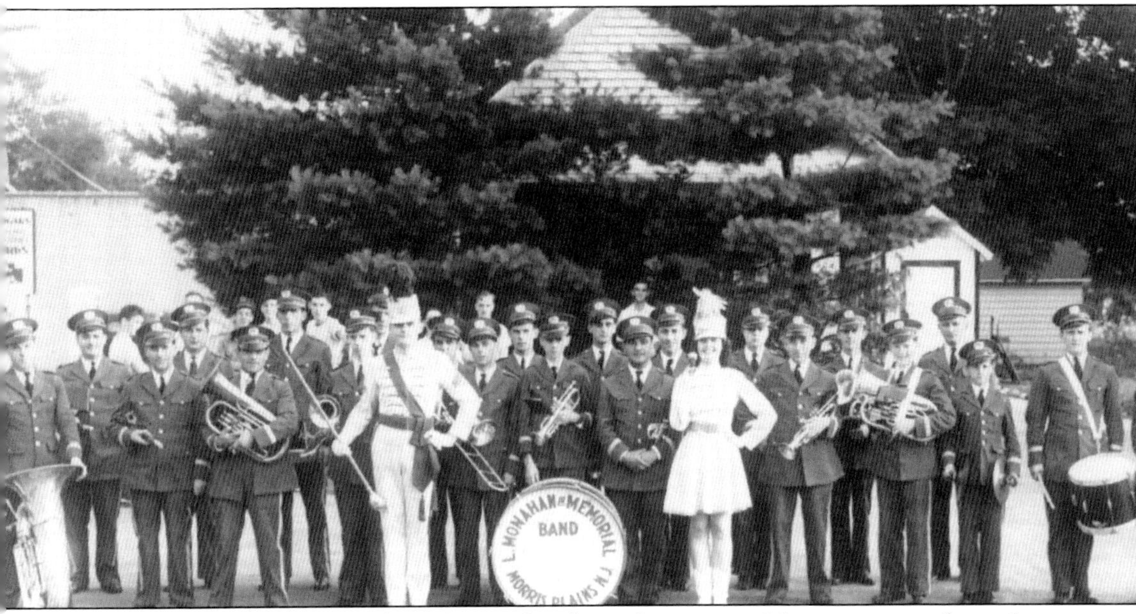

ON PARADE. The Morris Plains Cornet Band was the perennial favorite at parades and events everywhere. To finance new uniforms, Monahan had the boys serenade the town's rich estate owners under the windows of their mansions, hoping for donations. It worked. The Morris Plains Museum has one of those bright blue, gold-braided uniforms on display. The young lady in the front is Ann McManus McKean, an all-state twirler, who was sometimes hired to march with the all-male band.

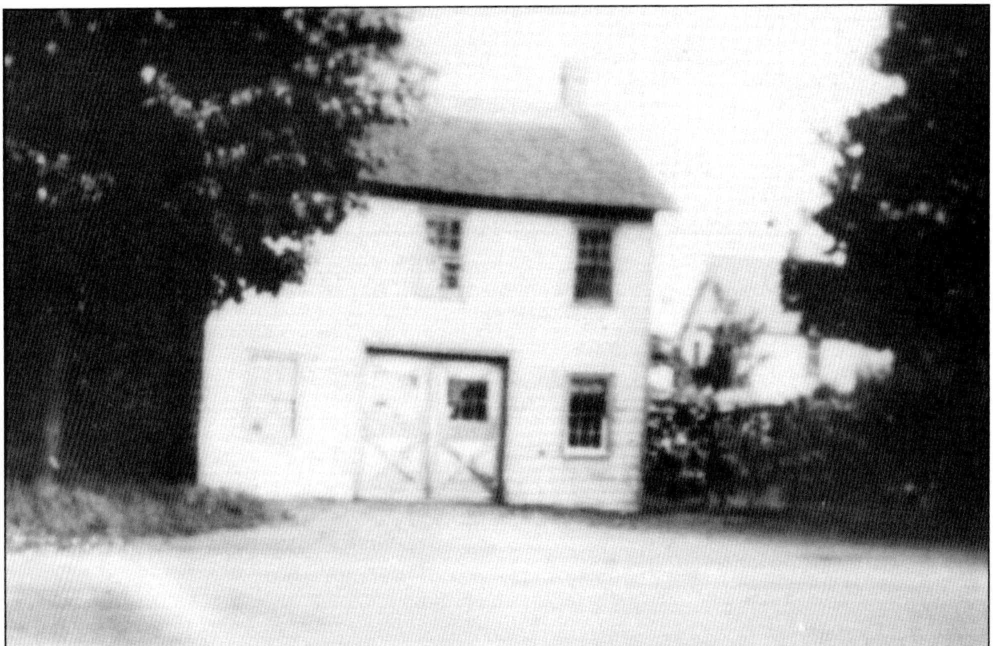

THE HOME OF THE MORRIS PLAINS CORNET BAND. Rehearsals were held in Monahan's "smithy" on Stiles Avenue. "A band keeps a town on the map," Monahan claimed, and so it did for more than 50 years.

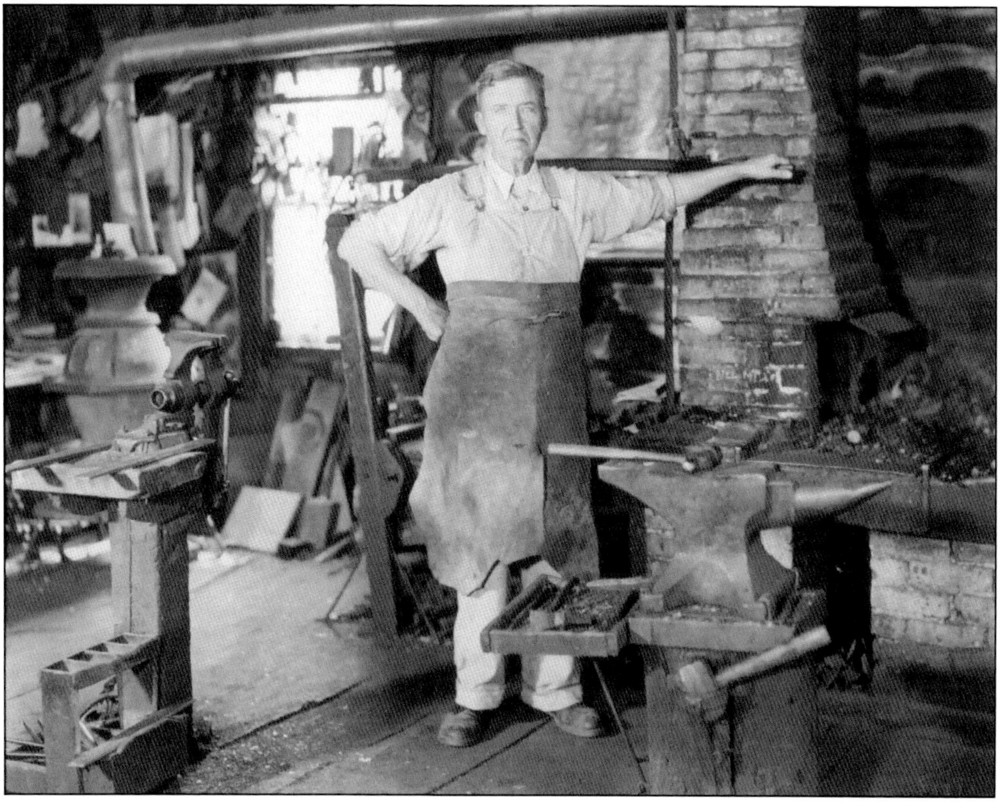

LARRY MONAHAN, MORRIS PLAINS'S MUSICAL BLACKSMITH. The tough but tuneful Monahan stands astride the tools of his trade. Monahan's blacksmith shop still exists, now a private residence. The open fire pit and anvil are long gone. Sometimes, on a warm summer night, you can almost hear the stirring cornet riffs of Monahan's Cornet Band floating on the breeze.

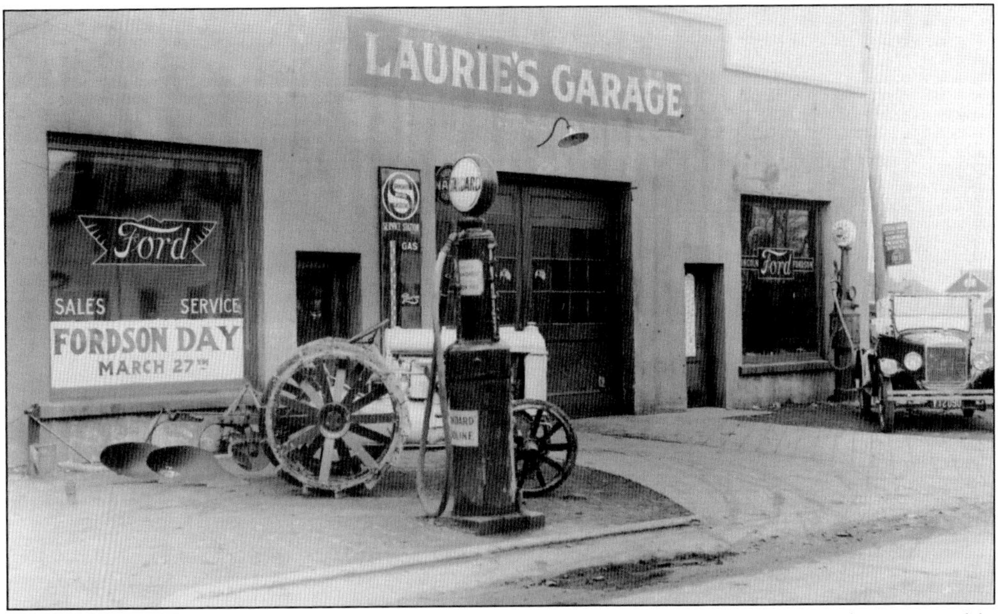

The Future Meets the Past. This 1923 photograph of Laurie's Garage captures the irreversible shift from the farm-dominated 19th century to 20th-century suburbia. In the photograph the tractor and the automobile are given equal space, but less and less farm equipment would be sold as housing developments rapidly replaced the old farms. Dozens of new businesses that sold or serviced the automobile sprang up in and around Morris Plains. Barns were turned into garages, and Joe Tunis's and Larry Monahan's blacksmith shops became obsolete in the blink of an eye.

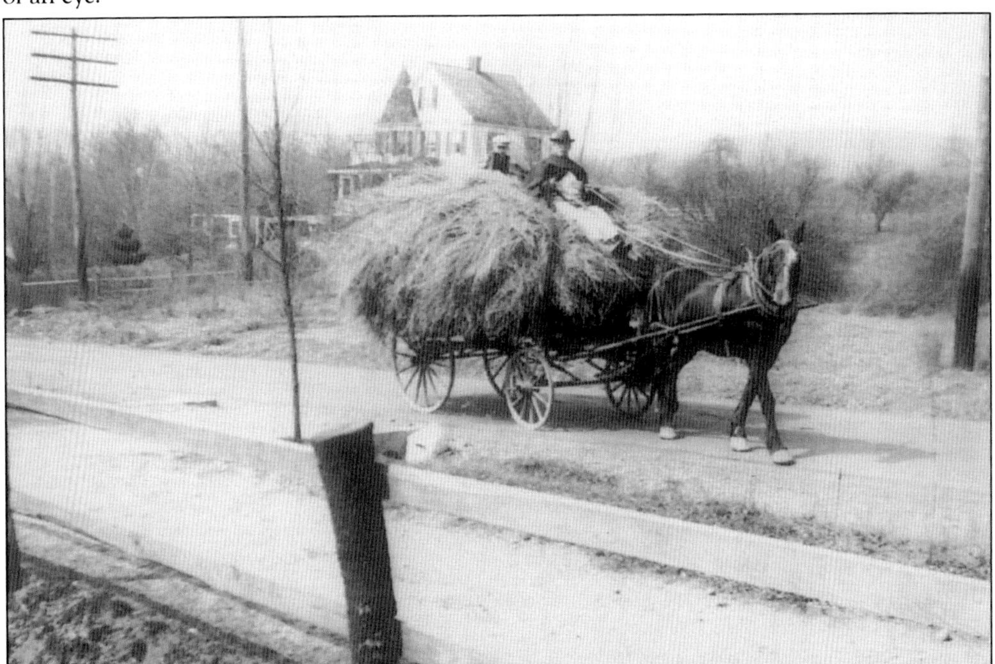

On Its Way to Extinction. A haywagon passes by the Norton house on West Hanover Avenue, its days numbered.

Seven

CASTLES OF ANOTHER TIME

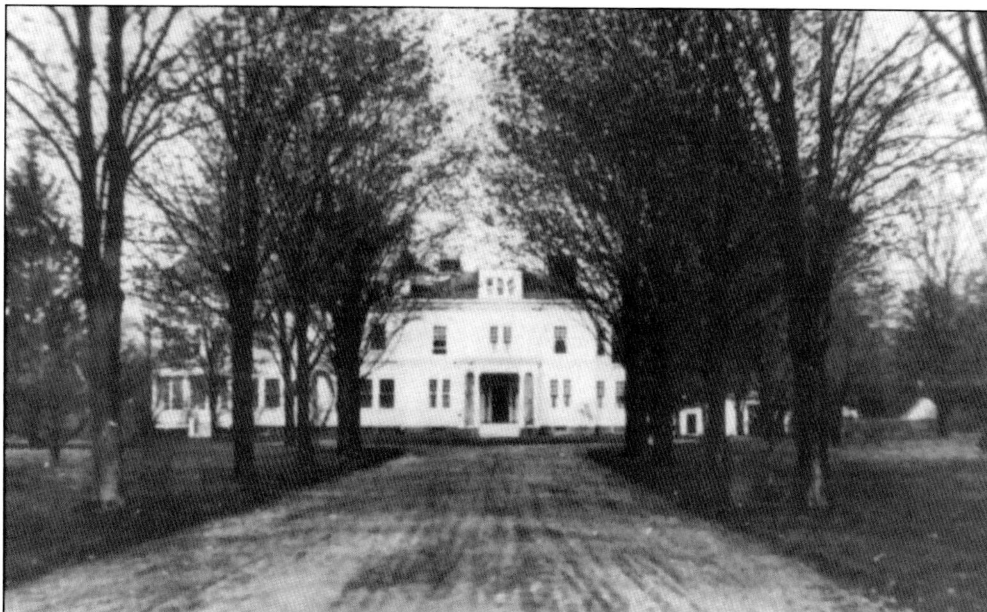

THE APPROACH TO IDLEWILD. The late 19th century was a golden time, full of progress and optimism. Great fortunes were made, and many of the wealthiest Americans lived lavishly. War and the Great Depression would come later, but for a brief time Morris Plains offered an unspoiled country setting for the wealthy to play Lord of the Manor. The Morris & Essex Railroad made New York City easily accessible from Morris Plains, and the "Millionaire's Special," a luxuriously appointed, by-invitation-only railroad car, made the trip singularly appealing. Idlewild, shown here, was the home of Louis A. Thebaud.

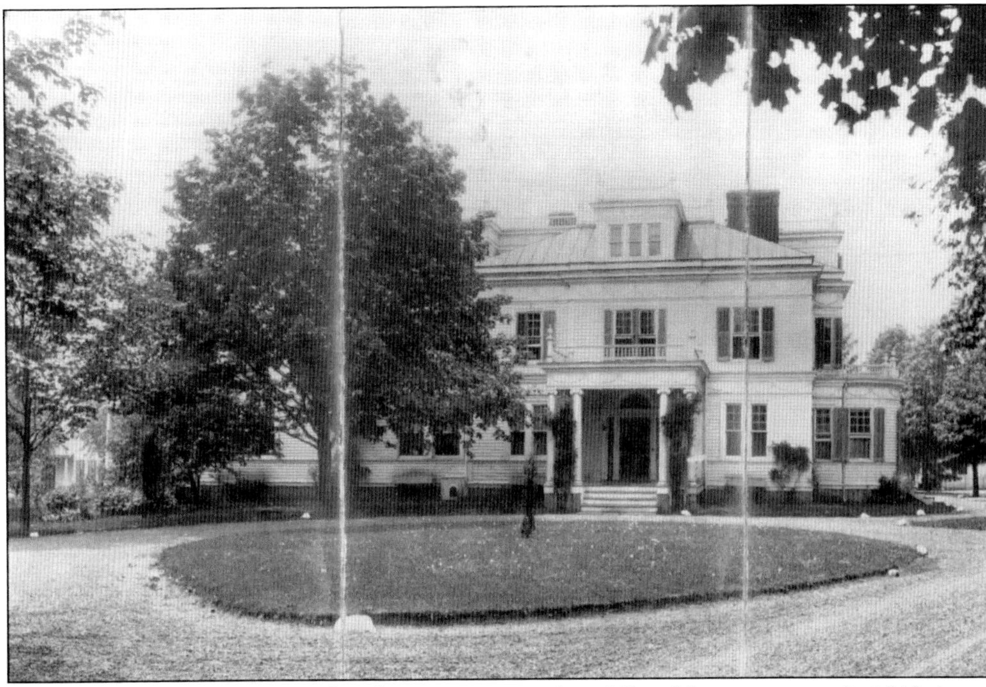

IDLEWILD IN ITS PRIME. Soon after this picture was taken, Idlewild was no more. In 1919, it was sold to Lewis Grove, a local developer, who lived there with his family until Idlewild burned to the ground one night in 1925 after an American Legion party.

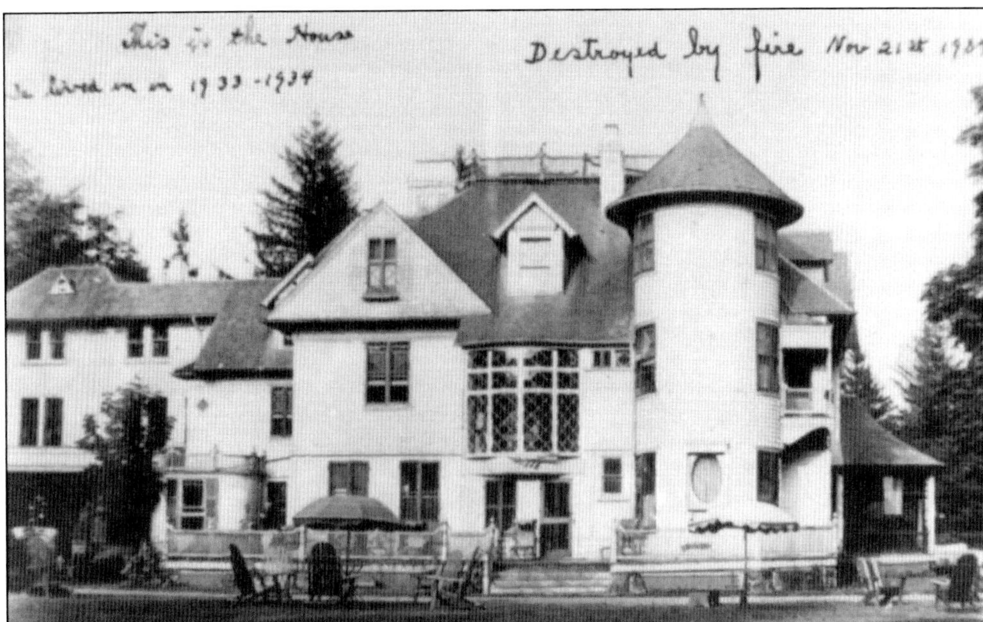

DOVER RIDGE. This magnificent estate stood at the end of a tree-lined road, today's Sylvan Drive. It was built in 1884 by Richard A. McCurdy, president of the Mutual Life Insurance Company, the most powerful financial institution in America at the time. Dover Ridge was the nucleus of several other mansions built with Mutual Life money.

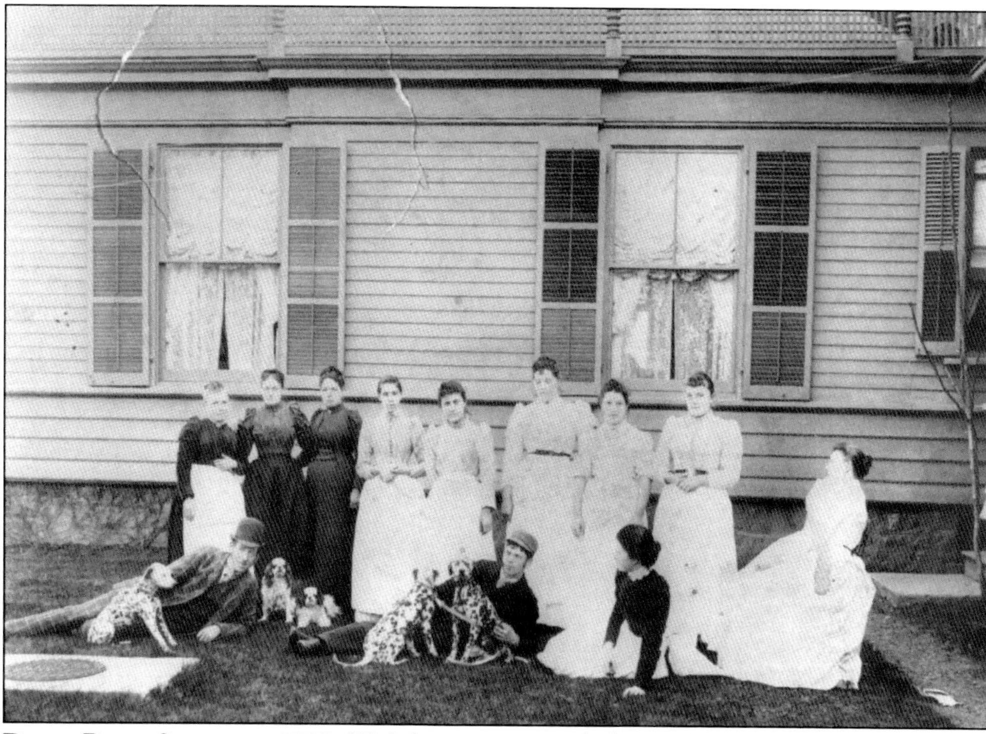

DOVER RIDGE SERVANTS, 1888. With banquet rooms, ballroom, billiard room, a huge kitchen and 36 other rooms, Dover Ridge required a lot of upkeep. Here, some of the servants pose with the household dogs. Later, the 475-acre estate became the Idlewild Country Club under the ownership of Lewis Grove. Virginia Grove Kenworthy, who lived at Dover Ridge with her family, remembers the ceiling-height stone fireplace in the reception room. After Dover Ridge was destroyed by fire in 1934, Lewis Grove built a large real estate development on the grounds.

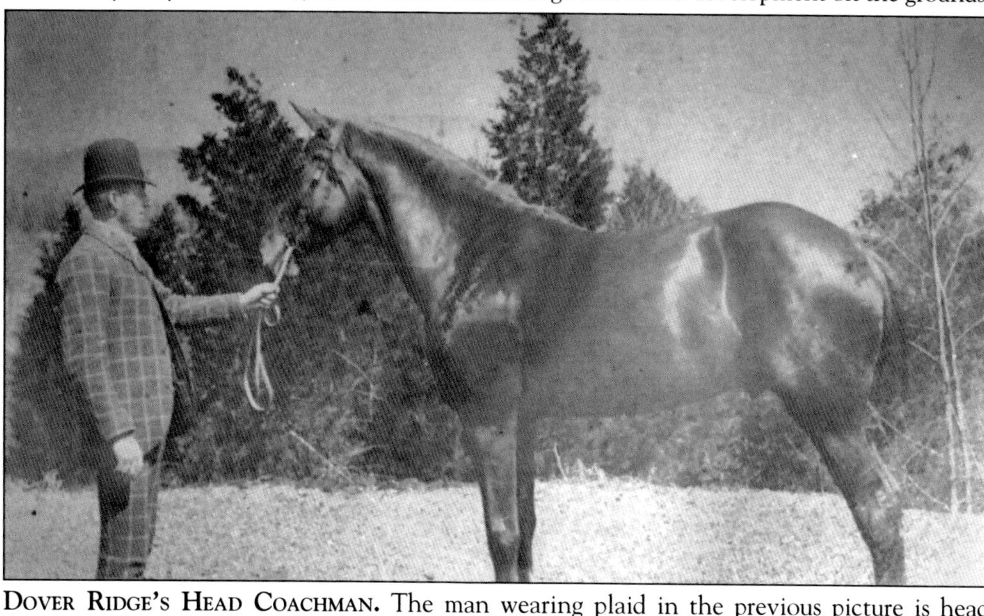

DOVER RIDGE'S HEAD COACHMAN. The man wearing plaid in the previous picture is head coachman Patrick Morris, shown again here with one of his charges.

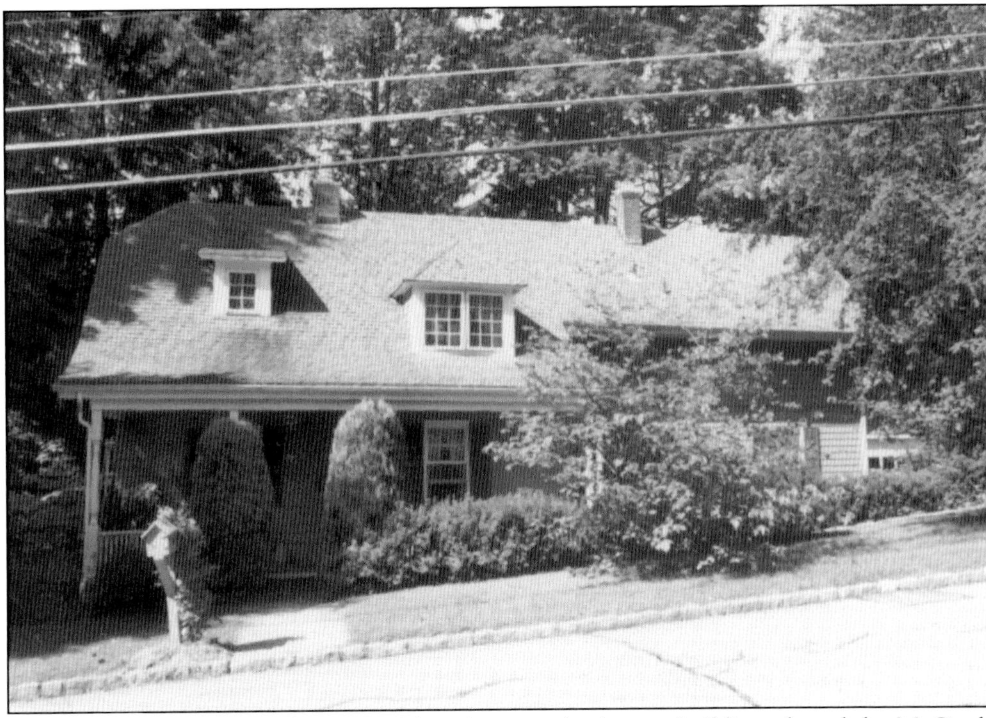

McCurdy's Coachman's Cottage. Many barns and other outbuildings dotted the McCurdy estate. This is the coachman's cottage, now a private home at 200 Mountain Way. Another nearby home on Overlook Trail was originally the McCurdy carriage house.

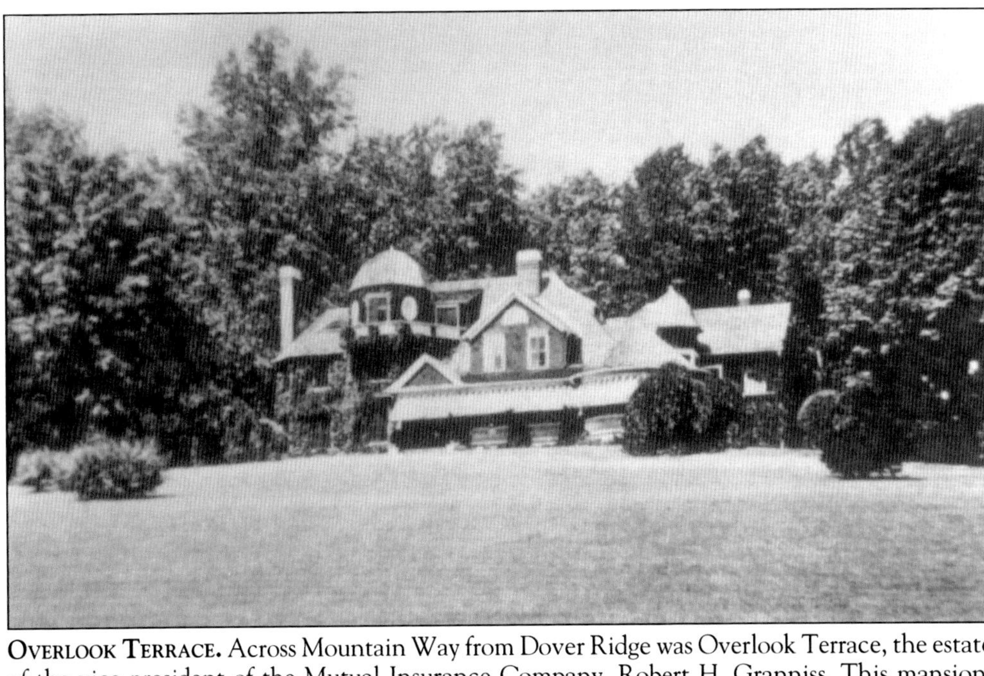

Overlook Terrace. Across Mountain Way from Dover Ridge was Overlook Terrace, the estate of the vice president of the Mutual Insurance Company, Robert H. Granniss. This mansion, built in 1886, sat where Mountain Way School is now located. It was razed in 1962.

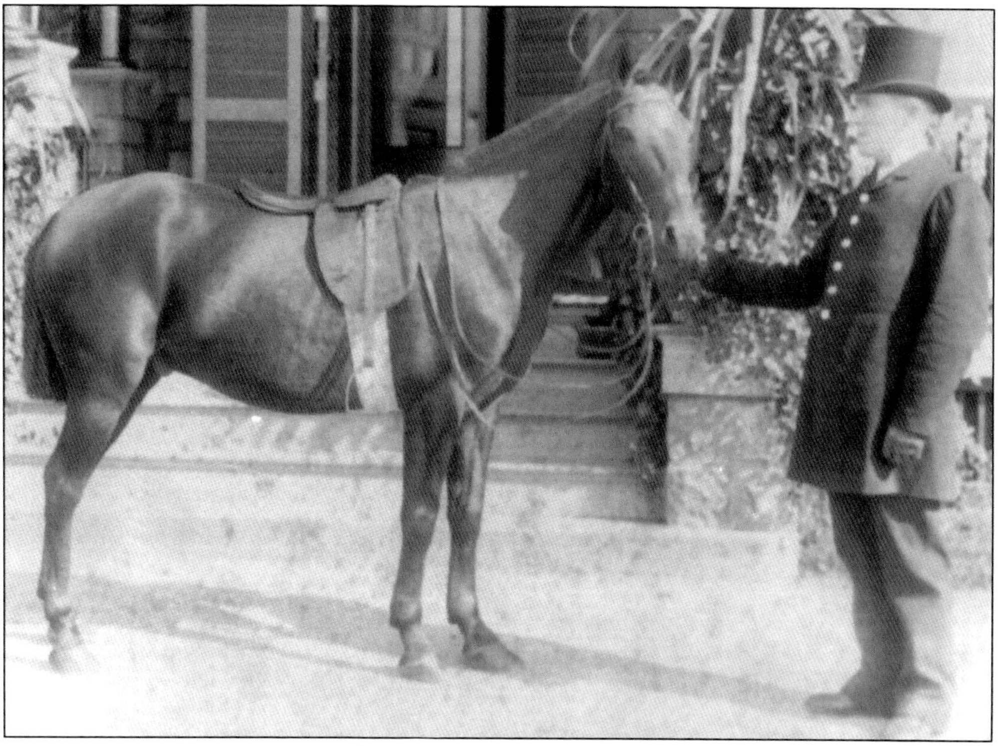

Coachman Michael Byrnes. Robert Granniss was enamored with all things English and spent a lot of money on fancy horses, carriages, and colorful servants' uniforms. The competition among Granniss and other estate owners was most evident each evening when richly appointed carriages vied to outdo each other as they picked up their owners arriving at the train station on the Millionaire's Special. Mr. Granniss played polo at the Whippany River Club.

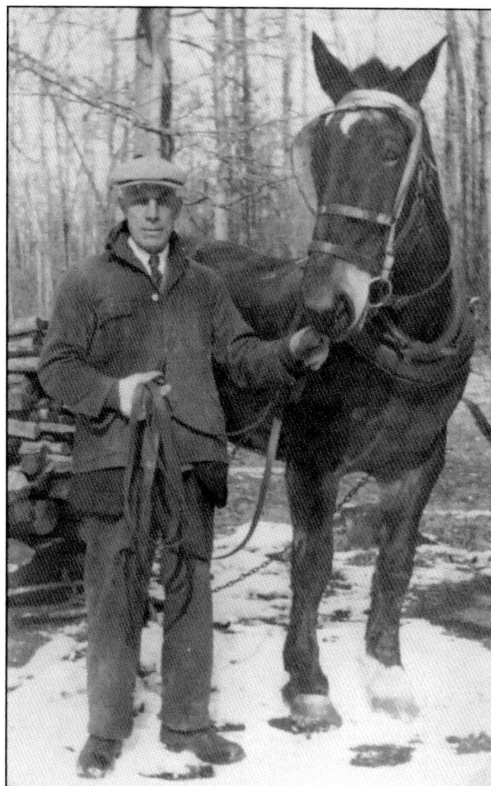

Caretaker Edgar Miller. Obviously not a polo pony, this powerful-looking horse is harnessed to a sled piled with logs. It looks as if Mr. Miller is wearing a tie and jacket despite the nature of his task. Mr. Miller was caretaker at the Granniss estate.

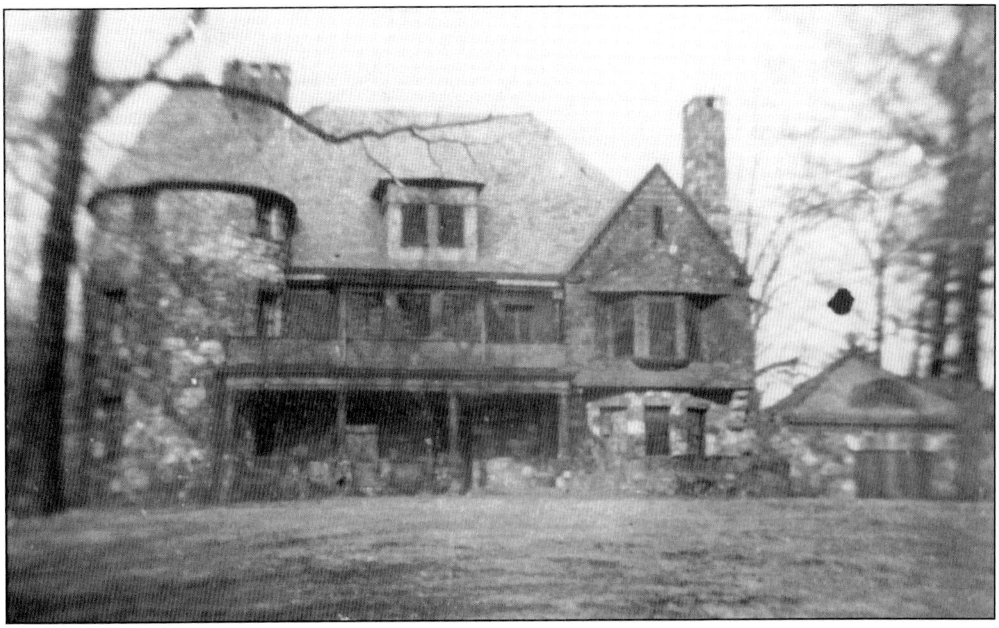

GONE WITHOUT A TRACE. Annie McClymond's stone mansion stood near the intersection of Littleton and Tabor Roads, high up on a hill. Today, there is nothing left of it—not even the hill. The house stood empty until the 1940s, when it was sold to Tom Landi. Landi disassembled the mansion and sold all the stone, metal, gravel, and even the soil that made up the hill. The property is completely level today.

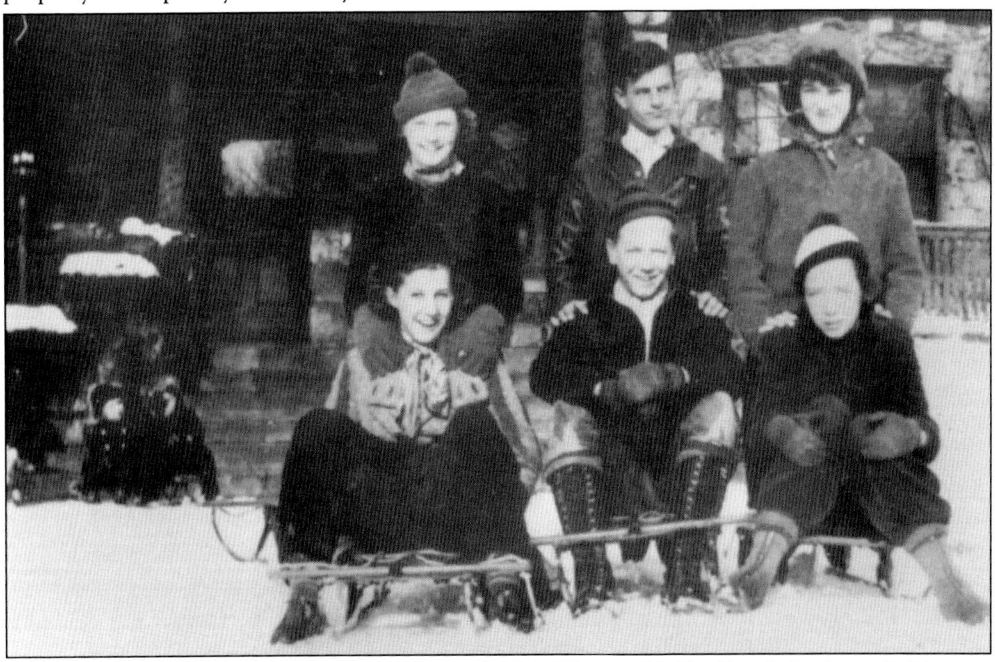

SLEDDING AT MCCLYMOND'S, 1933–1934. The McClymond hill offered the best sledding in town. With the mansion as a backdrop, these children get ready to fly. They are, from left to right, as follows: (front row) Helen Maines, William Mahon, and Bernadette Mahon; (back row) Betty White, Robert Brown, and Winifred Peach.

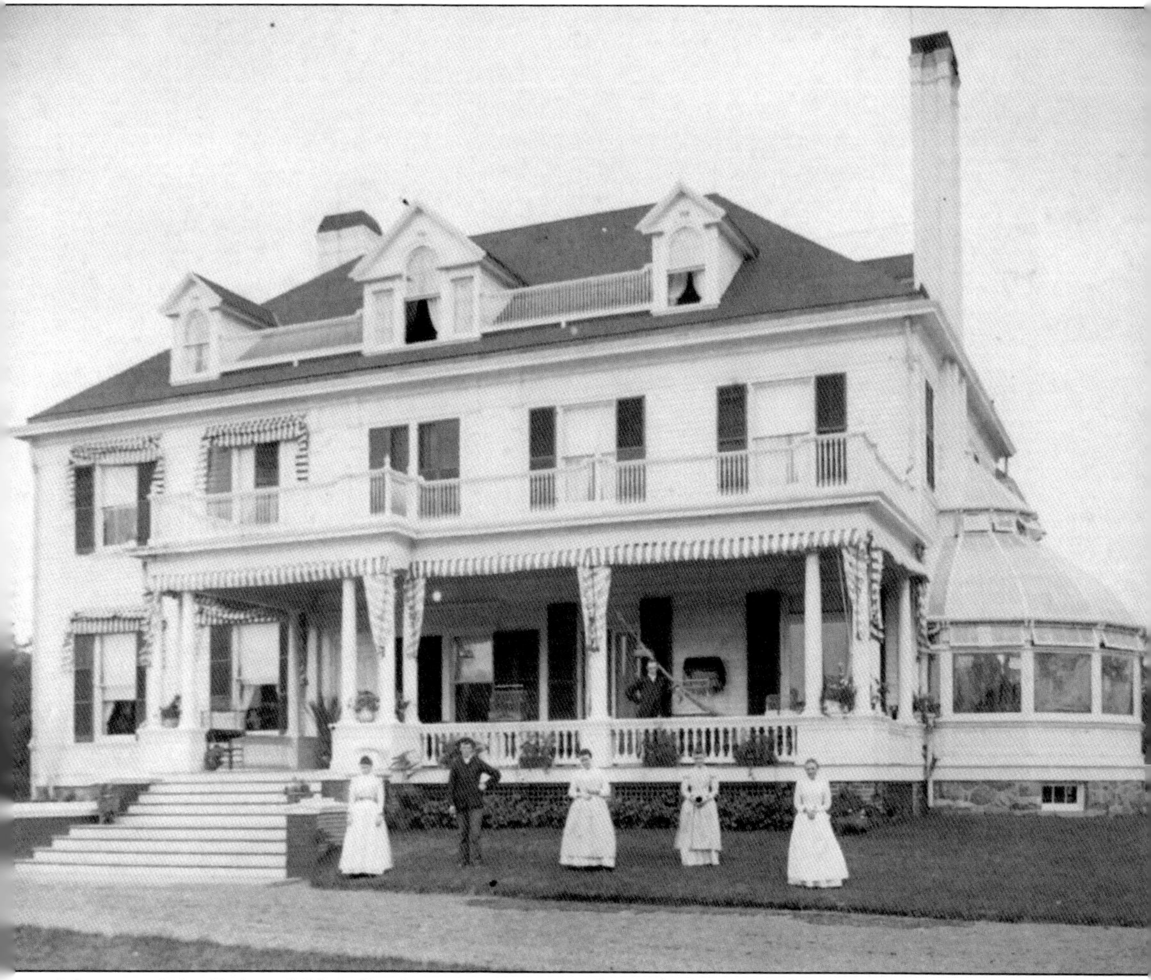

MAYFAIR. The Robert H. McCurdy mansion was at the end of present-day Mayfair Road. Robert H. McCurdy was the son of Richard A. McCurdy. In this picture, five unidentified people pose at arm's length while another looks on. By 1928, Mayfair was deserted and, after a fire, was razed for yet another real estate development.

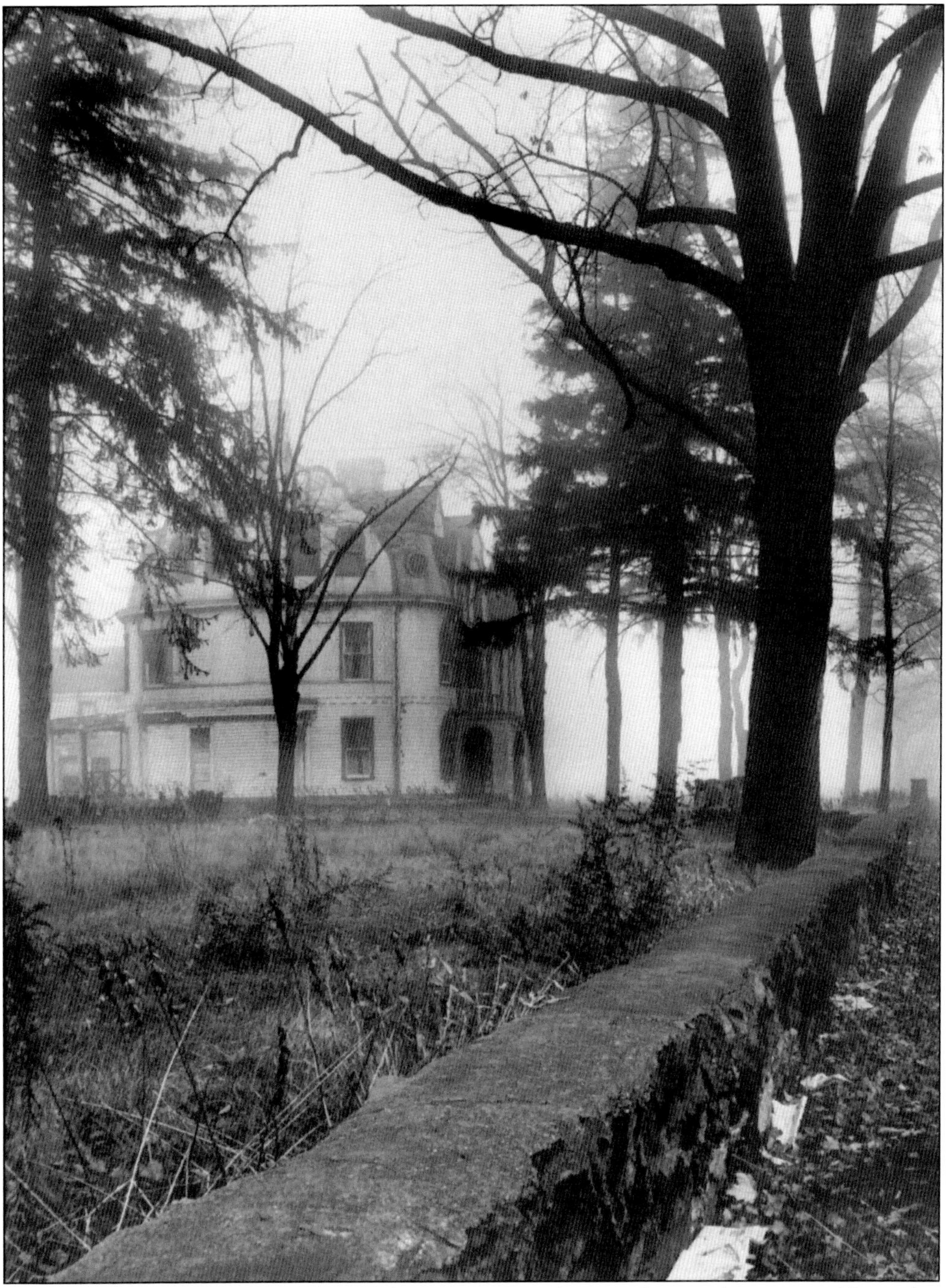

The End of an Era. Lost in mist and time, its trees dying and stone fences crumbling, this was Benjamin Sire's Maplehurst in the 1930s, some 50 years after it was built. Nicknamed "the Castle" in happier times, the mansion was the scene of many a "gay nineties" party. During Prohibition, it housed a high-end bootlegging operation, including expert counterfeiting of Canadian liquor labels. In 1941, it was razed after being abandoned and partially destroyed by several fires. And so a unique era in Morris Plains history came to an end.

Eight

The Man Who Got Teddy Roosevelt Elected

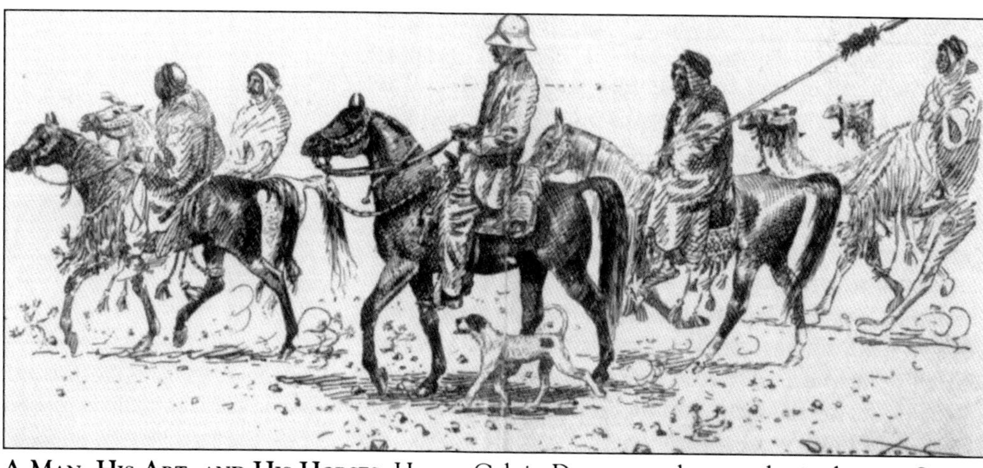

A Man, His Art, and His Horses. Homer Calvin Davenport, born and raised on an Oregon farm, became one of the most powerful and highly paid political cartoonists of his day. He had a passion for horses and introduced the legendary Arabian steed to America. His famous Arabians lived in palatial barns at his Morris Plains farm. He was a master raconteur and a friend to the famous, but it amused him to affect the manner of a simple "country boy," the words he would later choose as the title of his autobiography.

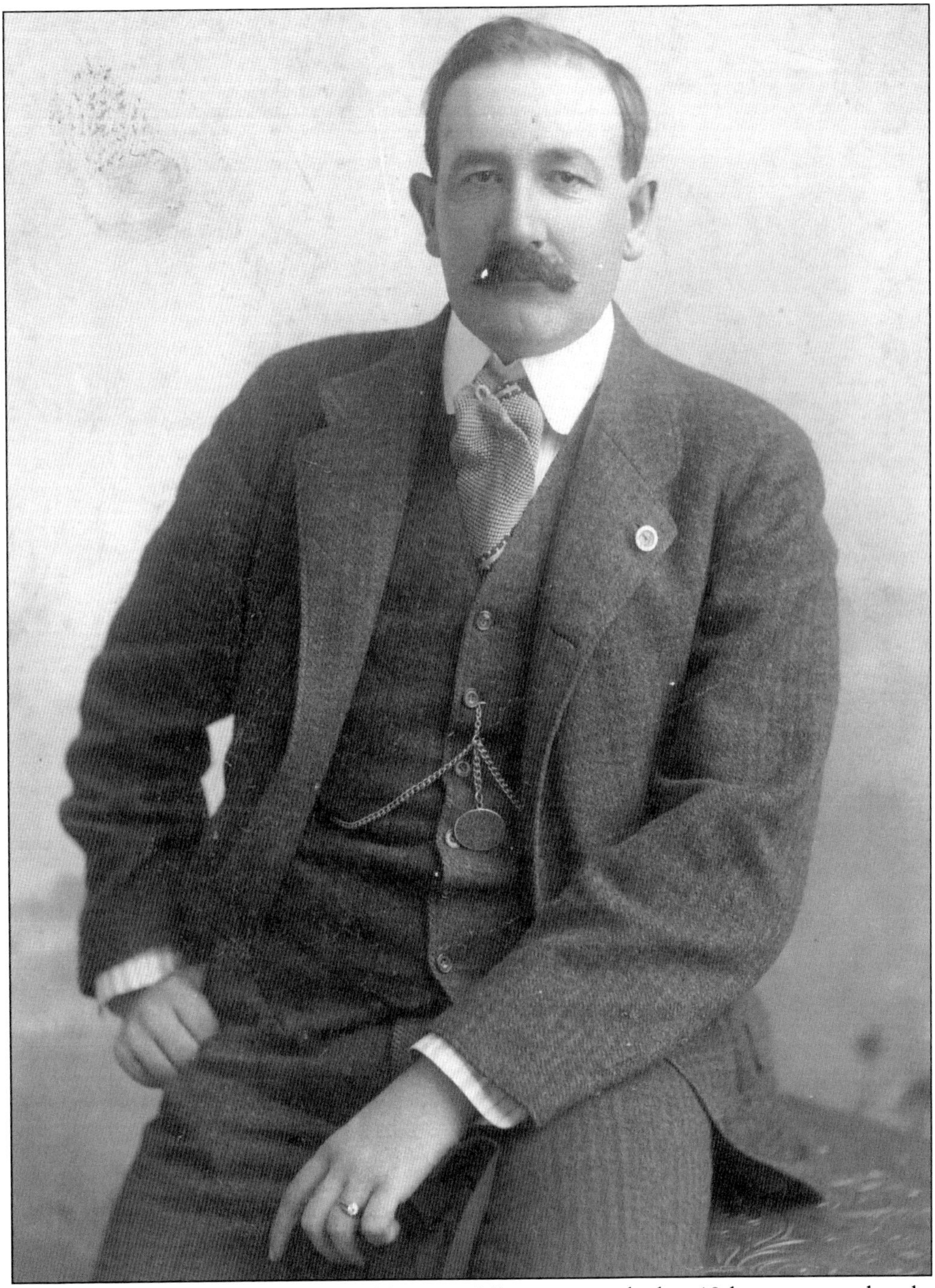

The Power of His Pen. America's golden age of illustration in the late 19th century produced a small circle of artists who honed the political cartoon into the most powerful social commentary of the time. Statesman and editor John Engles described the extraordinary power of two of the leading illustrators of the day: "There is no weapon so potent as the pencil of Thomas Nast and Homer C. Davenport . . . . Sinners may be indifferent to God and the Devil, but they shrink from the pillory of the cartoon." (Courtesy JFPLMMT.)

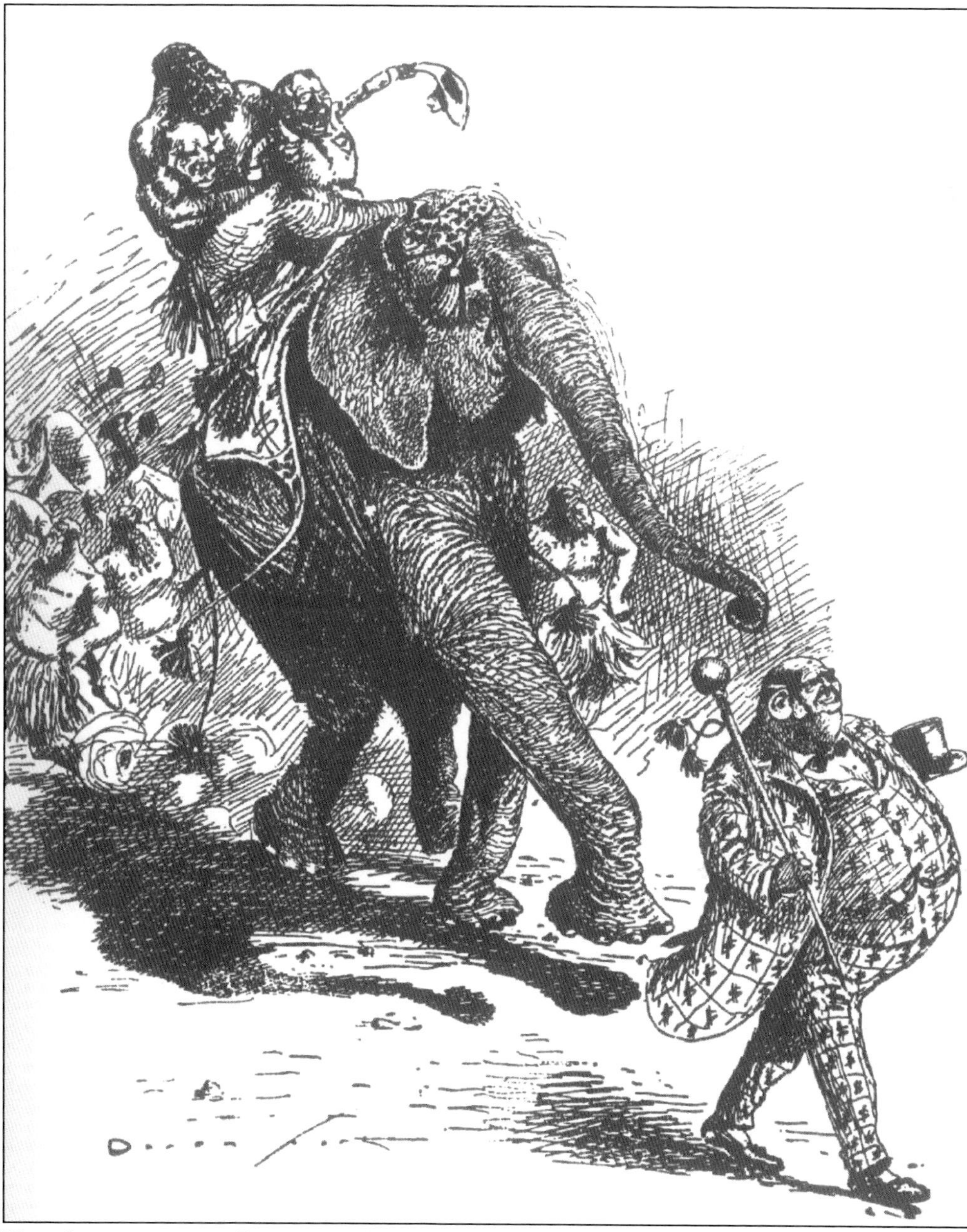

The Shorthand of Political Cartoons. The readers of late-19th-century newspapers would understand the symbols in this cartoon. The Republican elephant follows "Dollar Mark" Hanna, a leading influence-peddler of the day. Riding the elephant, but locked in the arms of the "Trust Goon" are Pres. William McKinley and Vice Pres. Theodore Roosevelt. Influence-buying by large corporations is still a major issue today. Mark Hanna so detested Davenport's characterization of him that he had the Anti-Cartooning Act introduced in the New York legislature. The effort failed, and Davenport continued to flog Hanna in William Randolph Hearst's newspapers.

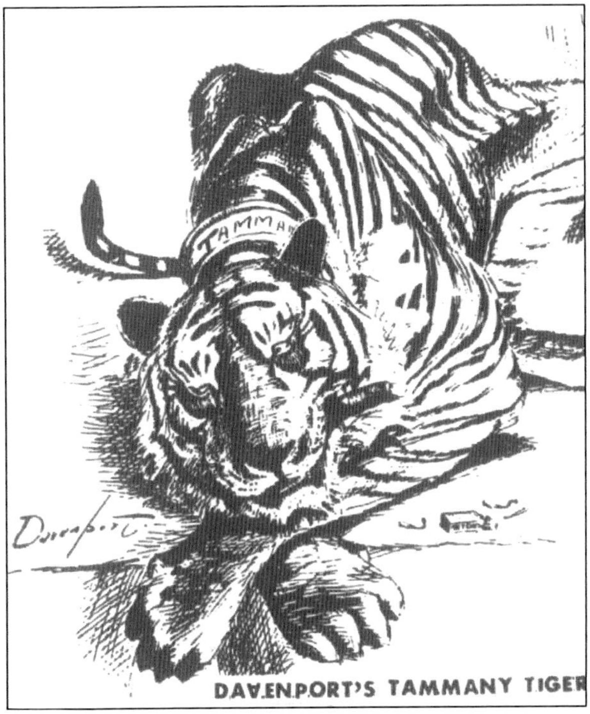

THE "TAMMANY TIGER." The voracious tiger symbolized the corrupt politicians beholden to William "Boss" Tweed, whose New York headquarters was in Tammany Hall. Tweed said of Davenport's work, "I don't care what the papers write—the voters don't read. But they can see those damn pictures."

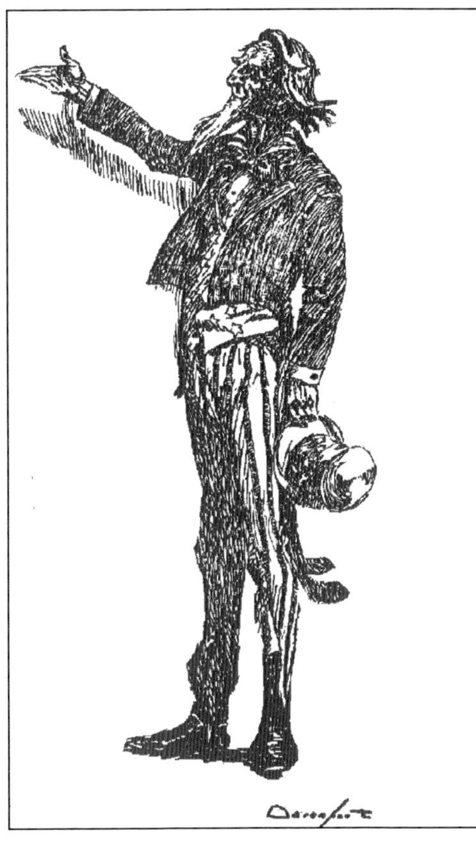

DAVENPORT'S UNCLE SAM. Davenport used his characterization of Uncle Sam to comment upon the great social and political issues of the day. This familiar image soon came to symbolize the soul and conscience of America.

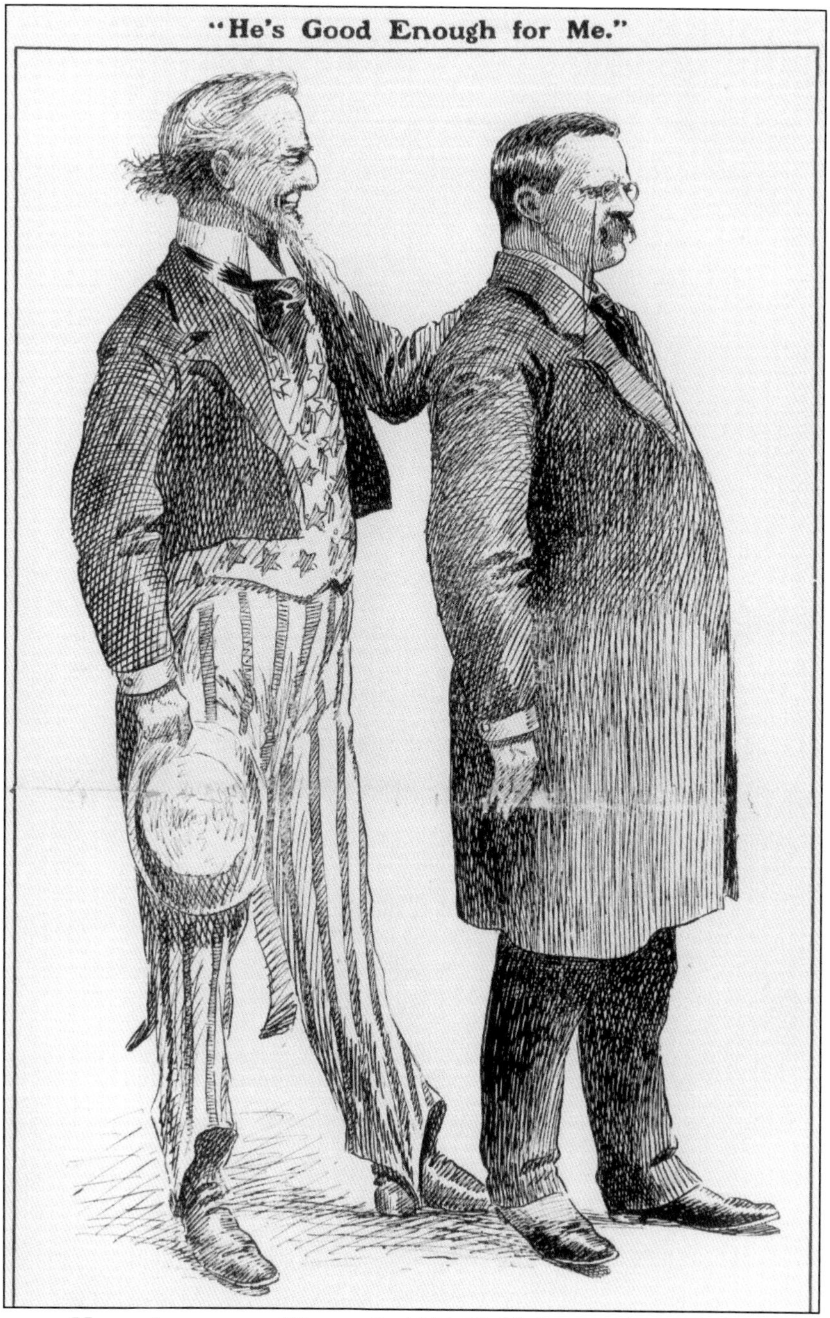

THE CARTOON HEARD 'ROUND THE WORLD. In 1904, Teddy Roosevelt was feeling the ill effects of Davenport's poison pen in Hearst's Democratic newspapers. He deliberately cultivated Davenport's friendship, inviting him to the Roosevelt family estate to ride and shoot. Soon afterward, the cartoonist received a huge offer to leave Hearst for the rival Republican New York paper. Davenport accepted the offer, switched political sides, and soon produced "the greatest vote-getting cartoon of all time," wherein Uncle Sam taps Roosevelt for the presidency. He smiles affectionately while declaring, "He's good enough for me." Roosevelt, who had been the underdog in the race, won handily.

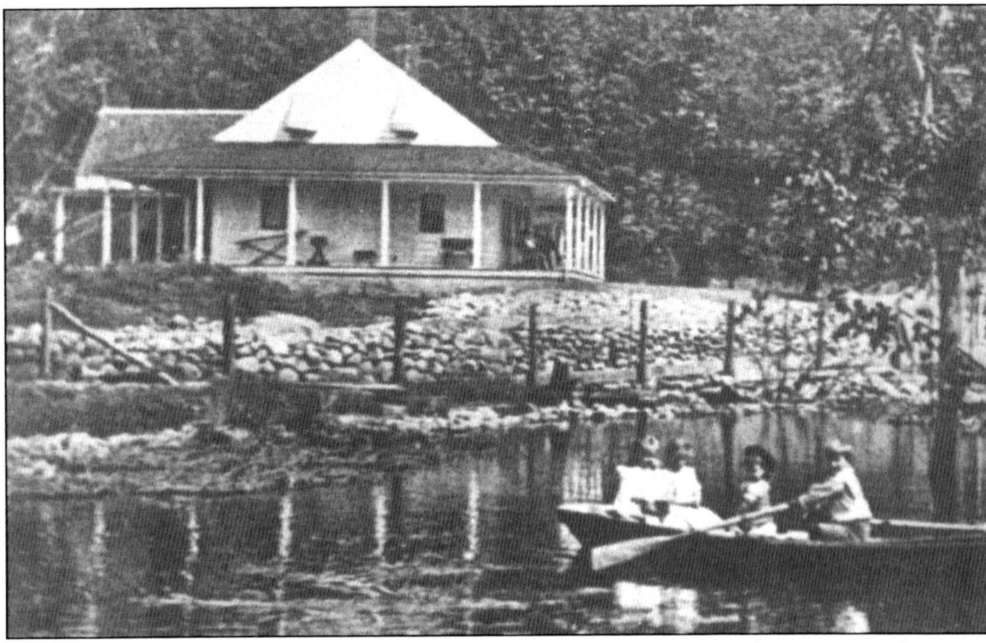

DAVENPORT'S HOME IN MORRIS PLAINS. In 1901, Davenport wrote to his cousin, "I have just bought a farm of 27 acres, with two nice streams through it." He packed up his family and moved to the old Owens farm on the west side of Tabor Road in Morris Plains. There, Davenport let his love of animals run rampant. He assembled a veritable zoo: Chinese ducks, Sicilian donkeys, English pheasants (from William Gladstone), Persian sheep (from the shah of Iran), Angora goats, and the largest collection of rare pheasants in the world.

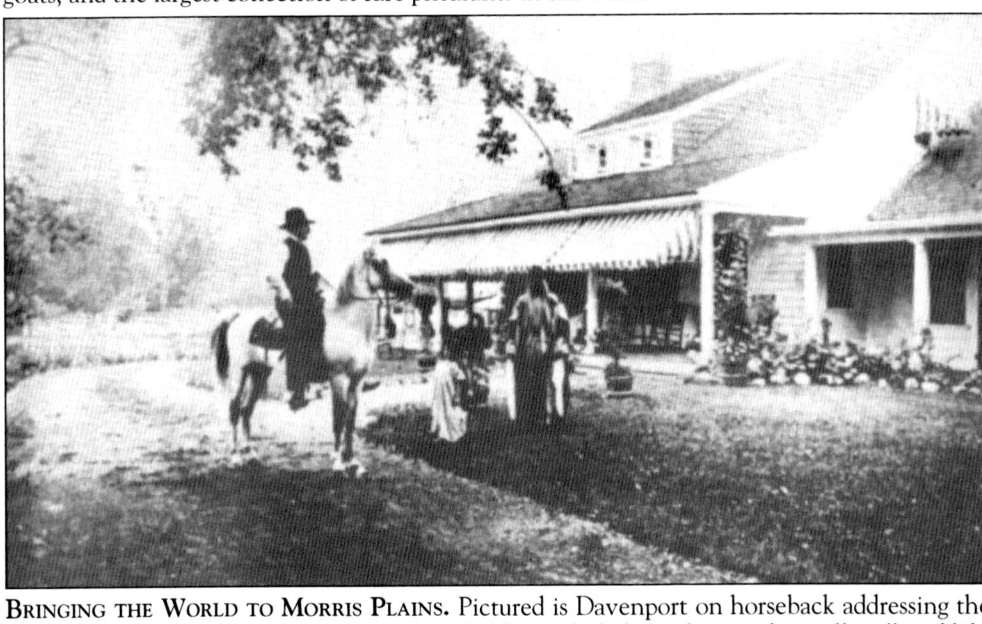

BRINGING THE WORLD TO MORRIS PLAINS. Pictured is Davenport on horseback addressing the Bedouin groomsman. Large parties at Red Gables included the famous from all walks of life: Thomas Edison, William Jennings Bryan, Buffalo Bill, Lillian Russell, Frederick Remington, the Flora Dora girls, and many others. Davenport asked visitors to sign his unique "guestbook"—the white clapboard siding of Red Gables.

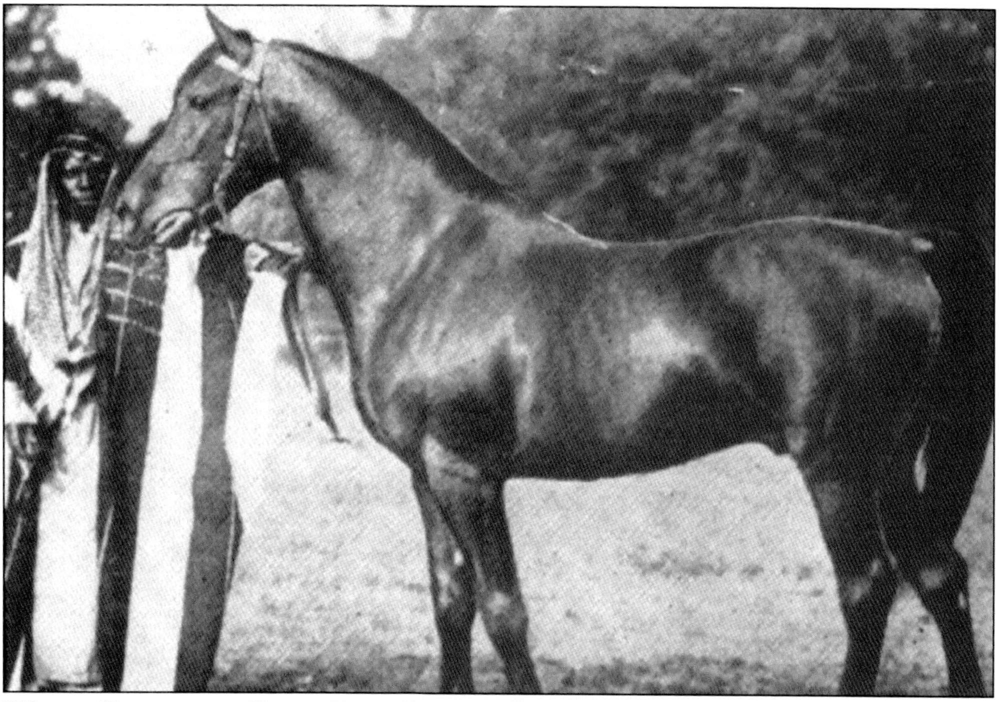

"Haleb, Pride of the Desert" and Bedouin Groom. Davenport had first seen and coveted Arabian horses at the 1893 World's Fair, but ownership by foreigners was forbidden by the sultan. However, with Roosevelt's help, Davenport traveled to the Arabian Desert and obtained a number of the fabled Arabian steeds. Davenport's Arabian horses were housed in huge barns at Red Gables, and from there the breed spread far and wide.

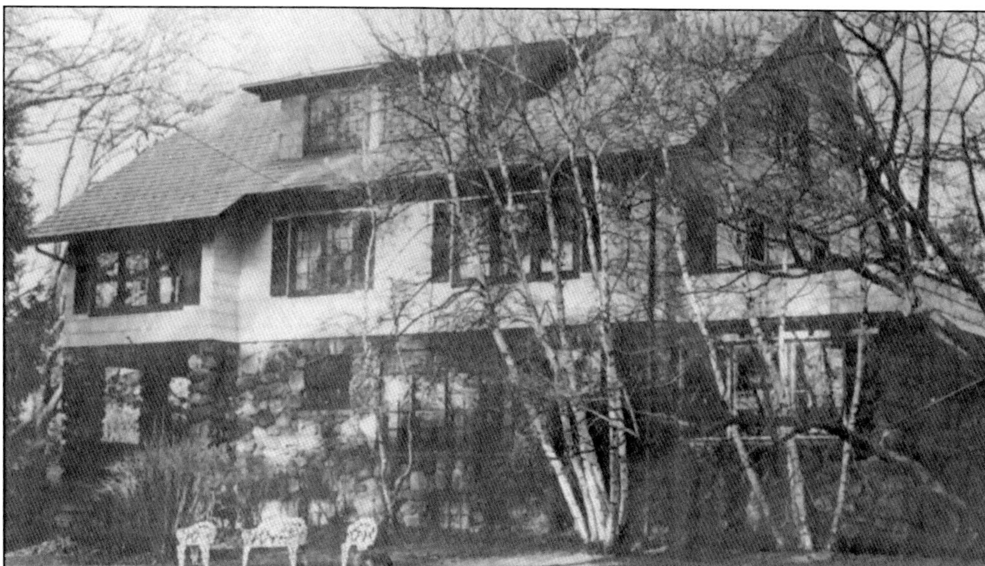

Designed by Gustav Stickley. Stickley, founder of the mission style in America, decided to locate his home and workshop to be near his friend Davenport. In 1913, Stickley designed this Craftsman-style home built of local natural materials on Court Road for William C. Parker, the well-known Morristown photographer. It is now the home of Mr. and Mrs. John Harper.

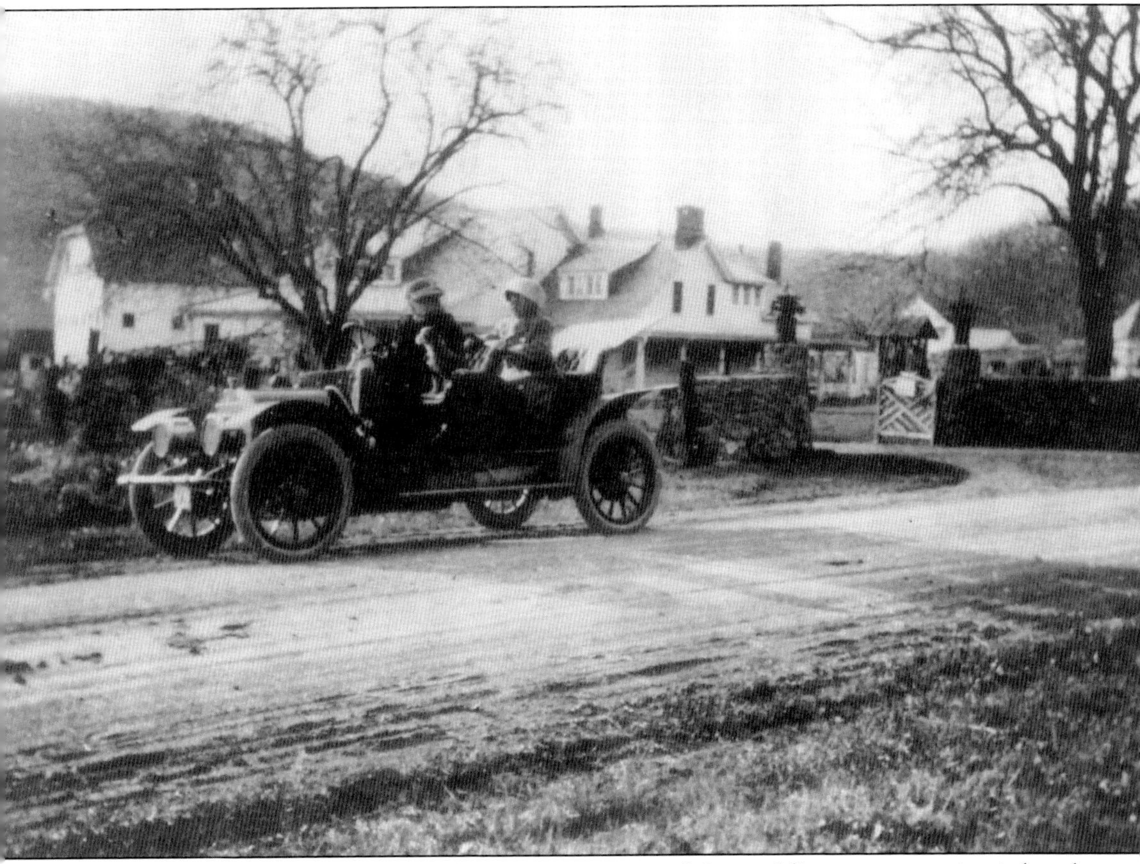

Red Gables, c. 1910. Davenport's reputation as one of the world's great cartoonists is largely forgotten today. He died early, at just 45, in a fever made worse by waiting in a cold rain for the *Carpathia* to bring home survivors of the *Titanic*. His beloved Morris Plains farm passed through a succession of owners, including Mr. and Mrs. Kyle Myers, who raised Irish setters there in the 1940s. In 1957, Davenport's house with its autographed clapboards, his barns, outbuildings and even his ponds were obliterated, buried under the pavement of Warner-Lambert's northwest parking lot. All that remains of Homer Davenport's presence in Morris Plains is a street called Davenport and, perhaps, (it was once rumored) the hidden grave of his favorite Arabian horse.

Nine

Morris Plains Comes of Age

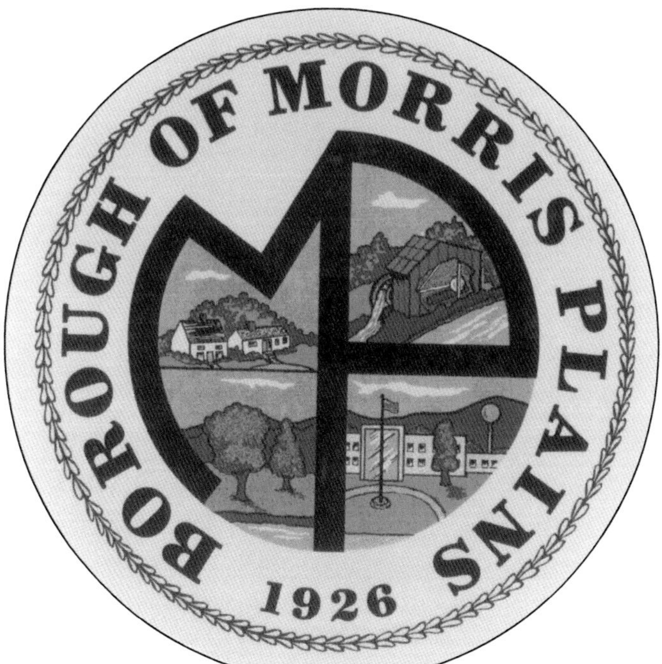

Morris Plains Declares Its Independence. The Great War ended the turn-of-the-century optimism and hopes for peace, and all else was put on hold for the duration. After the terrible storm passed, the people of Morris Plains turned back to domestic affairs. In 1926, the battle cry was "home rule for the home town" as the little town decided whether to break away from Hanover Township. Nearly 250 years after its birth, independence was declared, and the Borough of Morris Plains came into being. Government would be by elected mayor and council.

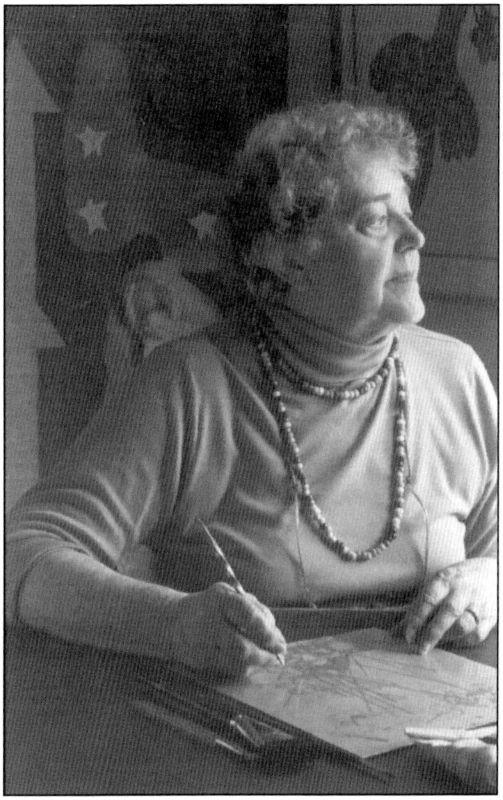

ARTIST SHIRLEY CAMPBELL. In 1970, many years after the borough was incorporated, artist Shirley Campbell created the official seal of Morris Plains. The three pictorial sections represent Thomas Pierson's 1685 sawmill, Morris Plains's natural beauty and residential character, and modern industry—tributes to the past, present, and future.

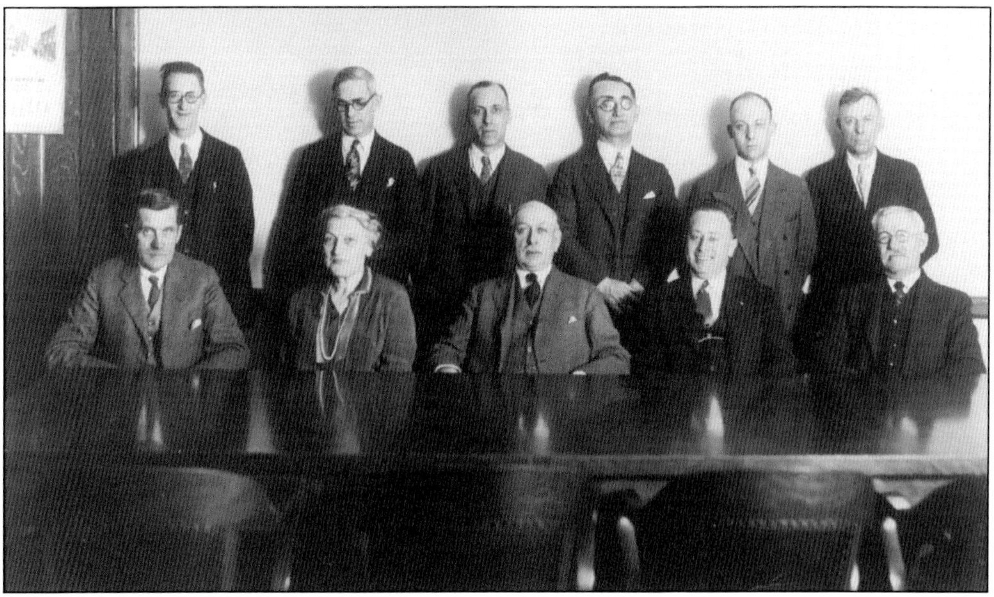

THE MAYOR AND COUNCIL OF 1927. The town government officials shown, from left to right, are as follows: (front row) L.S. Young, Margaret Stang, Mayor D.M. Merchant (elected by popular acclamation), H.G. Vorburger, and Edward Connelly; (back row) E.N. Babington, James Fear, Frank Millen, L.H. Burch, John Yawger, and Atty. David Barkman. (Burch and Fear replaced original council members Arthur VanWinkle and Richard Lindabury.)

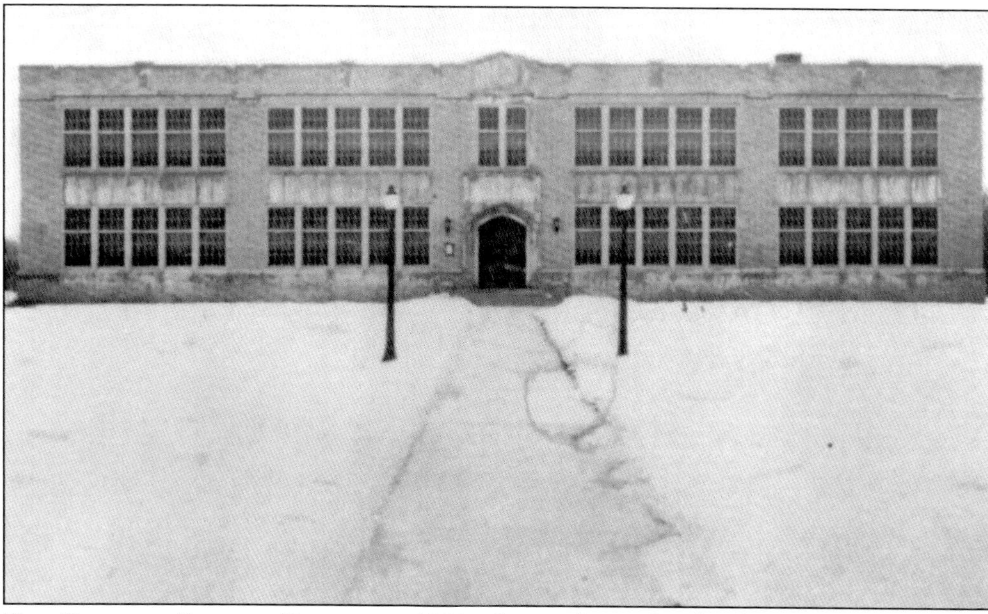

The Borough School, Dedicated 1923. A new borough school was built in Jonathan Roberts's former cow pasture in a Gothic Revival style. Richard Simmonds thought the school to be somewhat austere and soon donated trees.

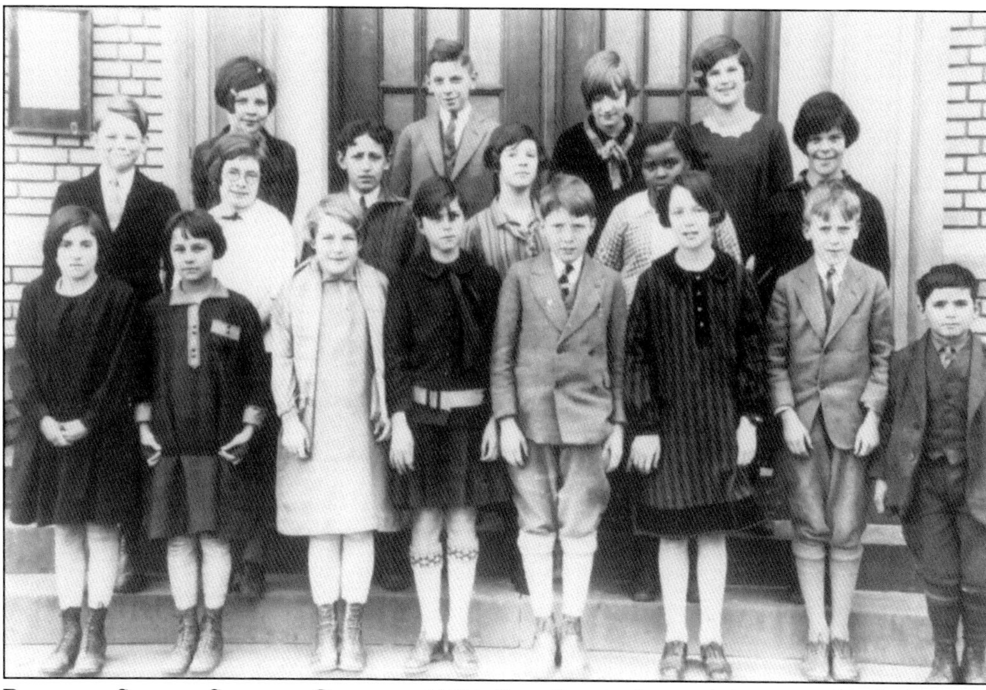

Borough School Seventh Graders, 1927. Standing in front of the new school, from left to right, are the following: (first row) Marion Call, Alice Kay, Gertrude Christenson, Margery Cronshey, Frank Stietz, Virginia Dobbins, Wilfred Breare, and Wesley Jacobus; (second row) Kenneth Vroom, Mary Louise Clark, Joe Lombardi, Ruth Higgins, May ?, and Edith Jones; (third row) Evelyn Howard, David Wehman, Evelyn Eakley, and Florence Dallenger.

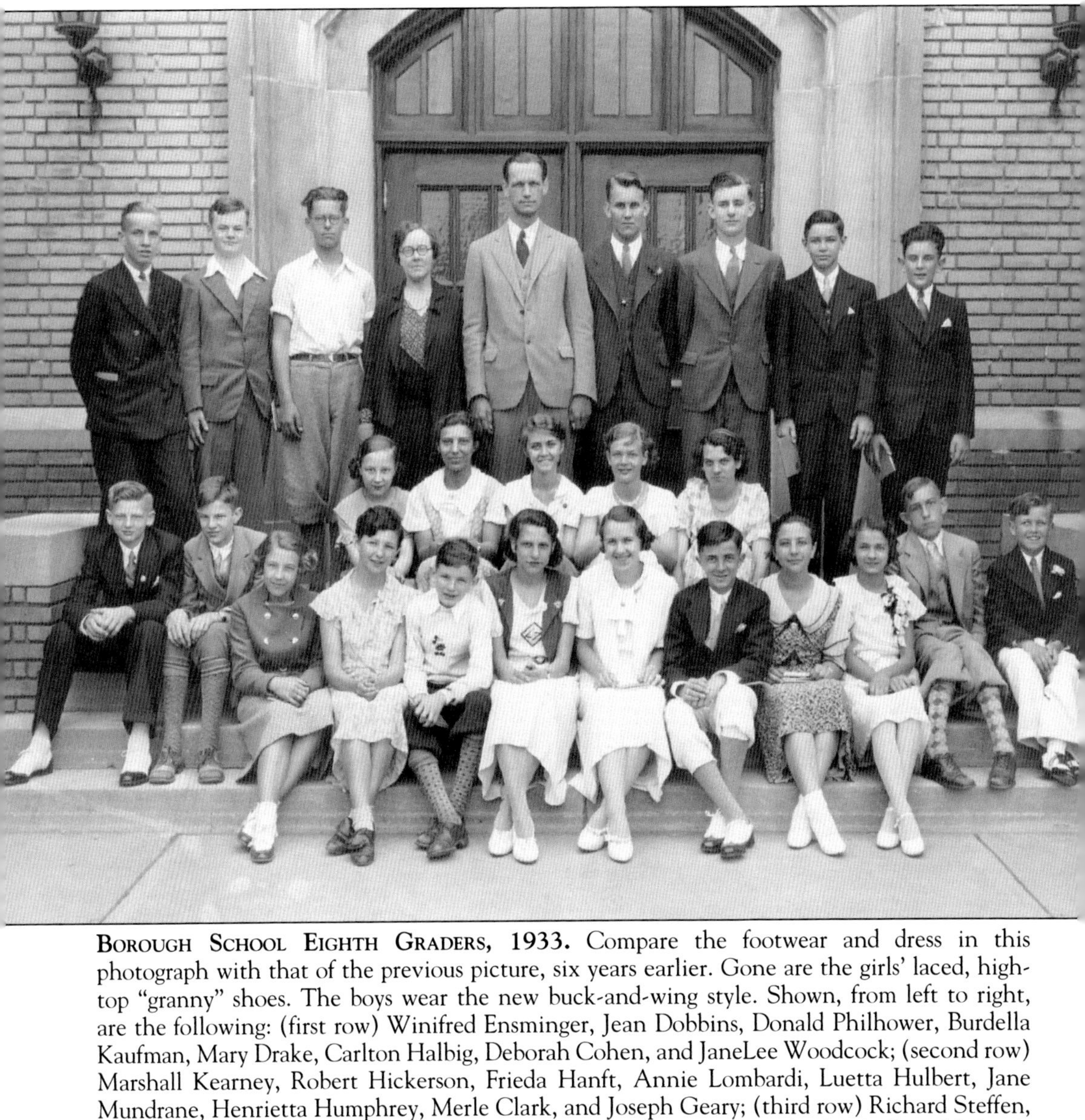

BOROUGH SCHOOL EIGHTH GRADERS, 1933. Compare the footwear and dress in this photograph with that of the previous picture, six years earlier. Gone are the girls' laced, high-top "granny" shoes. The boys wear the new buck-and-wing style. Shown, from left to right, are the following: (first row) Winifred Ensminger, Jean Dobbins, Donald Philhower, Burdella Kaufman, Mary Drake, Carlton Halbig, Deborah Cohen, and JaneLee Woodcock; (second row) Marshall Kearney, Robert Hickerson, Frieda Hanft, Annie Lombardi, Luetta Hulbert, Jane Mundrane, Henrietta Humphrey, Merle Clark, and Joseph Geary; (third row) Richard Steffen, Gerald Matthews, Raymond Mills, Florence Ayers (eighth-grade teacher), Mr. Donald Smith (principal), Mrs. Harold Green (seventh-grade teacher), Edward Barry, Robert Edwards, and Robert Bartron.

ALEXANDER PATTERSON, LONGTIME POLICE CHIEF. Being independent meant that the town must provide more of its own essential services. The Public Safety Committee was formed in 1926, and Alexander Patterson was appointed the first chief of police. A full-time police department would not be formed until 1948. Chief Patterson was tough when he had to be; on November 29, 1929, he reported that he had ordered two miscreants to "get out of the borough within 24 hours and to stay out."

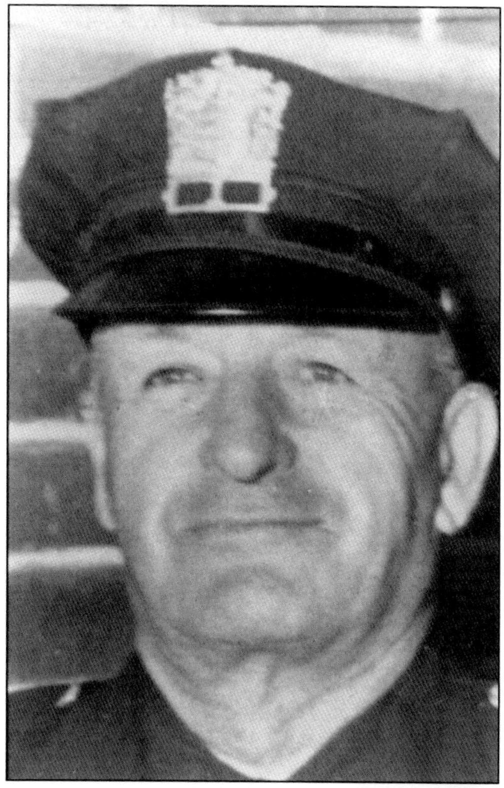

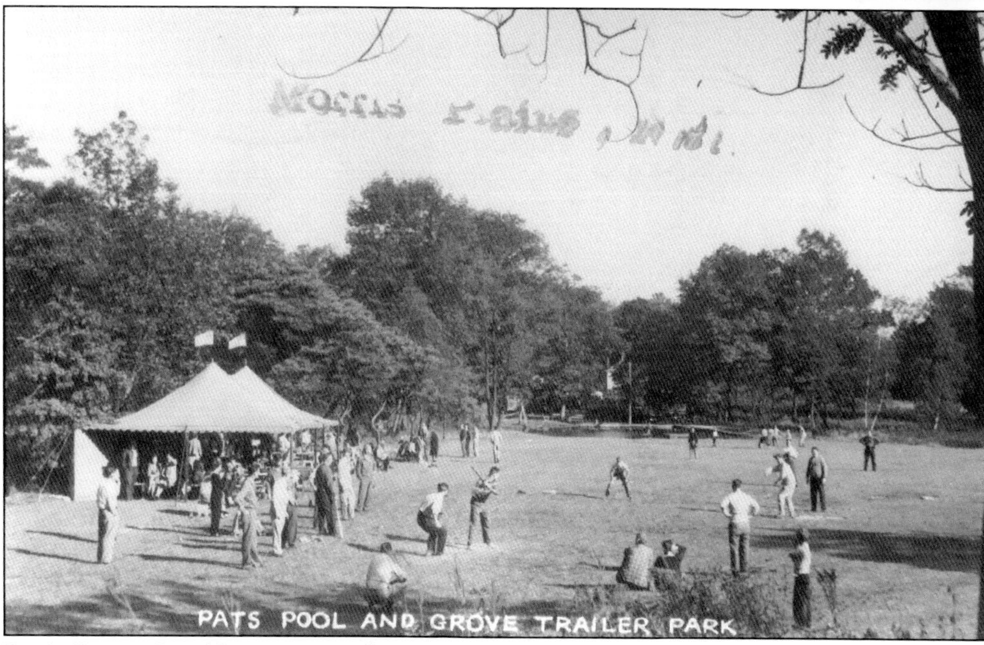

PAT'S GROVE. In addition to patrolling and investigating crimes, Chief Patterson also served as building inspector, school bus driver, and forest fire warden. In the 1940s, he also ran Pat's Pool, a popular swimming hole and trailer park on Tabor Road. After his death, police badge No. 1 was retired in his honor.

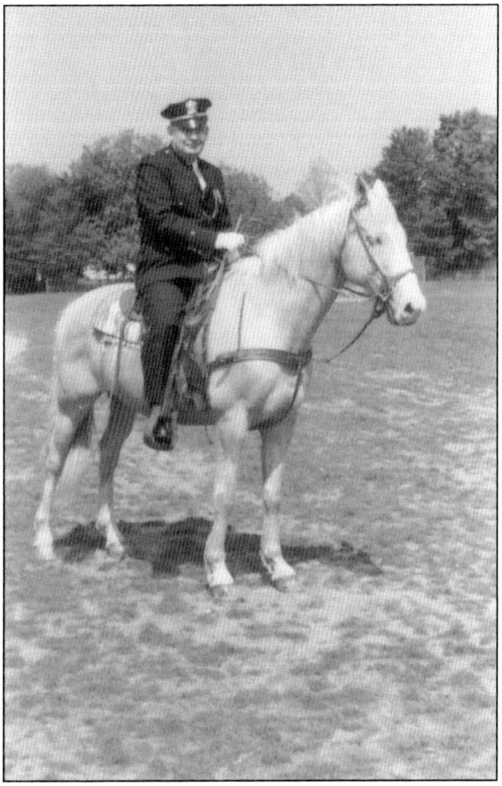

CHIEF GEORGE BURNS RIDES AGAIN, 1963. As a joke, Dr. James Weisert, the chief organizer of the 1963 Memorial Day parade, spread the rumor that the chief of police would lead the parade on a white stallion. Chief George Burns (who, unbeknownst to Dr. Weisert, had extensive riding experience) called Weisert's bluff and went on to lead the parade in grand style, much to the surprise of the good doctor and many others.

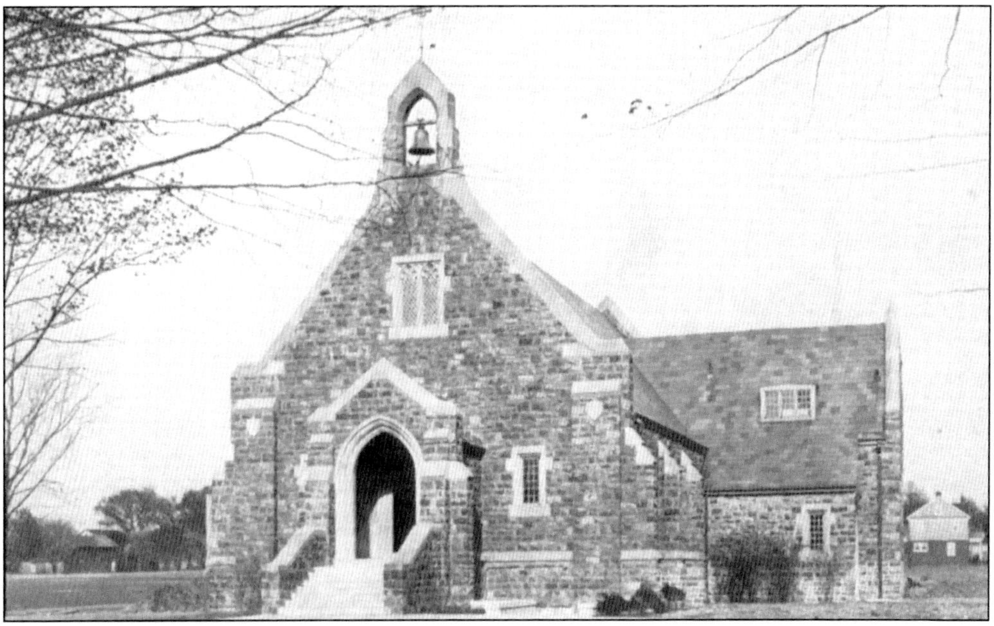

ST. PAUL'S EPISCOPAL CHURCH. This stone edifice was built in 1928 and was dedicated on a fall day in 1929 by Fr. John C. Lord. Thus the organizational meetings and strawberry festivals at the Cronshey home on Speedwell Avenue bore fruit nearly a decade later.

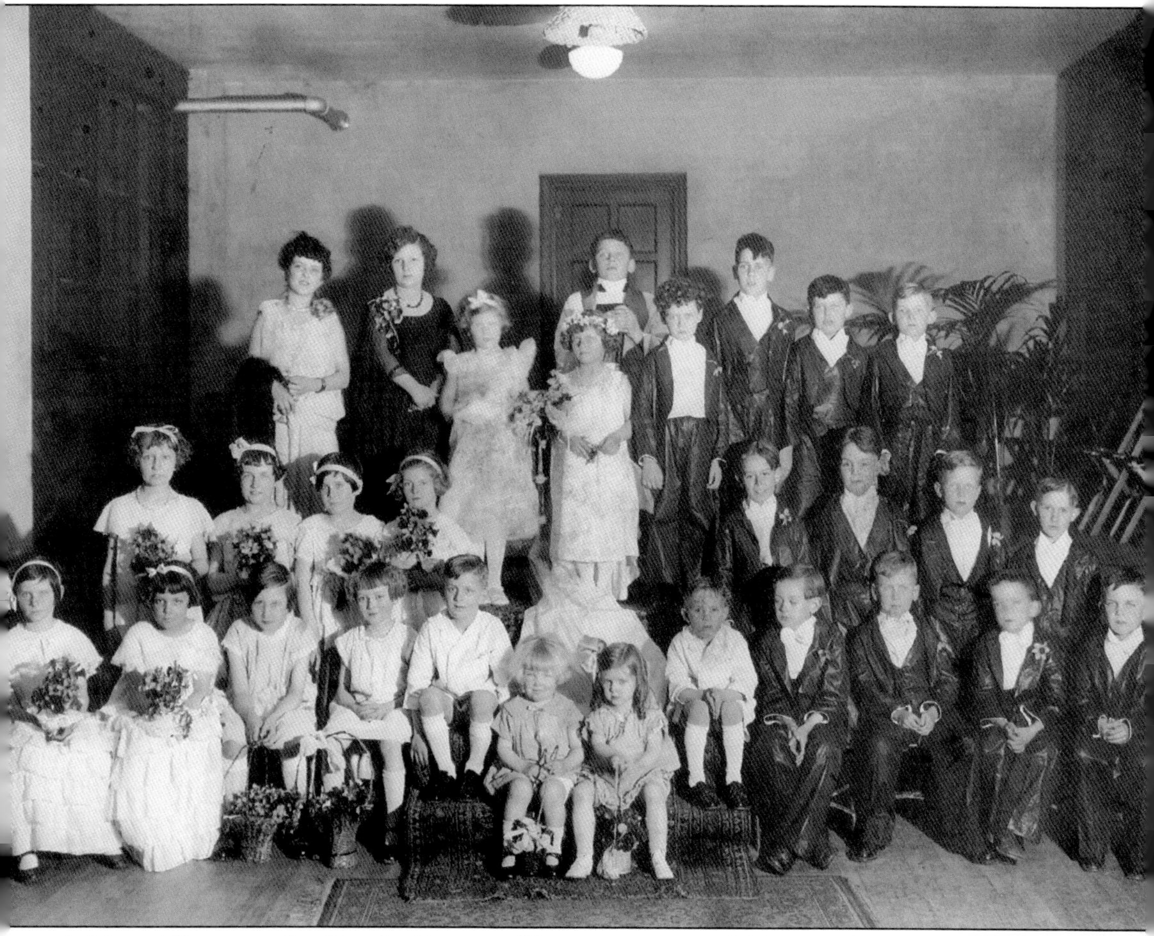

A Mock Wedding, St. Paul's Church. These very young children took part in a Sunday school play in 1928. One has to wonder how these little boys were made to don suits and ties and escort girls to a "wedding." Looking at the groom (center), all does not bode well for the marriage.

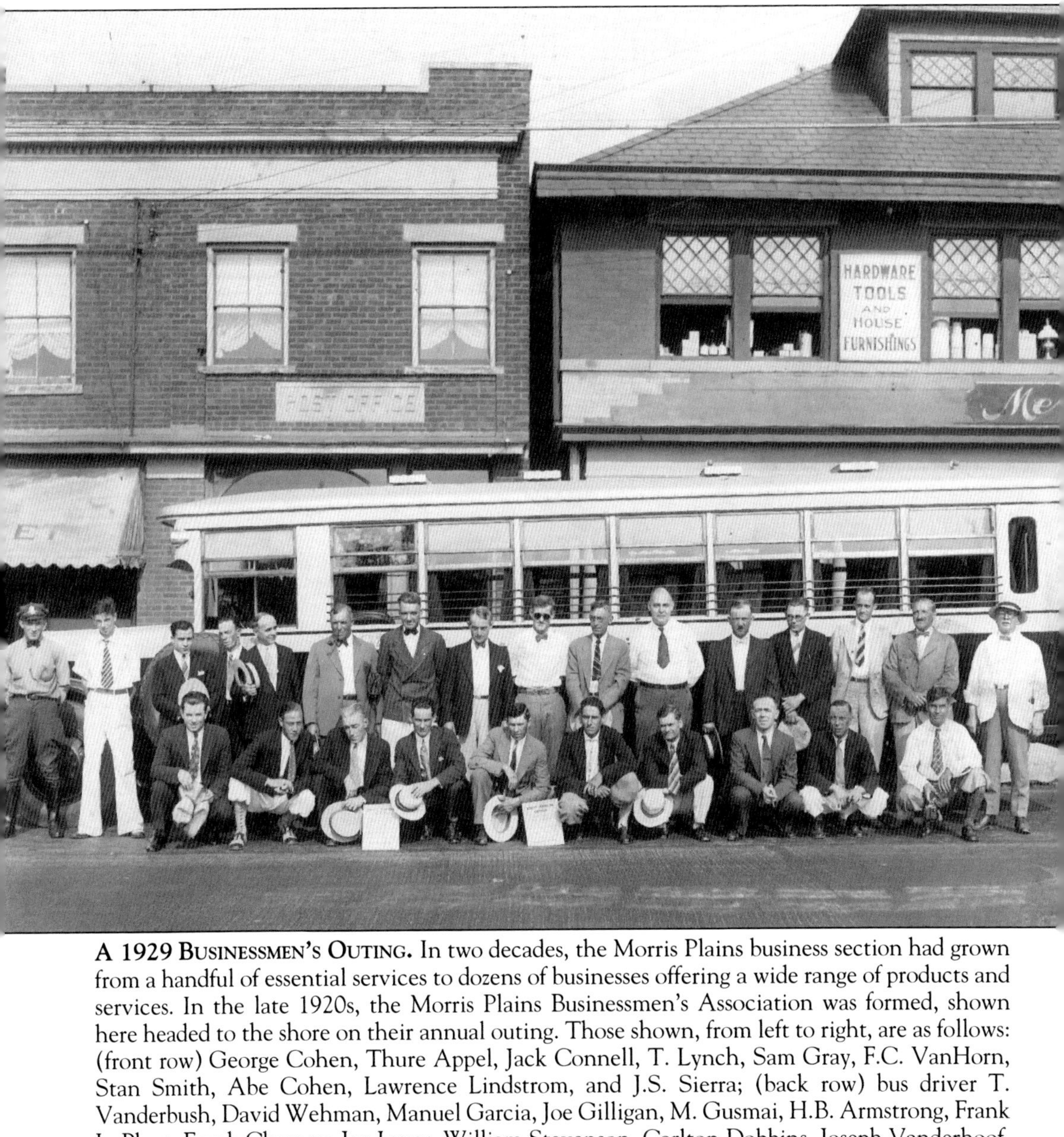

A 1929 Businessmen's Outing. In two decades, the Morris Plains business section had grown from a handful of essential services to dozens of businesses offering a wide range of products and services. In the late 1920s, the Morris Plains Businessmen's Association was formed, shown here headed to the shore on their annual outing. Those shown, from left to right, are as follows: (front row) George Cohen, Thure Appel, Jack Connell, T. Lynch, Sam Gray, F.C. VanHorn, Stan Smith, Abe Cohen, Lawrence Lindstrom, and J.S. Sierra; (back row) bus driver T. Vanderbush, David Wehman, Manuel Garcia, Joe Gilligan, M. Gusmai, H.B. Armstrong, Frank L. Plant, Frank Chesney, Joe Layer, William Stevenson, Carlton Dobbins, Joseph Vanderhoof, Bob Florin, G.F. Hutchinson, Dr. R.V.D. Totten, and Dan Merchant.

JAMES MCERLANE, POSTMASTER. For some reason now lost in time, the first post office in Morris Plains was named Lathrop when it opened in 1876 at Littleton on the Mount Pleasant Turnpike. A month later, it was moved into town and its name changed to Morris Plains. James McErlane was appointed postmaster by Franklin D. Roosevelt in 1934. He served for 32 years.

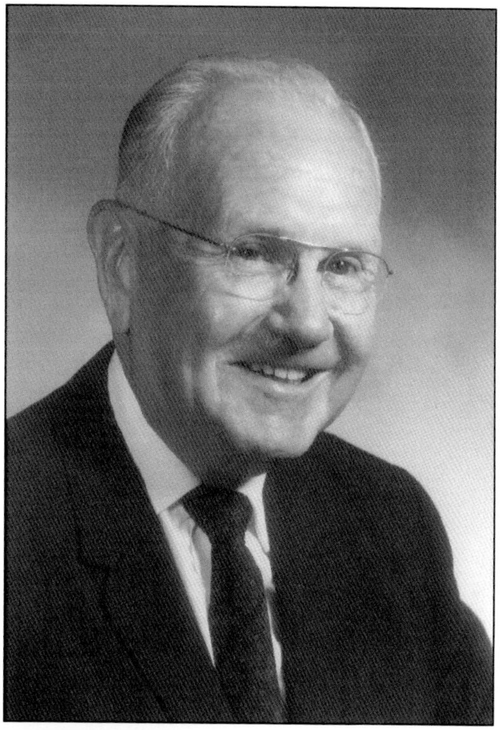

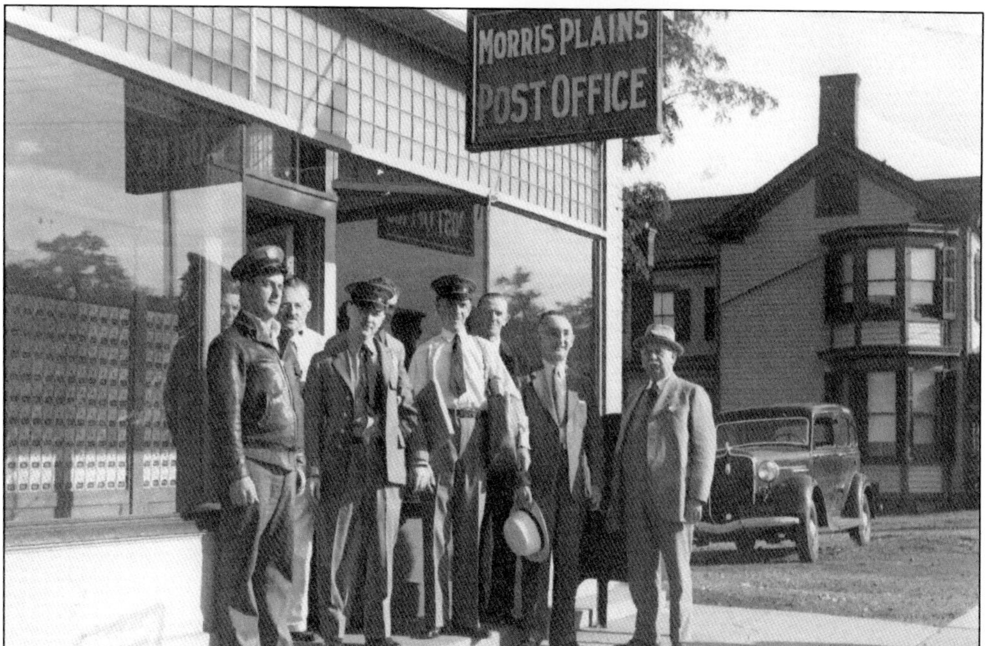

THE POST OFFICE ON FIRST DAY OF HOME DELIVERY, 1936. Standing in front of the post office are, from left to right, Frank Byrnes, Dr. R.V.D. Totten, Fred McGrath, James McErlane, Walter Coss, William Gilligan, Mayor Louis Burch, and Dan Merchant. William Dugan and Willard Youngs are in back and are hard to see. Postmaster McErlane asked that the public "bear with us until such time as all houses are numbered."

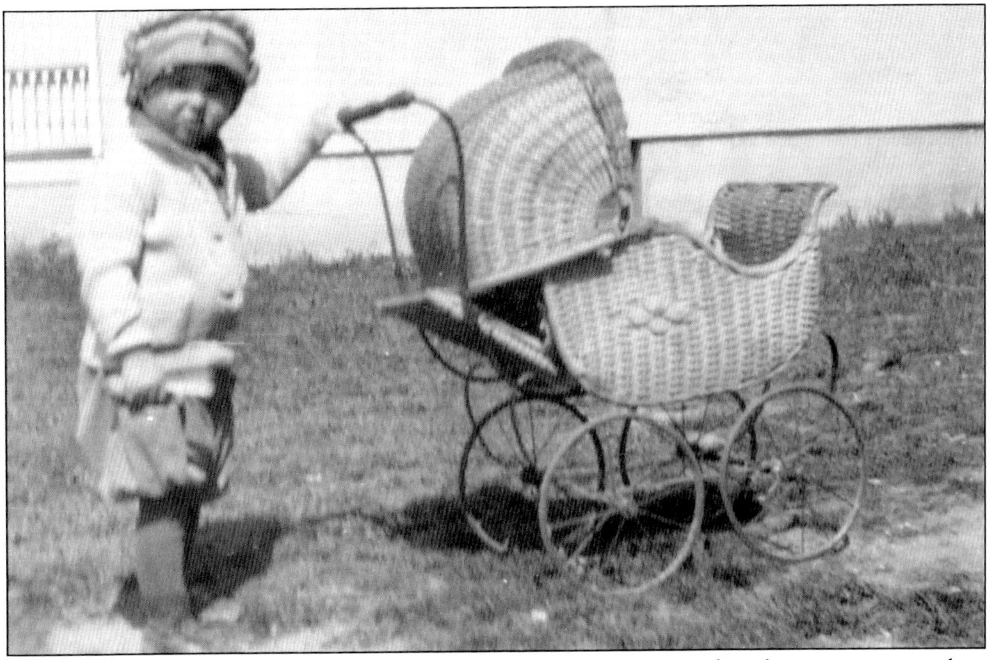

Jean Dobbins Osborne, Female Pioneer. In 1944—many years after this picture was taken at her family's Academy Road home—Jean "Bunny" Osborne was hired to be the first woman parcel post carrier in New Jersey. "It'll never work. A woman isn't strong enough for the job," cried her male colleagues. But Dobbins did the job as well as a man, and a longstanding barrier to women, one of many at the time, was broken. Later, Bunny Osborne was Morris Plains's tax collector, another former all-male domain.

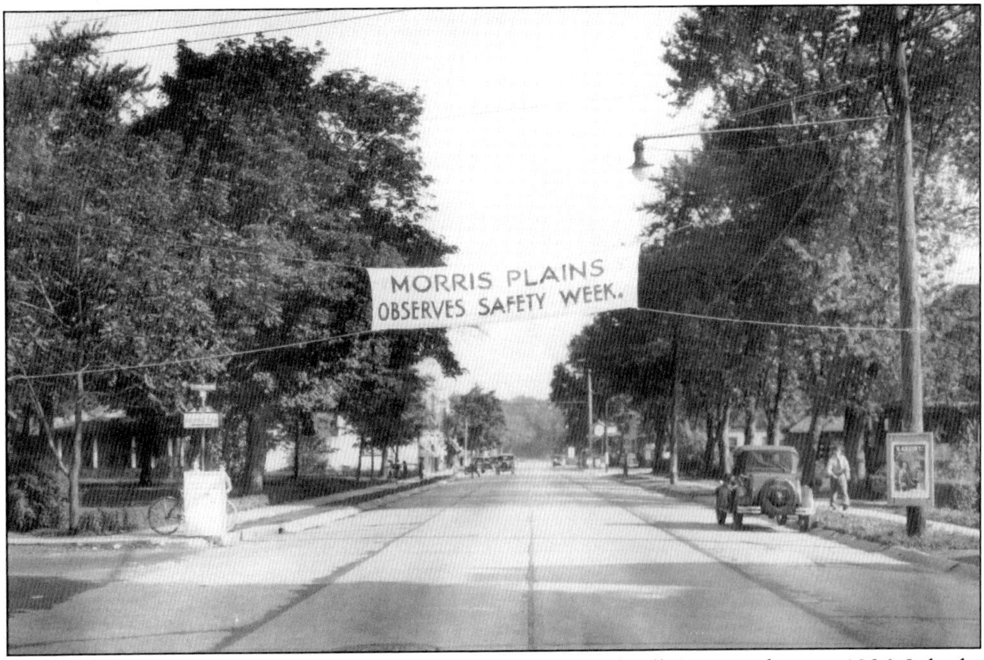

Morris Plains Observes Safety Week. This view of Speedwell Avenue dates to 1936. It looks north toward town from the corner of Glenbrook Road. (Courtesy JFPLMMT.)

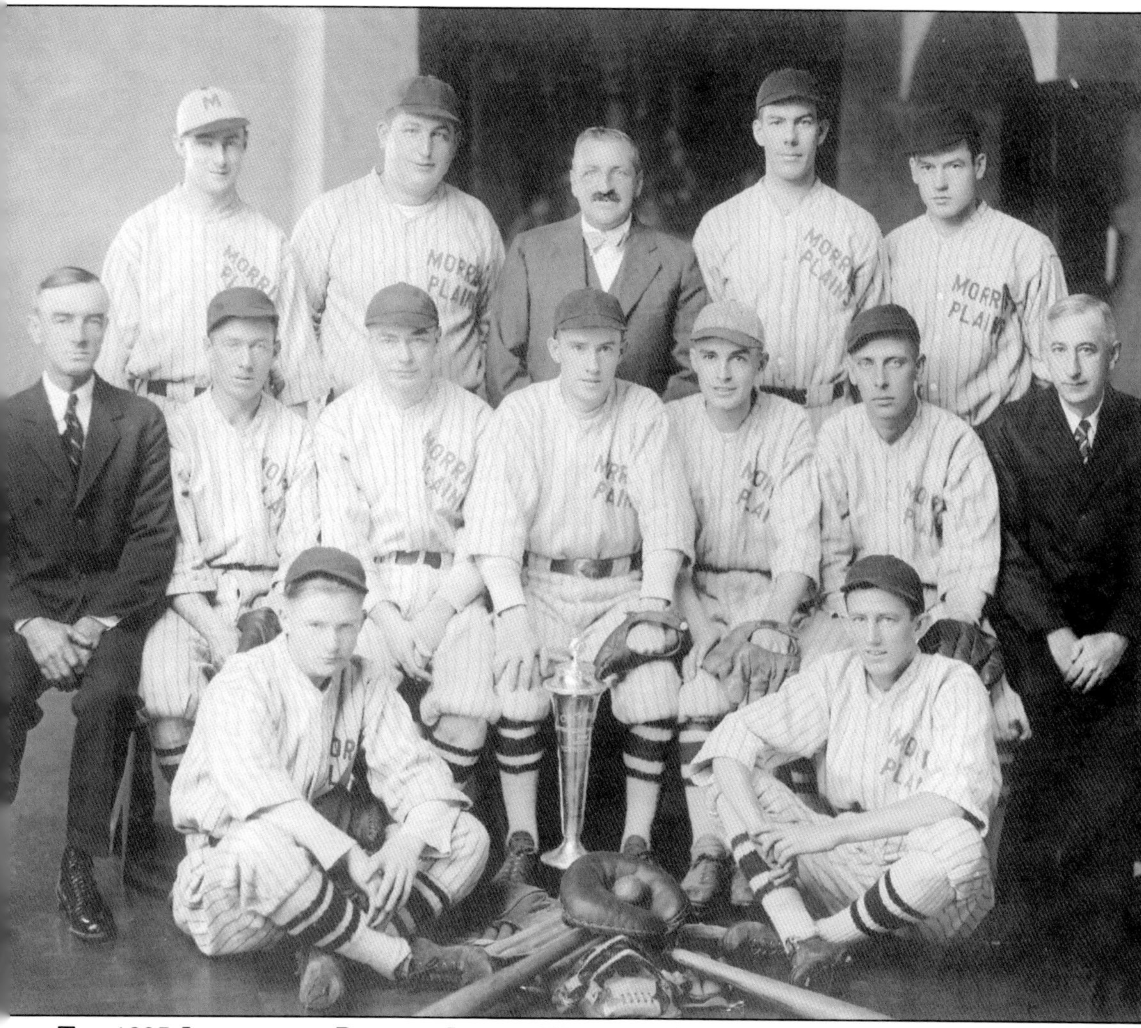

The 1927 Intercounty Baseball League Winners. This picture is remarkable in that it includes the then current Morris Plains mayor and three future mayors, whose terms of office are given in parentheses. Shown, from left to right, are the following: (first row) Tom Logan and "Peanuts" McCormack; (second row) Jim Fear (1954–1961), Frankie Lauenstein, Martin Franks, Bill Levick, Biddley Rogers, Biff Lindstrom, and Richard Lindabury (1927–1929); (third tow) Joe Murphy, Alex Laurie, manager R.V.D. "Doc" Totten (1929–1931), Gerald Coursen (1947–1953), and Eddie Mieninger.

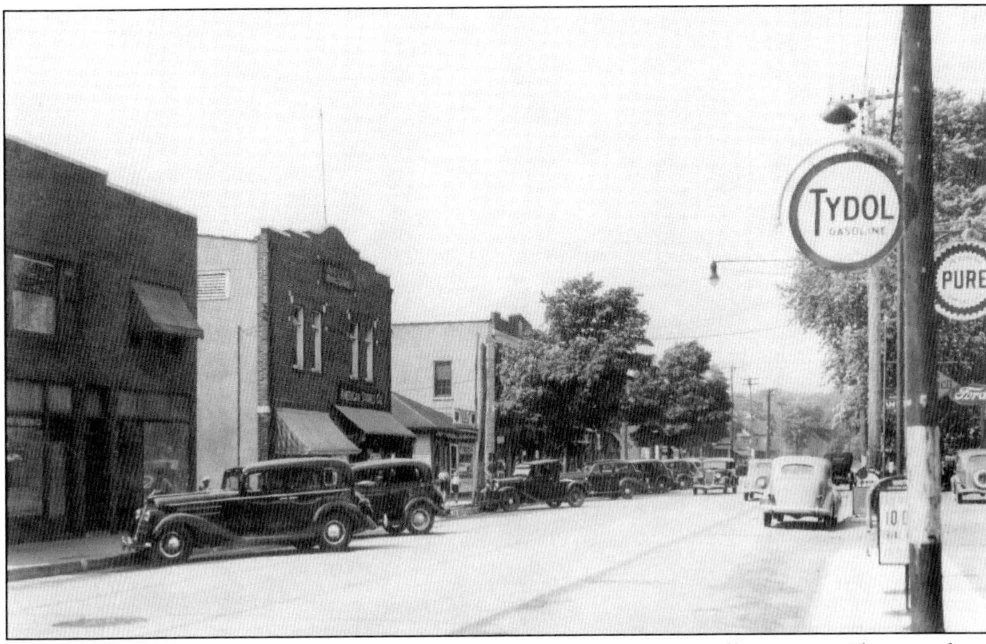

West Streetscape, 1936. Cars line the west side of upper Speedwell Avenue. The storefront at the far left, housing Hurley and McGough's Liquor Store and MacLean's Drug Store, was destroyed by a fire in 1994. The next building is the old Junior Order of United American Mechanics building, moved there 50 years previously from its original location on Franklin Place. (Courtesy JFPLMMT.)

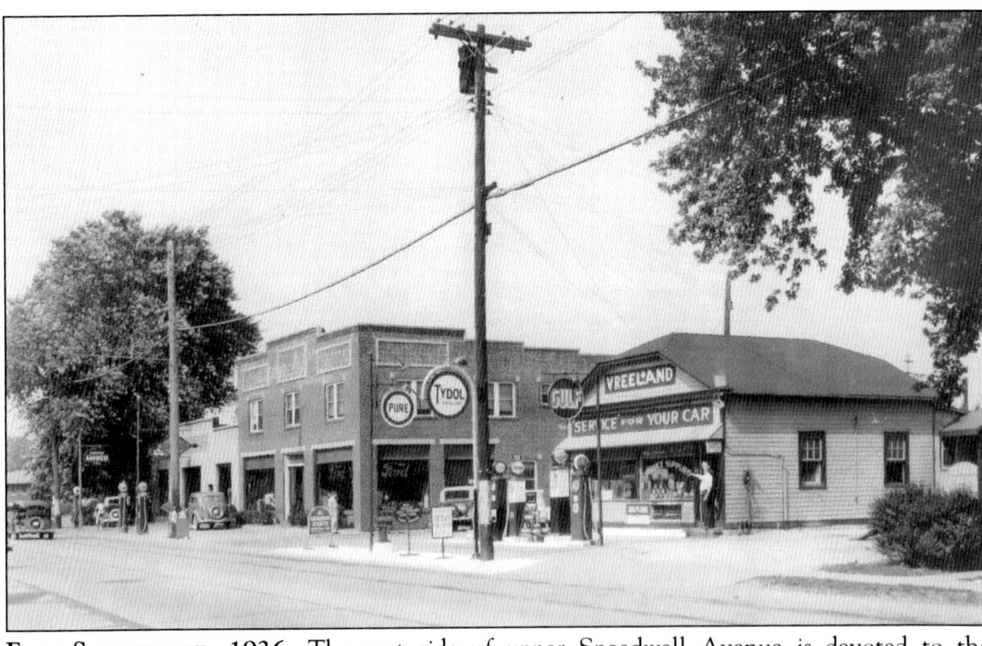

East Streetscape, 1936. The east side of upper Speedwell Avenue is devoted to the automobile, with Laurie Motors flanked by a gas station on each side. The Vreeland Garage in the forefront is now a Chinese restaurant. (Courtesy JFPLMMT.)

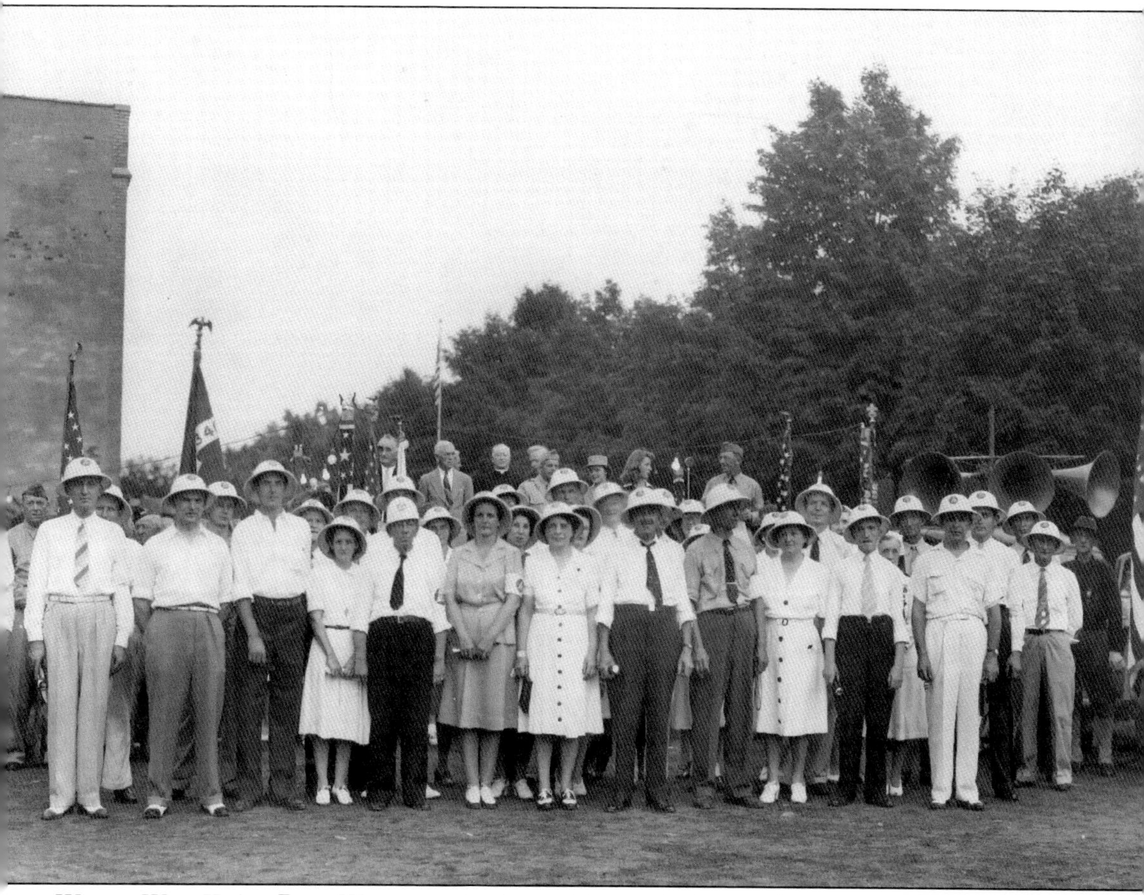

World War II Air Raid Wardens. As the world exploded in war for the second time in the century, Morris Plains put aside normal small-town life to learn the principles of civil defense. Every citizen had a job to do. Air raid wardens looked to the skies for enemy planes. Doctors and nurses made plans for heavy casualties. Air raid shelters were provisioned. First aid classes were given. Every family had a victory garden as they faced war shortages. It was a time that forced small-town America to come of age and face once again the grim reality of war.

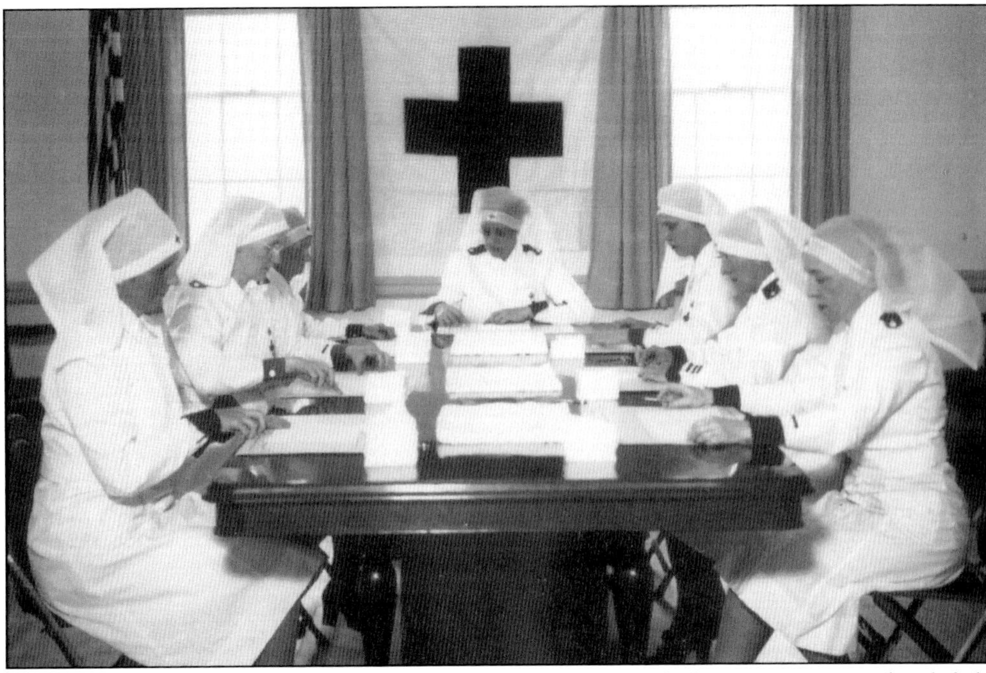

MORRIS PLAINS SURGICAL DRESSING UNIT. These unidentified women prepare battlefield dressings to be shipped overseas. The table they are working on is the original Morris Plains council table, now being used in the Rotary Room at the Morris Plains Museum.

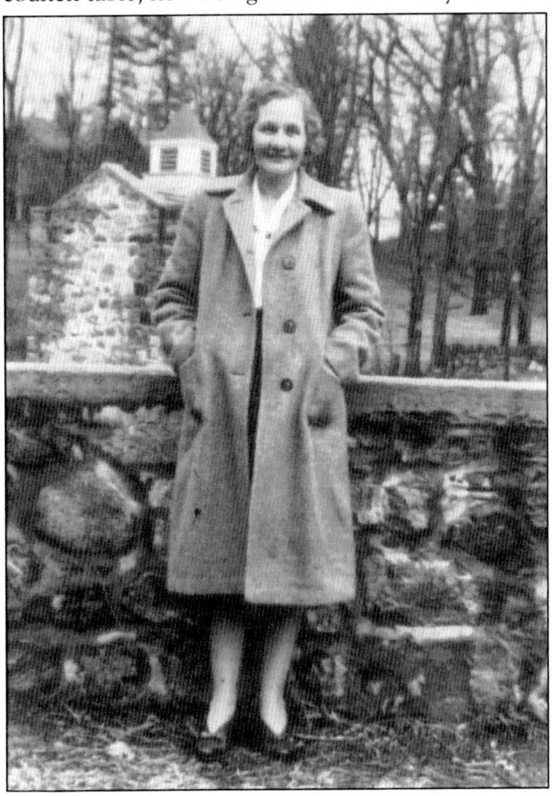

EDNA MING. During the war, the Morris Plains Service Corps made sure that Morris Plains's servicemen and women were not forgotten. The corps published a hometown newsletter, and gifts were sent to soldiers on Christmas and birthdays. Mrs. Ming won the VFW Outstanding Citizen award for keeping track of constantly changing addresses so those at the front would receive news, encouragement, and cheer from the home front.

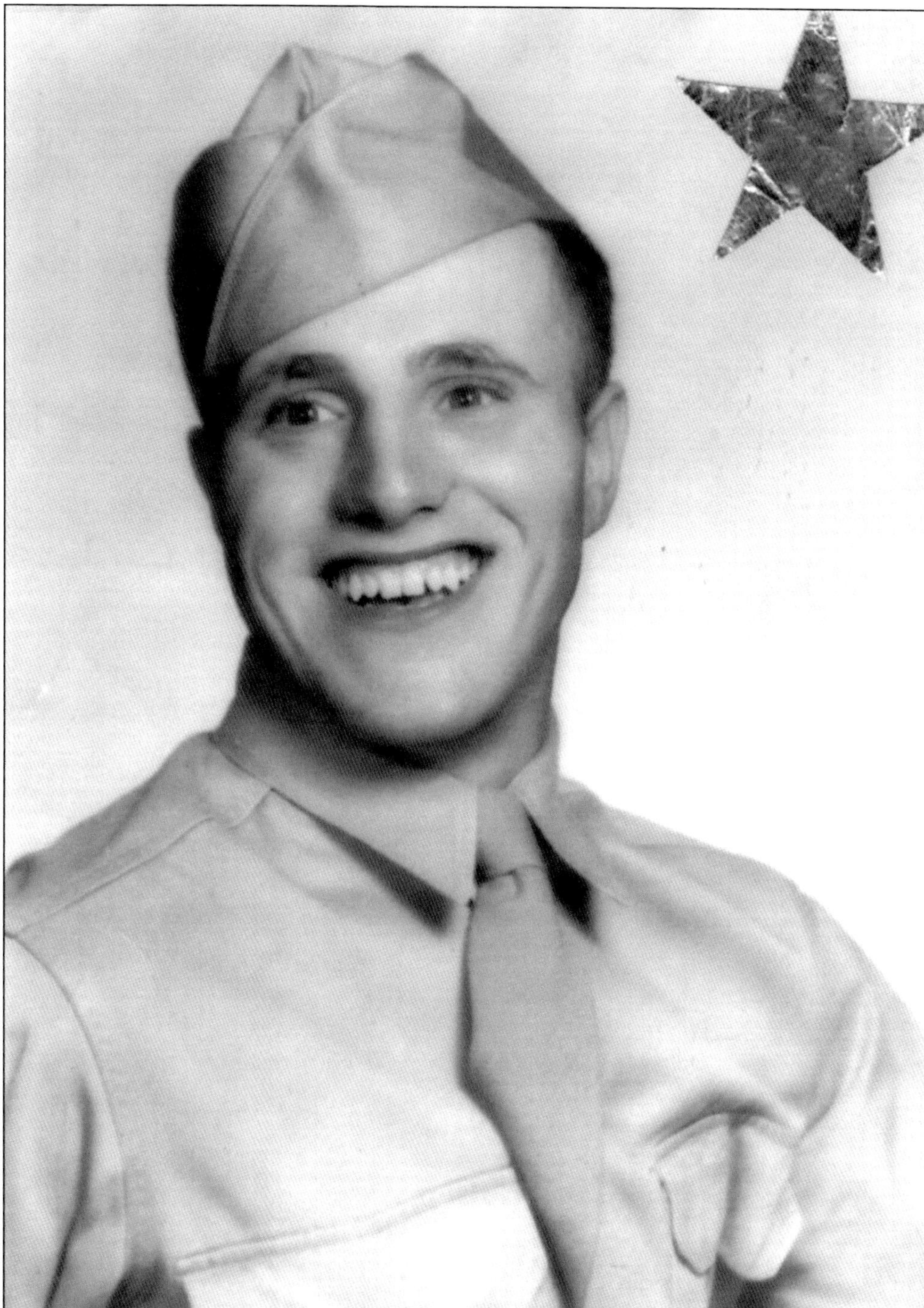

Morris Plains's Fallen Heroes. This is Benjamin "Benny" Signorelli, who died in the Battle of the Bulge, mortally wounded after going to the aid of a soldier pinned down by artillery fire. Benny was 18 years old when he was killed. He is one of ten young men from Morris Plains who went to war and never returned. Benny's family still lives in Morris Plains and helped unveil a new memorial in Roberts Garden on Memorial Day 2000.

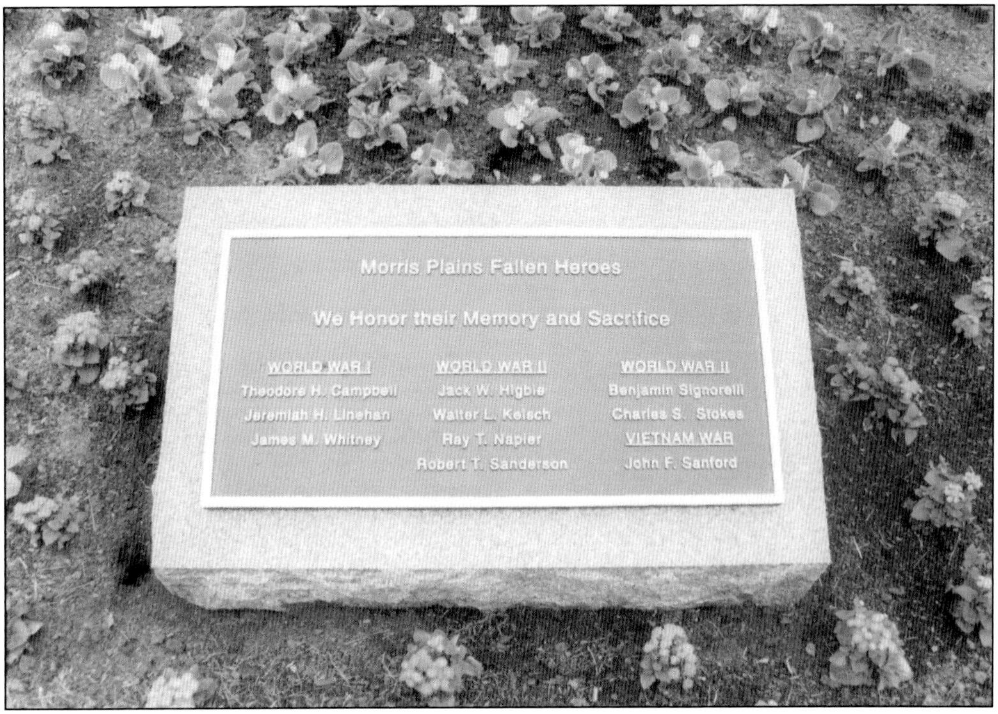

A NEW MEMORIAL IN ROBERTS GARDEN. The bronze soldiers' memorial commemorating Morris Plains's fallen heroes was suggested by the Morris Plains Museum, sponsored by the Morris Plains Rotary Club and directed to completion by rotarian and assistant town historian Hank Sawoski.

World War I:
Theodore H. Campbell
James M. Whitney
Jeremiah H. Linehan

World War II:
Jack Higbie
Walter L. Kelsch
Ray T. Napier
Robert T. Sanderson
Benjamin Signorelli
Charles S. Stokes

Vietnam War:
John F. Sanford

Ten

PROMISE AND POSSIBILITY

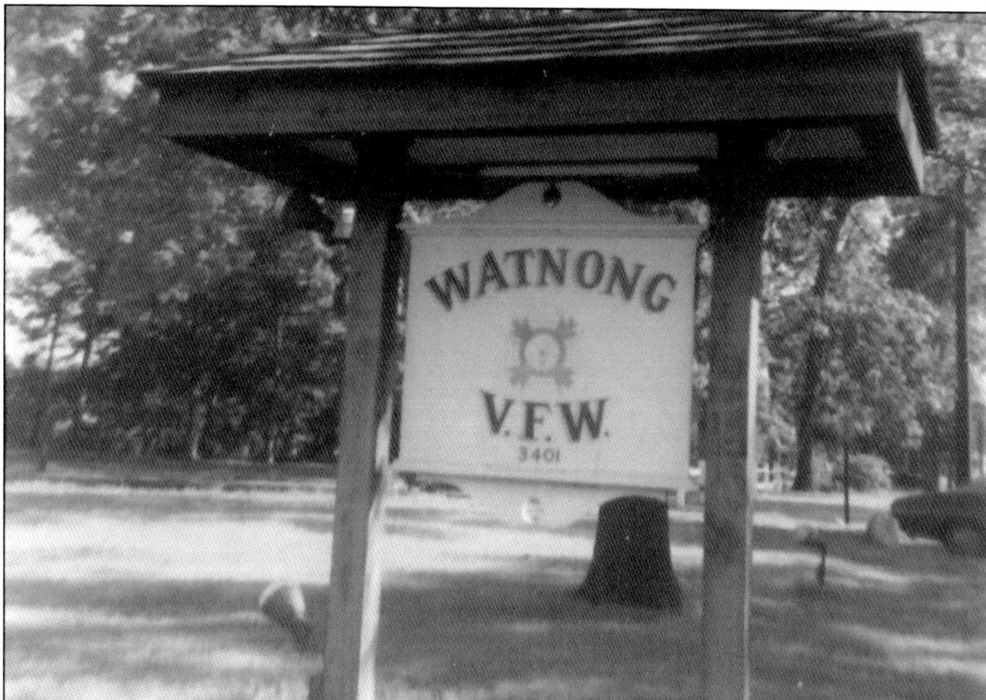

VFW POST 3401. World War II was over, the boys came home, and Morris Plains picked up the pieces. War survivors found Watnong Post 3401 of the Veterans of Foreign Wars, chartered in 1935, waiting to welcome and honor them for their bravery and sacrifice. In 1981, Post 3401 moved to its new facility on Tabor Road provided by Warner-Lambert in exchange for the land on which the old post stood.

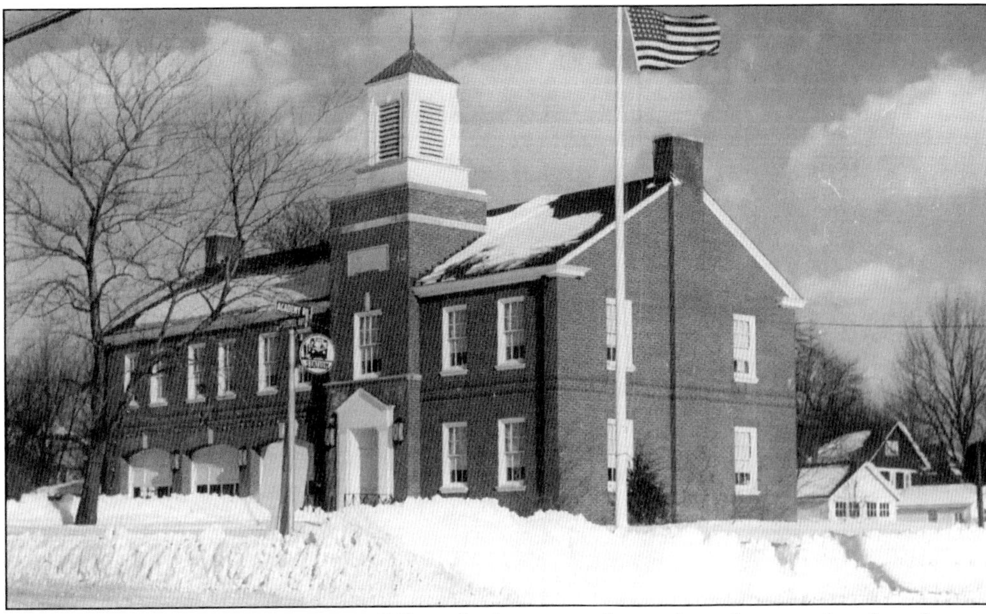

Municipal Building, Built 1942. When the boys came home from the war, they found a new brick municipal building on Speedwell Avenue. It replaced the old wooden structure destroyed by fire in 1940 and served the needs of both fire department and local government. In 1990, a new wing was added.

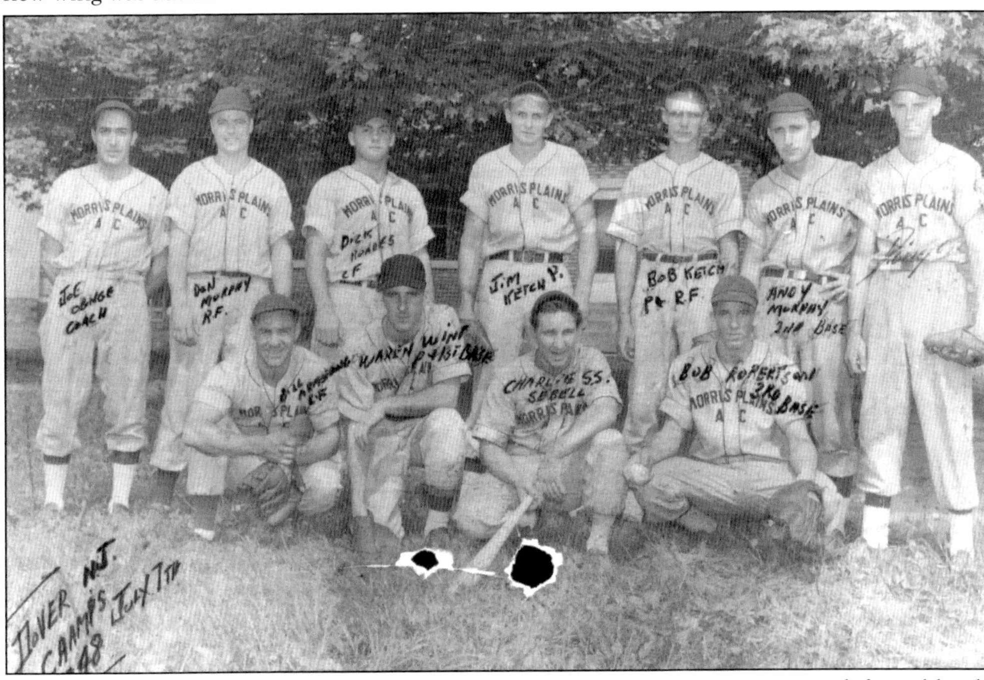

The Morris Plains Athletic Club. In the postwar years, attention turned from bloody battlefields to grass-covered athletic fields. The MPAC won the Dover Twilight League championship in 1948. The winners, from left to right, are as follows: (front row) Bill Armstrong, Warren Windt, Charlie Sebelle, and Bob Roberson; (back row) manager Joe Ognibene, Don Murphy, Dick Rhoades, Jim Ketch, Bob Ketch, Andy Murphy, and Fred Davis.

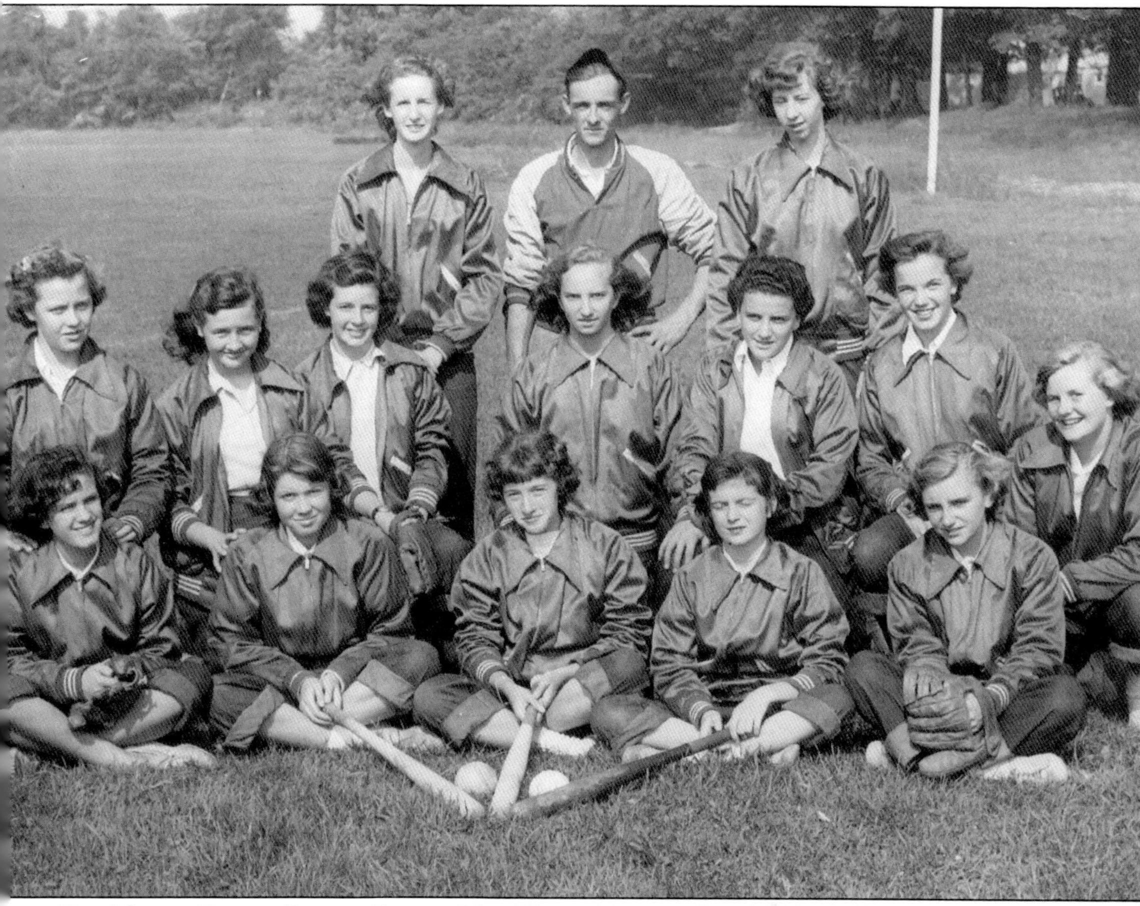

The Morris Plains Sports Club, 1950. The girls' team played basketball and softball; the boys' team played basketball and baseball. They traveled to games in the Backes Floor Covering truck. The players, from left to right, are as follows: (front row) Shirley Stewart, Dona Scoble Hausser, Carla Capuano, June Meeker Peterson, Jane Wilhelm, and Shirley Hansen Ford; (middle row) Kathryn Youngs Elgood, Pat Cullen Dorflinger, Jackie Gorry Markey, Helen Myers Dower, Joyce Heinhold, and Rita Kapinos Brown; (back row) Sue Gorry Edwards, Jim McIntyre (coach), and Doris Campbell Riddle.

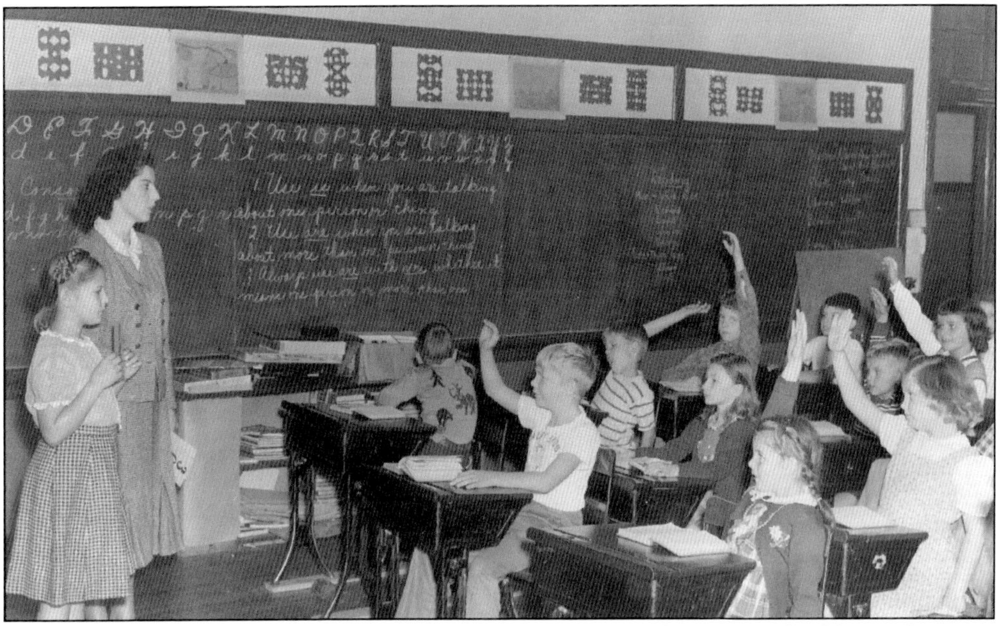

Borough School, 1948. Miss Madeline Glaab (later Mrs. Carleton Bruen) addresses her class of fourth graders. As is true of schoolchildren everywhere, some are eager and responsive and others less so. On this long-ago day, a young man in the front row may have missed out on the lesson in progress.

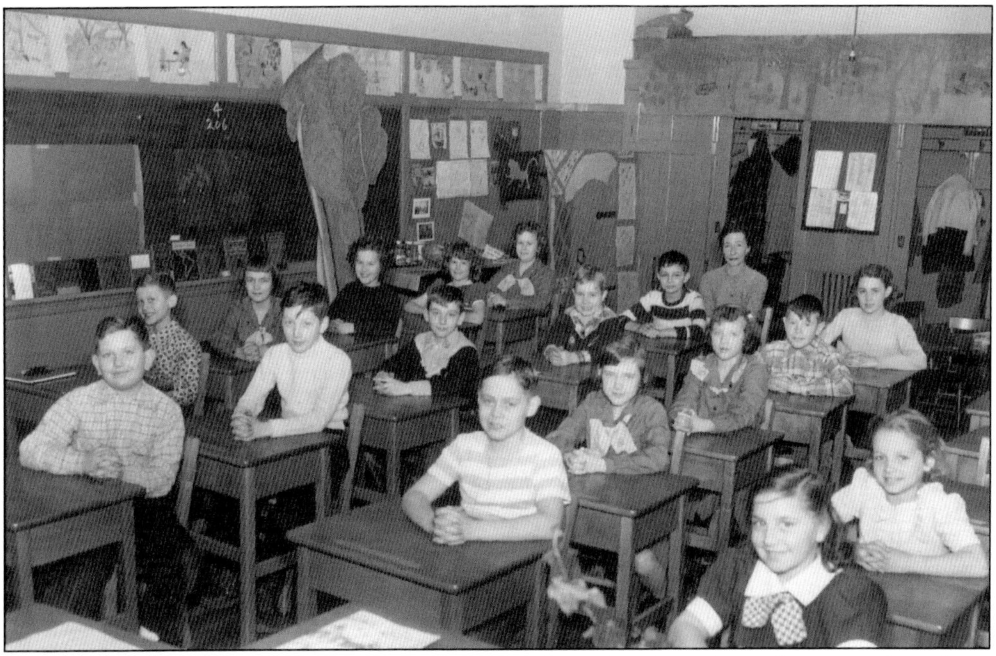

Fourth Graders, 1951. Starting from the right, these fourth-grade students are, from front to back, as follows: (first row) Geraldine Signorelli and Eleanor Meeker; (second row) Robert Volbrek, Deborah Munsel, Christine Olin, Richard Ross, and Lois Otterbein; (third row) John Wrubel, Bill Wilson, Dick Smith, John Trompen, Bill Stewart, and teacher Mrs. Briant; (fourth row) Neil Marek, Mary Melvin, Linda Patton, Jill Newirth, and Judy Sagert.

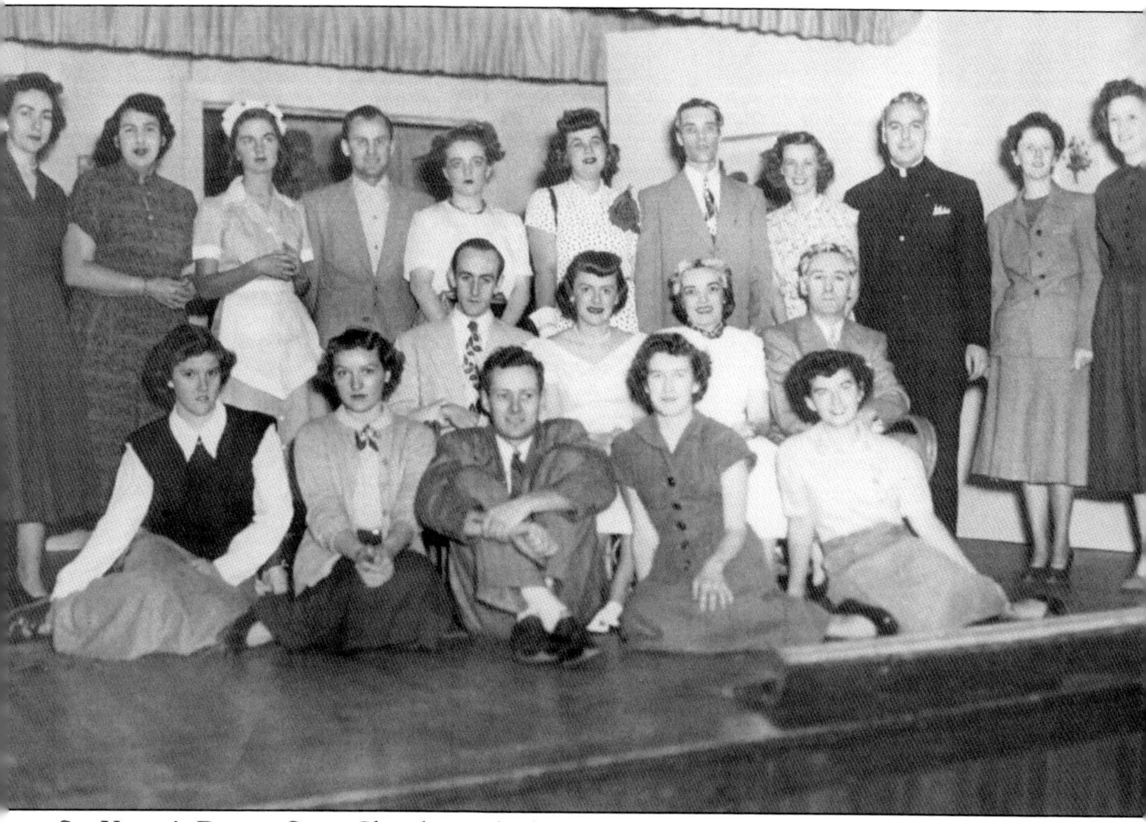

St. Virgil's Drama Club. Churches and other institutions picked up where they had left off before the war, as men and women settled into a life free of the obligations of wartime. In 1950, St. Virgil's Drama Club put on the play *To Tell the Truth.* The dramatists are, from left to right, as follows: (front row) Gertrude Myers Nodoro, Kathryn O'Hara Hoehne, Harold Benz, Ann Myers Doherty, and Eileen Sweeney Doherty; (middle row) Al Nugent, Mary Lonergan Larkin, Anita Knight Dempsey, and Willard (Tic) Applin; (back row) Betty Nugent, Ann Palumbo Russo, Mary Huss Krozser, Frank Lojewski, Claire Hennessy Benz, Mary Bolger, Harry Young, Patricia Comeau, Gerald Palumbo, Mary Byrnes, and Helen Benz.

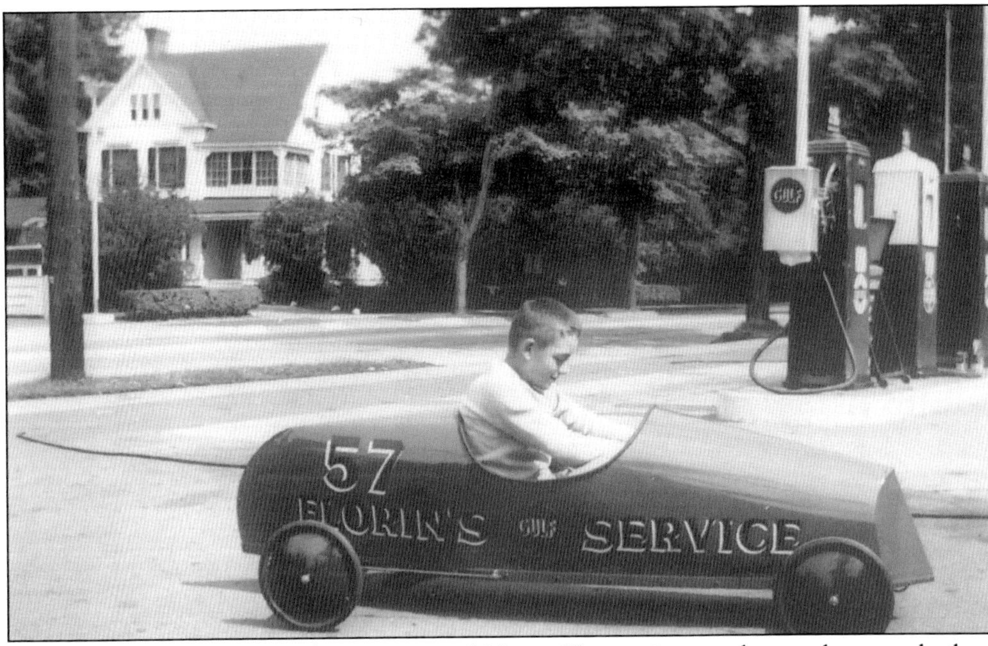

ALAN FLORIN, 1940s. This future mayor of Morris Plains tries out the soapbox car, built at his father's service station on Speedwell Avenue near Five Corners. Across the street is the Conklin-Ward house in better days.

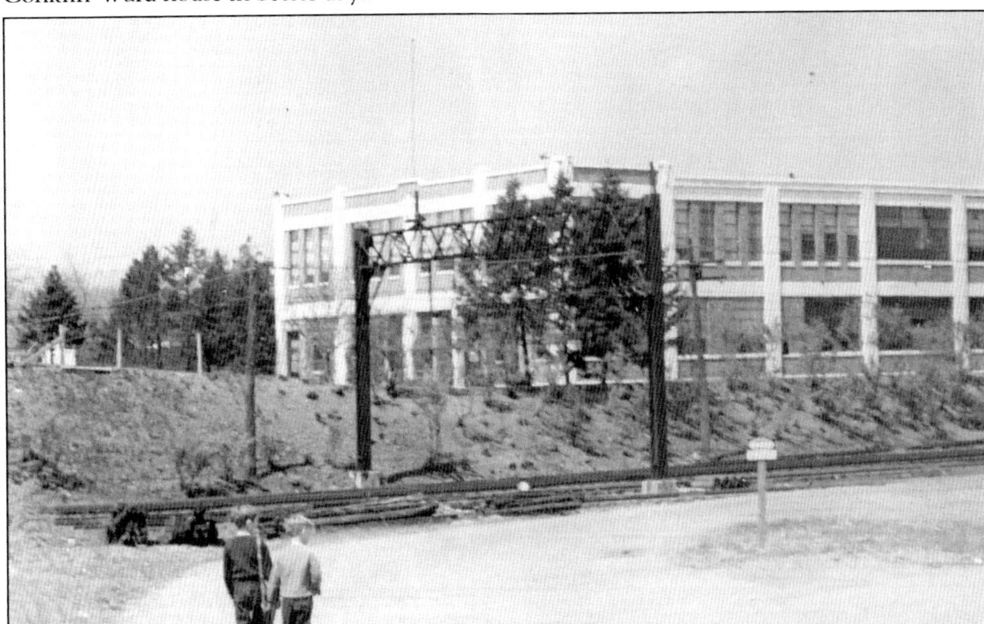

GONE FISHIN'. These two young boys are on their way home from the "sandpit" water hole after a day of fishing. Behind them is the G. Washington coffee refining factory. George Washington, the inventer of instant coffee, moved his business to Morris Plains in 1927 and operated until 1998.

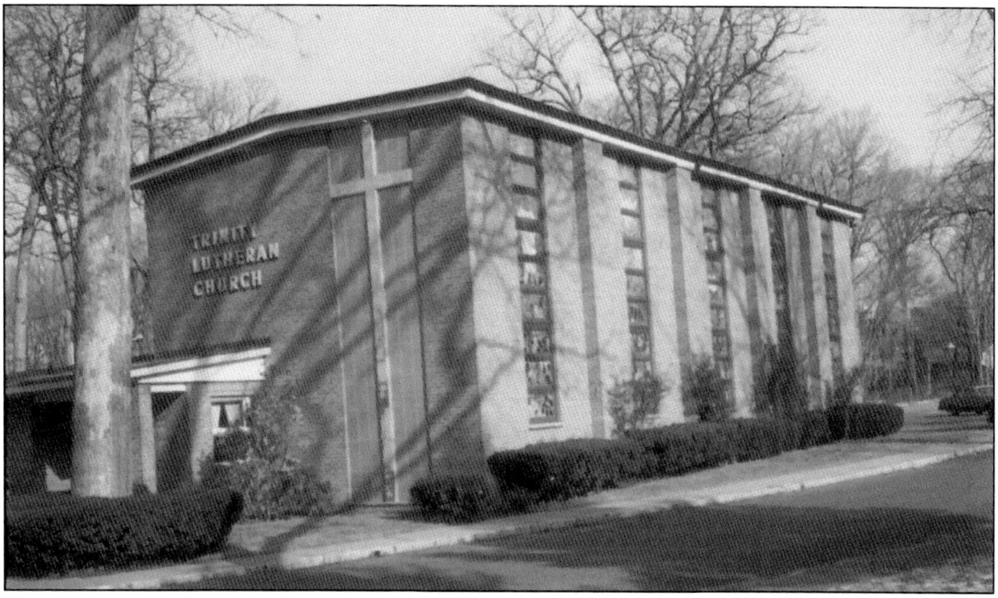

The Trinity Lutheran Church. Although Morris Plains Lutherans trace their beginnings to 1916, their new church was dedicated on February 21, 1954. The church sits beside the Watnong Brook on Mountain Way.

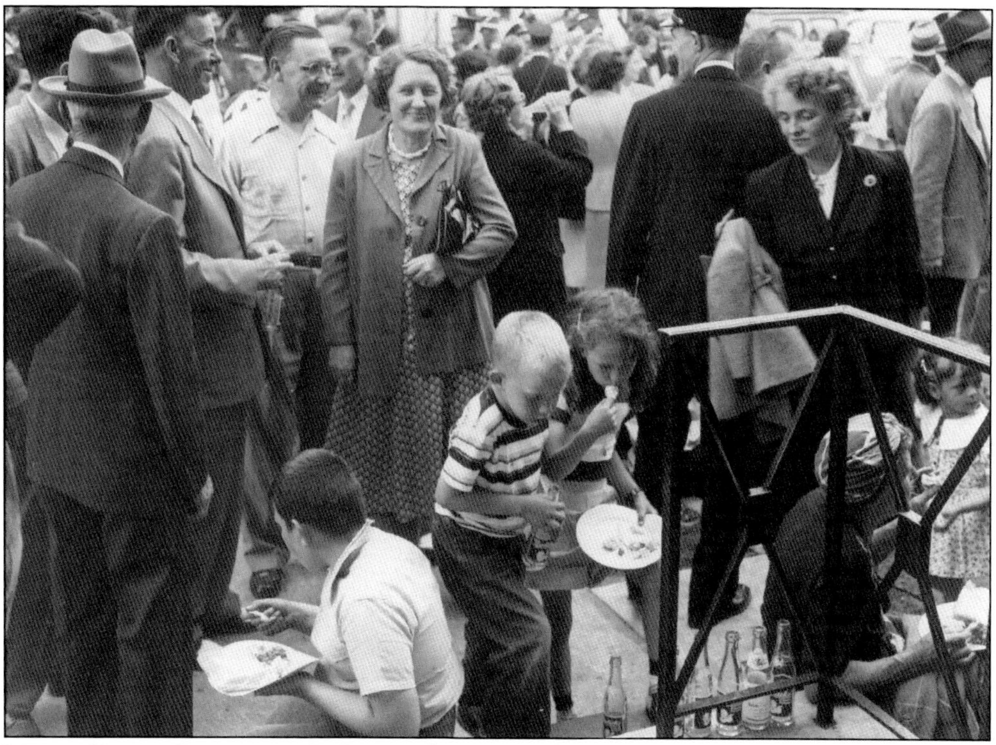

Morris Plains Celebrates. In June 1951, Morris Plains celebrated 25 years of independence from Hanover Township. The town had accomplished much in those years, and postwar optimism was still running high. The picture shows the crowd, young and old alike, enjoying themselves on the steps of the borough hall.

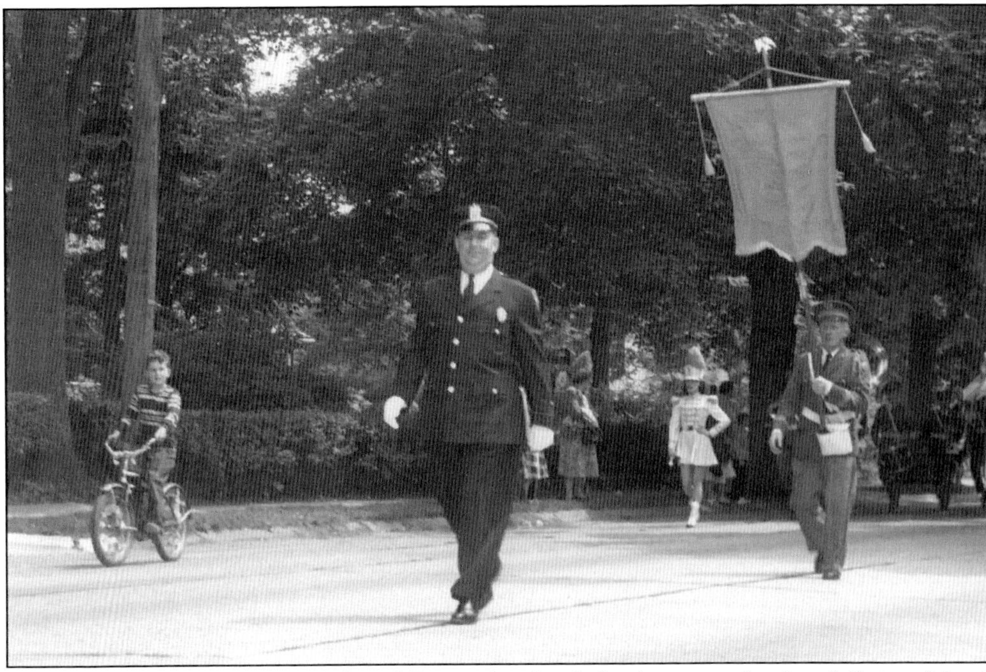

Celebration Parade, 1951. Edward Barry, the chief of police, was the first full-time Morris Plains policeman with formal police training. Here, he marches in the Morris Plains 25th anniversary parade.

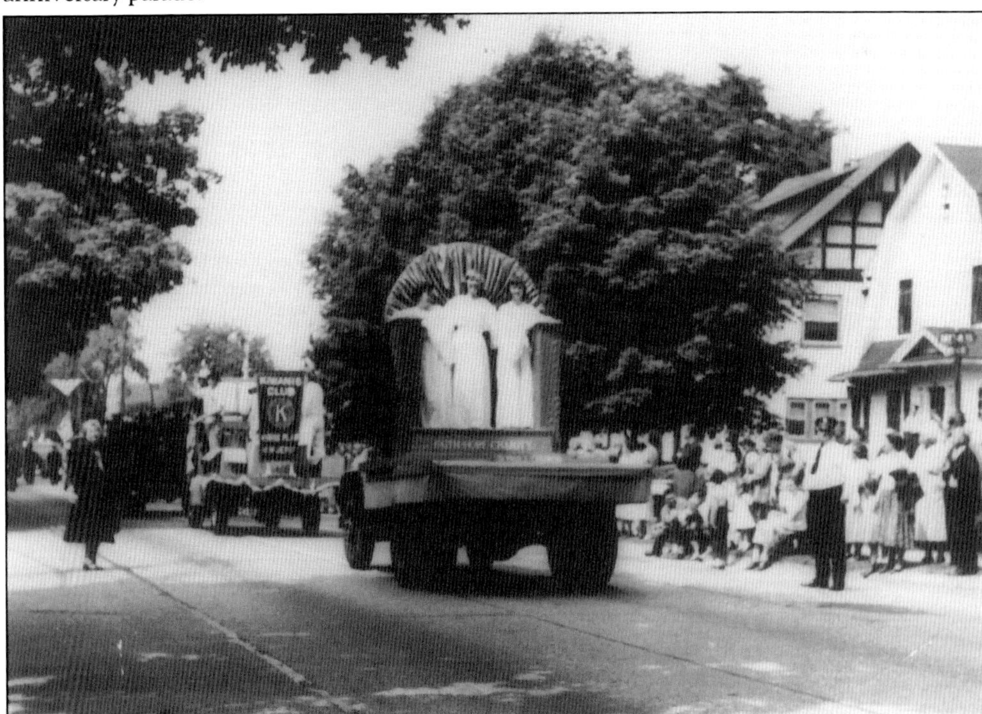

St. Paul's Float. Barbara Wikander, Vera Craig, and her sister pose as "Faith, Hope, and Charity" on a float constructed by Emil Possi and Carl Ahlfield for the 1951 anniversary parade.

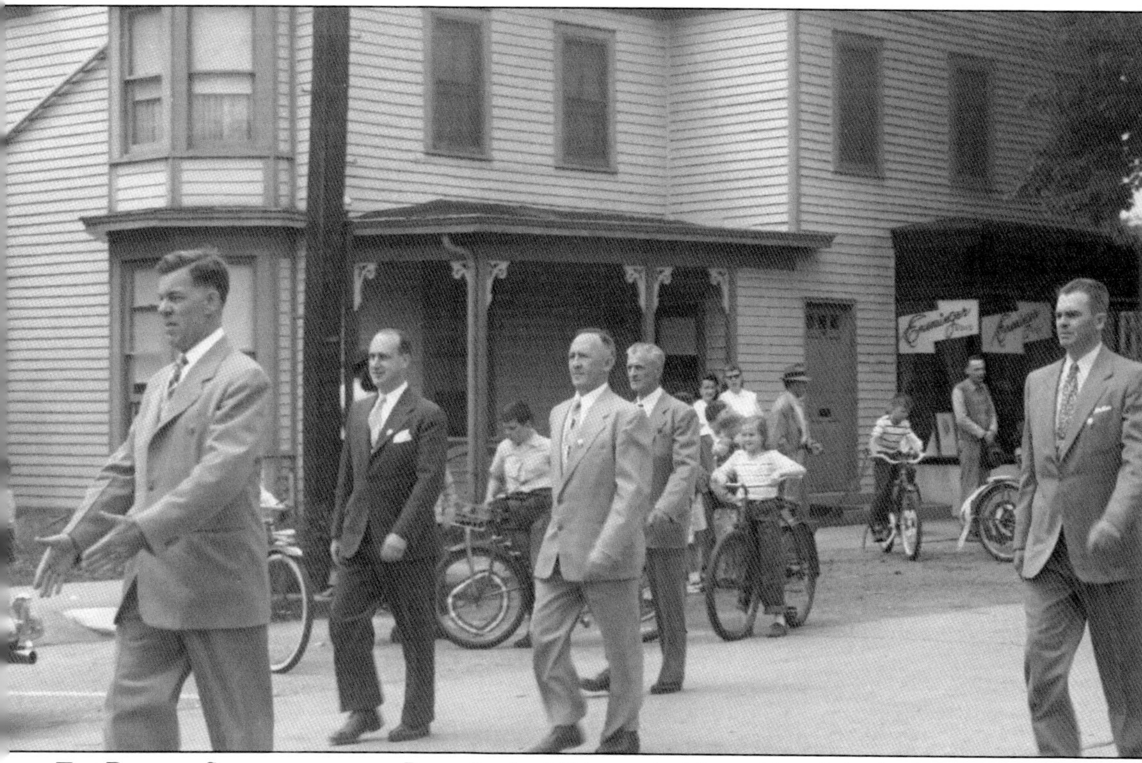

THE PRESENT SHADOWED BY THE PAST. In the 1951 parade, Morris Plains's leaders were caught by the camera as they marched past the 200-year-old Young-Clark building on the corner of Jaqui Avenue. The old structure survived three fires while Morris Plains grew from a handful of rural farms to a thriving 20th century modern community. The marchers, from left to right, are Gerald Coursen (mayor), Milt Trompen (councilman), Fred Reeves (councilman), Herbert Ueltz (borough clerk, and Griff Humphrey (councilman).

Today, Morris Plains has managed to preserve the best of small-town life while capitalizing on its location in one of the world's most culturally rich metropolitan areas. Morris Plains offers something for everybody: Morris Plains Days, Memorial Day parades, Labor Day block parties, fishing contests, townwide holiday celebrations, scout programs, senior citizen programs, high quality schools, town sports and recreation, a library, museum, garden club, public swimming pools, playgrounds, and much more. Churches and civic organizations such as the Veterans of Foreign Wars, the Knights of Columbus, and Rotary enhance adult life.

Wherever the citizens of Morris Plains roam, they will always find that their hometown, the unique "community of caring," will be waiting for them when they return.

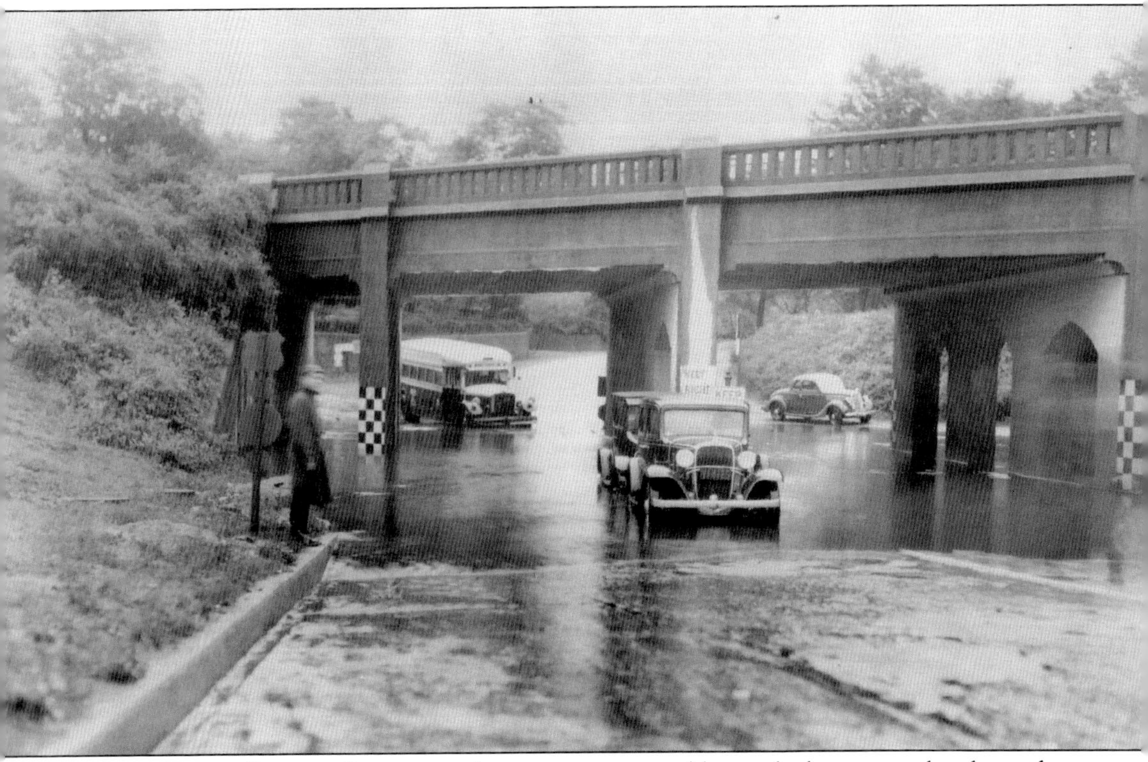

Some Things Remain. Despite steady progress, some problems take longer to solve than others. The railroad underpass at Littleton Road was built in 1915, but decades later it still flooded after a heavy downpour, leaving cars and buses stranded. Today, a pump has eliminated the problem—except when there is a power failure.

For those who worry that change endangers all that is dear and familiar, read the following lines penned by a Morris Plains native, then note the date they were written. You can take comfort in knowing that the more things change, the more they remain the same.

Morris Plains—My Home Town

I've lived for many a tedious year,
On grand old Morris Plains;
And seen the changes which occurred
On broad street and its lanes.

You'd scarcely recognize the place,
Nor know that you were back;
Unless some old familiar friend
Should tell you of that fact!

—Author unknown, written in 1867
in the *Morris Plains Argosy*.